D1823141

Gender in the Middle Ages

Volume 12

THE UNSPEAKABLE, GENDER AND SEXUALITY IN MEDIEVAL LITERATURE 1000–1400

Gender in the Middle Ages

ISSN 1742-870X

This series investigates the representation and construction of masculinity and femininity in the Middle Ages from a variety of disciplinary and interdisciplinary perspectives. It aims in particular to explore the diversity of medieval genders, and such interrelated contexts and issues as sexuality, social class, race and ethnicity, and orthodoxy and heterodoxy.

Proposals or queries should be sent in the first instance to the editors or to the publisher, at the addresses given below; all submissions will receive prompt and informed consideration.

Professor Jacqueline Murray, Department of History, University of Guelph, Guelph, Ontario, N1G 2W1, Canada

Professor Diane Watt, School of English and Languages, University of Surrey, Guildford, Surrey GU2 7XH, UK

Boydell & Brewer Limited, PO Box 9, Woodbridge, Suffolk IP12 3DF, UK

Previously published volumes in the series are listed at the end of this book.

THE UNSPEAKABLE, GENDER AND SEXUALITY IN MEDIEVAL LITERATURE 1000–1400

Victoria Blud

D. S. BREWER

First published 2017
D. S. Brewer, Cambridge

ISBN 978-1-84384-468-6

D. S. Brewer is an imprint of Boydell & Brewer Ltd
PO Box 9, Woodbridge, Suffolk IP12 3DF, UK
and of Boydell & Brewer Inc.
668 Mt Hope Avenue, Rochester, NY 14620–2731, USA
website: www.boydellandbrewer.co.uk

A CIP catalogue record for this book is available
from the British Library

CONTENTS

ACKNOWLEDGEMENTS

This book has been with me for a long time, and I would like to thank everyone who has sustained the relationship between me and it along the way. This work could not have been completed without the support of the English departments at King's College London and the University of York, and the funding of the Arts and Humanities Research Council. I must first thank Clare Lees and Bob Mills, who introduced me to medieval literature as an undergraduate and later mentored me both during and beyond my doctoral studies, for years of advice and inspiration. I am also grateful to the editors of this series, in particular Diane Watt, for encouraging me to write this book in the first place. Many thanks are due to the anonymous readers at Boydell & Brewer, whose comments and feedback made this a better book, and especially to the indefatigable Caroline Palmer for her unstinting support and guidance. Chapter 3 is derived in part from 'Wolves' Heads and Wolves' Tales: Women and Exile in *Bisclavret* and *Wulf and Eadwacer*', published in *Exemplaria* 26.4 (2014), 328–46;[1] I am grateful to the editors and publishers of this journal for permission to reproduce this material.

I feel very fortunate to have had the support of many friends and colleagues from the University of London and the Centre for Medieval Studies at York (as well as the unspeakable miscreants of Woking!) through this process. Amid the ups and downs of writing I've been the grateful recipient of much professional generosity, and in particular I would like to thank John Arnold, Laura Bailey, Joshua Burson, Ardis Butterfield, Michele Campopiano, Laura Crombie, Josh Davies, Gillian Galloway, Daniel Gerrard, Jeremy Goldberg, Linne Mooney, Emilie Morin, Laura Reid, Brittany Scowcroft, Kathleen Walker-Meikle, Christine Williamson and Claudia Wittig, for offering the benefit of their expertise, feedback on drafts, previews of unpublished work, checks to translations (any remaining errors are of course my own), practical help, moral support, and/or wine. Special thanks to Emilie and to Laura Crombie for reading the whole manuscript – you were wonderful, and we can talk about something else now. Finally, love and thanks to Sandy, Rob and Tom Blud for making sure I didn't starve or go too strange before I'd finished.

1 Available online: http://www.tandfonline.com/ [http://www.tandfonline.com/doi/abs/10.1179/1041257314Z.00000000057]

ABBREVIATIONS

ASPR	The Anglo-Saxon Poetic Records
Bosworth-Toller	Bosworth, Joseph, *An Anglo-Saxon Dictionary*, ed. T. Northcote Toller et al. (Oxford: Clarendon Press, 1898)
CA	Gower, *Confessio Amantis*, in G. C. Macaulay, ed., *The English Works of John Gower*, 2 vols, EETS e.s. 81, 82 (Oxford: Oxford University Press, 1900–01)
EETS	Early English Text Society
e.s.	extra series
o.s.	original series
s.s.	supplementary series
JEGP	*Journal of English and Germanic Philology*
JMEMS	*Journal of Medieval and Early Modern Studies*
LGW	Chaucer, *Legend of Good Women*, in Larry D. Benson, gen. ed., *The Riverside Chaucer*, 3rd edn (Oxford: Oxford University Press, 1988)
MED	Kurath, Hans, and Robert E. Lewis, eds, *Middle English Dictionary* (Ann Arbor, MI: University of Michigan Press, 1999)
PL	*Patrologia Cursus Completus, series Latina*, ed. J.-P. Migne (Paris: Garnier, 1841–55)
PMLA	*Publications of the Modern Language Association of America*
RES	*Review of English Studies*

INTRODUCTION: WORDS AND OTHER FRAGMENTS

> There is not one but many silences, and they are an integral part of the strategies that underlie and permeate discourses.
>
> Michel Foucault.[1]

> What I seek in speech is the response of the other.
>
> Jacques Lacan.[2]

What do we mean when we speak of the unspeakable? From the ineffable glories of the divine, plunging down to the murky depths of the 'unspeakable sin', some things cannot be put into words – but these are often, paradoxically, those things about which there is an abundance of discourse. Alongside everything that is spoken (or written) there also exists an unspoken: as Pierre Macherey insists, a text will inevitably expose its ideological crises, and say what it does not say.[3] For medievalists, the failure of communication often takes a material aspect, for along with the textual evidence there is a textual void: the missing, damaged, incomplete or lost manuscripts that expose the fragmentary nature of medieval records, and whose exploration delves into the spaces between the fragments, looking for the unknown, the unsaid, the silenced and the unspeakable. As Foucault and Lacan suggest, such silence may be calculating, or inviting; the unspeakable may be gruesome or awesome, and often, those acts described as 'unspeakable' in contemporary reports are also those described as 'medieval'. In this book, I examine the idea of the unspeakable in the Middle Ages as an important concept with respect to medieval texts in general, and in constructions of medieval gender and sexuality in particular. Who gets to speak, and why, and how? And who doesn't, and why, and how?

1 Michel Foucault, *The History of Sexuality I: The Will to Knowledge*, trans. Robert Hurley (London: Penguin, 1998), p. 27.

2 Jacques Lacan, 'The Function and Field of Speech and Language in Psychoanalysis', in Écrits: A Selection, trans. Alan Sheridan (London and New York: Routledge, 1977), pp. 33–125 (p. 94).

3 Pierre Macherey, 'The Text Says What It Does Not Say', trans. G. Hall, in *Literature in the Modern World*, ed. Dennis Walder (Oxford: Oxford University Press, 1990), pp. 215–22.

The unspeakable and the unsayable have become prominent in contemporary theory, particularly in the work of Giorgio Agamben, who (in common with many medievalists) draws on Foucault for the philosophical basis of his best-known and most controversial work, *Homo Sacer*,[4] and William Franke, who builds a philosophy of apophatic language that addresses negative theology through an encounter with Hegelian and Platonic debates.[5] For Franke, the limit of language is the crucial philosophical question of the age; for Agamben, too, the question of humanness and the political condition of living, of being permitted to live, is intimately bound up with the question of language. Wittgenstein famously concludes that, 'Whereof one cannot speak, thereof one must be silent.'[6] Yet, as Derrida shows in his late work, if we aim to be silent this does not mean we should be secret: translating the Freudian *Verneinung*, Derrida deconstructs the mechanism of the secret by showing how the initial negation – the assurance that what is secret will not be repeated – is itself negated when the person who possesses this knowledge repeats and represents it for themselves. 'There is a secret of denial [*dénégation*] and a denial [*dénégation*] of the secret. The secret as such, *as secret*, separates and already institutes a negativity; it is a negation that denies itself. It de-negates itself.'[7] To ensure something is not spoken of becomes a guarantee that it must be spoken of.

A growing body of scholarship interrogates the unspeakable as it is encountered in modern and postmodern history and culture, focusing especially on obscenity, pornography, torture, genocide and atrocity.[8] The body of potential

4 Giorgio Agamben, *Homo Sacer: Sovereign Power and Bare Life,* trans. Daniel Heller-Roazen (Stanford: Stanford University Press, 2001). See also Agamben, *Language and Death: The Place of Negativity*, trans. Karen E. Pinkus and Michael Hardt (Minneapolis: University of Minnesota Press, 1991); Agamben, *Potentialities: Collected Essays in Philosophy*, ed. and trans. Daniel Heller-Roazen (Stanford: Stanford University Press, 1999).

5 See William Franke, *On What Cannot Be Said: Apophatic Discourses in Philosophy, Religion, Literature, and the Arts*, 2 vols (Notre Dame: University of Notre Dame Press, 2007); Franke, *A Philosophy of the Unsayable* (Notre Dame: University of Notre Dame Press, 2014).

6 'Wovon man nicht sprechen kann, darüber muss man schweigen', Ludwig Wittgenstein, *Tractatus Logico-Philosophicus*, trans. C. K. Ogden (London: Kegan Paul, Trench, Trubner & Co., 1922), pp. 90, 162.

7 Jacques Derrida, 'How to Avoid Speaking: Denials', in S. Budick and W. Iser, eds, *Languages of the Unsayable: The Play of Negativity in Literature and Literary Theory* (New York: Columbia University Press, 1997), pp. 3–70 (p. 25, original emphasis).

8 See especially Peter Michelson, *Speaking the Unspeakable: A Poetics of Obscenity* (Albany, NY: SUNY Press, 1992); Naomi Mandel, *Against the Unspeakable: Complicity, the Holocaust, and Slavery in America* (Charlottesville: University of Virginia Press, 2006). Among other recent scholarship associating the unspeakable with torture and with the legacy of the Holocaust, see Sonja Boos, *Speaking the Unspeakable in Postwar Germany: Toward a Public Discourse on the Holocaust* (Ithaca: Cornell University Press,

critical works on the unspeakable is extensive: as a term, it attracts diverse theoretical interest and weight from different disciplines and critics. Franke's extensive work *On What Cannot Be Said* provides a broad and engaging account of both the scope of an intellectual endeavour whose participants range from Plato to John Cage, and the importance of this discussion to Western culture. At this point, he declares, apophatic discourse is 'assuming the role of a common language, a *koiné*, like Hellenistic Greek, for many expressions of the postmodern predicament'.[9] The medieval period is indeed found in these discussions: studies of negative theology and apophatic language that draw on medieval thinkers and mystics from Plotinus and Pseudo-Dionysius to Duns Scotus, Meister Eckhart and Marguerite Porete, have been re-examined and used to reconfigure psychological, sociological, philosophical and literary methodologies. Elizabeth Scala has shown how the particular rhetorical, editorial and material concerns and conditions of production obtaining in the Middle Ages give rise to a creative culture predicated on an '*other* text', in which 'the present text – presented here as the effect of an irretrievable, precursory text – displaces and replaces the absent narrative'.[10] However, with the notable exception of Karma Lochrie's *Covert Operations*, on the uses and abuses of secrecy in the Middle Ages, the place of the medieval unspeakable and its relation to the literature, popular theology and social texts of the Middle Ages has been less frequently studied. The many varieties of the medieval unspeakable and its tropes have not been examined as a focus so much as a characteristic element of other phenomena, principally apophatic mysticism on the one hand, and the suppression of same-sex eroticism on the other.

This book is not a history of the unspeakable, nor another philosophy of the unsayable. It is partly an attempt to intervene in critical discussions of apophatic language that co-opt from the medieval traditions of negative theology but do so for the illumination of contemporary texts and concerns, and tend not to engage with medieval culture or literature; it is also an attempt to explore the medieval unspeakable as it relates to the literary and the quotidian, as well as to the philosophical and the elevated. Lochrie deals with secrecy as 'a cultural operation [...] not limited to sexual constructions, acts, or identities but [which] travels freely among medieval and postmodern discourses alike'.[11] In as much as it develops a gendered reading

2014). I am very grateful to Emilie Morin for several discussions about this field of scholarship and for sharing her insights.

9 Franke, *On What Cannot Be Said*, vol. 2 (p. 11). Franke explores the work of poets, musicians, artists and architects in this second volume (pp. 37–48, 211–344).

10 Elizabeth Scala, *Absent Narratives: Manuscript Textuality, and Literary Structure in Late Medieval England* (New York: Palgrave Macmillan, 2002), p. 13.

11 Karma Lochrie, *Covert Operations: The Medieval Uses of Secrecy* (Philadelphia, PA: University of Pennsylvania Press, 1999), p. 5.

of the 'unspeakability topos', this book also owes a debt to Carolyn Dinshaw's *Getting Medieval* (1999), which extends the ground of late medieval literature almost up to the present day and employs a methodology of 'touch' in order to stimulate connections between the medieval and the (post)modern, as well as to Lochrie's theorised reading of secrecy in the light of medieval sources.[12] Though the concept of inexpressibility or ineffability as it applies to religious texts is the subject of wider scholarship,[13] this is an idea that emerges in relation to both the very good and the very bad in medieval literature, which manifests as places and spaces as well as words (not) on the page, and which is used strategically even as it threatens to overwhelm the authors and readers who encounter it.

MANY SILENCES

How to speak of the unspeakable? This was the classic conundrum of the confessional. Even as it became a mechanism of tremendous importance both as an essential of religious practice and as the paradigmatic framework of self-expression and self-knowledge, the practice of confession was underpinned by the manoeuvres of the unspeakable. Even Margery Kempe, for whom John the Baptist appears when she seeks a priest to shrive her, has a regular confessor, the 'gostly fadyr' first mentioned at the start of the narrative. He is sometimes sharp with her: it is his hastiness that forestalls the telling of Margery's own unspeakable sin at the outset of the narrative – the 'þing whech sche had so long conselyd' and which appears to precipitate her dalliance, but which is never revealed.[14] The Foucauldian evocation of confessional discourse includes the role played by obligation, force and, in extreme circumstances, torture, in ensuring that when confession is not 'dictated by some internal

12 See Lochrie, *Covert Operations*; Carolyn Dinshaw, *Getting Medieval: Sexualities and Communities, Pre- and Post-Modern* (Durham, NC: Duke University Press, 1999).

13 See, for example, Robin Kirkpatrick, *Dante's Inferno: Difficulty and Dead Poetry*, Cambridge Studies in Medieval Literature, 1 (Cambridge: Cambridge University Press, 1987); Robert S. Sturges, *Medieval Interpretation: Models of Reading in Literary Narrative, 1100–1500* (Carbondale, IL: Southern Illinois University Press, 1991). The 'inexpressibility topos' – see Ernst Robert Curtius, *European Literature and the Latin Middle Ages* (London: Routledge & Keegan Paul, 1953), pp. 159–62 for a widely cited description – is also the subject of critical readings of medieval poetry, particularly *Pearl*, whose themes of both bereavement and celestial vision provide amply inexpressible subject matter. See Theodore Bogdanos, *Pearl: Image of the Ineffable. A Study in Medieval Poetic Symbolism* (University Park, PA and London: Pennsylvania State University Press, 1983); and Ann Chalmers Watts, 'Pearl, Inexpressibility, and Poems of Human Loss', *PMLA* 99.1 (1984), 26–40.

14 See *The Book of Margery Kempe*, ed. Sandford Brown Meech and Hope Emily Allen, EETS o.s. 212 (Oxford: Oxford University Press, 1940), I. 1 (p. 7). Margery nevertheless continues to visit him throughout the course of the *Book*, some forty years.

imperative, [it] is wrung from a person by violence or threat'.[15] Whilst it is certainly true that medieval confessors had ways of making you talk (as evidenced by, for instance, the scripts for interrogation provided in some – but not all – *summae* and manuals of confession), the difficulty for the priest lay in talking of and dispensing penance for sin without giving his flock ideas. This could prove especially tricky if the sin in question was deemed 'unspeakable'. Raymond of Peñaforte, for example, advises in his thirteenth-century summa that a priest 'in his questions [...] not descend to special circumstances and special sins; for many fall severely after such an interrogation who otherwise never would have dreamt of it'.[16]

The concern that speaking may be tantamount to acting is perhaps most acute in respect of heresy. The transgressions attributed to Lollards, for example, in the 1401 statute *De heretico comburendo* ('On the burning of heretics', a ban on English 'Wyclif Bibles'), include 'dissensions, divisions, hurts, slanders, and perils' and the wicked lot responsible for these crimes are referred to as the *nephande secta* – the wicked – in fact, unspeakable – sect.[17] This designation for heretics of all stripes is found much earlier, in Bernard of Clairvaux's sermon on the *Song of Songs*, where he insisted of heretics that they secretly practised 'nefanda et obscena' acts, and compared these to the hind end of a fox.[18] While the Latin *nefandus* is there to underline the iniquity of the heresy, it becomes strikingly apt when the finer details of the orthodox and the heretical become so numerous and diverse, so incoherent, that authorities cannot even articulate what this crime is. Heresy occurred in many guises, after all, and on each side there would always be denial – as Karen Sullivan observes, 'The heretic of the Middle Ages, it would seem, never existed as a heretic'.[19]

The trope of unspeakability, of course, also unites the mystic and the heretic: for the former it is evoked to describe their experience, for the latter it is brandished in the condemnation of their acts. The writings of Marguerite Porete are a case in point. Her spiritual practice developed around a self-directed apophatic mysticism, the desire for the unspeakable, and was eventually enough for the inquisition to condemn both her and her book for heresy. Her text's continued and anonymous circulation throughout Europe made 'Marguerite Porete' an unspeakable and unwriteable name, but a mystic writer of great significance nonetheless.

15 Foucault, *Will to Knowledge*, p. 59.

16 Raymond of Peñaforte, *Raymundina*; quoted in Thomas N. Tentler, *Sin and Confession on the Eve of the Reformation* (Princeton, NJ: Princeton University Press, 1977), p. 88.

17 *De heretico comburendo* (1401), quoted in Paul Strohm, *Theory and the Premodern Text* (Minneapolis: University of Minnesota Press, 2000), pp. 28–9.

18 Bernard of Clairvaux, *Sermones super Cantica Cantorum*, *PL* 183, col. 1090A.

19 Sullivan, *Truth and the Heretic: Crises of Knowledge in Medieval French Literature* (Chicago: University of Chicago Press, 2005), p. 1.

As the standard formulae of mystic writing show clearly, the difficulty of the unspeakable comes not with the inability to speak, but rather with the compulsion. Take the dilemma of Angela of Foligno, who declares that 'it seems that everything we are trying to say about this experience reduces it to a mere trifle, because what took place is so different from what can be said about it. I myself am very ashamed that I cannot find better words to describe it.'[20] The answer to Lacan's question, 'Who is speaking?', can hardly be more complicated than when it is the subject of the mystic unconscious that is at issue.[21] For the writer of the mystic text is always faced with a seemingly unworkable paradox: the task of putting the intangible, ineffable nature of God into words – of speaking the unspeakable. While the mystic experience is entirely predicated on a personal, unmediated dialogue with the divine, when the mystic attempts to communicate this experience the words get in the way. Even Augustine, the most celebrated of confessors, occasionally had cause to wonder if so much speech could ever be other than a cause of conflict and contradiction:

> Have I spoken something, have I uttered something, worthy of God? No, I feel that all I have done is to wish to speak; if I did say something, it is not what I wanted to say. How do I know this? Simply because God is unspeakable [*ineffabilis*]. But what I have spoken would not have been spoken if it were unspeakable. For this reason God should not even be called unspeakable, because even when this word is spoken, something is spoken. There is a kind of conflict here: if what cannot be spoken is unspeakable, then it is not unspeakable, because it can actually be said to be unspeakable. It is better to evade this verbal conflict silently than to quell it disputatiously. Yet although nothing can be spoken in a way worthy of God, he has sanctioned the homage of the human voice, and chosen that we should derive pleasure from our words in praise of him.[22]

Augustine ponders whether it is better to be silent in order to avoid this conclusion; yet God has nevertheless accepted praise from human voices – 'Hence the fact that he is called God [*Deus*]: he himself is not truly known by the sound of these two syllables, yet when the sound strikes the ear it leads all users of the Latin language to think of a supremely excellent and immortal being.'[23] The writing of such worship naturally entails further difficulties: not only does the process introduce mediation on at least one level, but it inevitably filters and narrows the meaning of the interlocuted speech. Yet if these

[20] *Angela of Foligno: Complete Works*, ed. and trans. Paul Lachance, The Classics of Western Spirituality (New York: Paulist Press, 1993), p. 148.

[21] See Jacques Lacan, 'Subversion of Subject and Dialectic of Desire', in Écrits, trans. Alan Sheridan, pp. 323–60 (p. 331).

[22] Augustine, *On Christian Teaching*, trans. R. P. H. Green (Oxford: Oxford University Press, 1997), pp. 10–11. Augustine, *De doctrina Christiana: de vera religione*, ed. J. Martin, Corpus Christianorum Series Latina, vol. 32 (Turnhout: Brepols, 1962), I. 6.

[23] Augustine, *On Christian Teaching*, p. 11; Augustine, *De doctrina Christiana*, I. 6.

determinedly loquacious subjects are to find any way of speaking themselves – of attaining the privileged site of what Luce Irigaray terms *la mystérique* – their only recourse is to describe or attempt in some way to convey the divine, to 'make' God with words before it is possible to make themselves, with all the unspeakably blasphemous pitfalls that will entail. Irigaray's concept of 'mystic language or discourse' is a convergence of four different positions,[24] a place in which the torments of the mystic or martyr are felt as language fails, and in pursuit of which the speaker 'cannot specify exactly what she wants. Words begin to fail her. She senses something *remains to be said* [*rester à dire*] that resists all speech, that can at best be stammered out. All the words are weak, worn out, unfit to translate anything sensibly.'[25]

The recourse to such a declaration, that language is insufficient and God ineffable, is the particular preserve of apophatic or negative mysticism, which (beginning with the text of Pseudo-Dionysius and continuing with Richard of St Victor, Marguerite Porete in the Low Countries, Meister Eckhart, Tauler and Suso in Germany, and later the *Cloud*-author in England) holds that one may only speak of God in terms of what God is not.[26] Apophasis – literally, *speaking away* – is the defining characteristic of the neoplatonic tradition of mysticism, which narrates and creates the attempt to approach God (the Good, or the One), who transcends names and is therefore approachable only in language that must be taken back again.[27] Studies of mysticism and the apophatic have been used to analyse and rethink issues in psychology, sociology, literary study and philosophy, drawing on a medieval tradition if not always making contact with medieval culture itself.[28] As scholars of mystic

24 Luce Irigaray, 'La Mystérique', in *Speculum of the Other Woman*, trans. Gillian C. Gill (Ithaca, NY: Cornell University Press, 1985), pp. 191–202. As Gill notes, the coinage incorporates the four elements of 'mysticism, hysteria, mystery, and the femaleness ["*la* mystérique"] fundamental to the previous three' ('La Mystérique', note, p. 191.)

25 Irigaray, *Speculum of the Other Woman*, p. 193. Quotations from French from Irigaray, *Speculum de l'autre femme* (Paris: Éditions de Minuit, 1974), pp. 238–52 (original emphasis).

26 On apophatic mysticism, see Michael A. Sells, *Mystical Languages of Unsaying* (Chicago: Chicago University Press, 1994); Bruce Milem, *The Unspoken Word: Negative Theology in Meister Eckhart's German Sermons* (Washington, DC: Catholic University of America Press, 2002); Carmel Bendon Davies, *Mysticism and Space: Space and Spatiality in the Works of Richard Rolle, 'The Cloud of Unknowing' Author and Julian of Norwich* (Washington, DC: Catholic University of America Press, 2008).

27 For histories and reconsiderations of apophatic discourse and mysticism, see Raoul Mortley, *From Word to Silence* (Bonn: Peter Hanstein, 1986); Bernard McGinn's trilogy of works, *The Foundations of Mysticism* (London: SCM Press, 1992), *The Growth of Mysticism* (London: SCM Press, 1995), *The Flowering of Mysticism* (New York: Crossroads, 1998); Jean-Luc Marion, *The Idol and Distance* (New York: Fordham Press, 2001); Denys Turner, 'How To Read the Pseudo-Denys Today?', *International Journal of Systematic Theology* 7.4 (2005), 428–40.

28 For a recent survey of the intersections of apophasis and psychoanalysis, see David

writing and apophatic speech have shown, the poetics of such a discourse draws on metaphors of emanation as well as negation, where self–other and here–there distinctions collapse. The refusal to name names reinforces the non-speaker's inability to grasp the One, and the One's unknowability and transcendence (and immanence).

Nevertheless, though the truth of such phenomena all but defies description, the fervent wish to disclose and share even this non-transferable gift compels the mystic to make the effort anyway. If it is impossible to speak or write the truth of God, this is evidently not a good enough reason to stop trying. Carmel Bendon Davis, writing on both apophatic and affective mystics of the late Middle Ages, suggests that 'Ineffability [...] may have troubled the mystics in theory but it had minimal effect on them in practice', arguing that the concept 'had more to do with their acknowledgement of God's inexpressible "essence" than with any limits that language may have seemed to impose on their ability to explain the human experience of God'.[29]

The medieval apophatic tradition is very important to the long history of apophatic discourse and to thought about the unspeakable, and mystic discourse and writing may, of course, enter (and, indeed, drive) a discussion of the medieval unspeakable in fascinating and gendered ways. Likewise, its study does reflect on and intersect with awareness of gender and sexuality when the erotics of a text written by a male or female contemplative evokes a gendered experience of the ineffable.[30] As Sigridur Gudmarsdottir summarises, for feminist theologians writing on the challenges of mysticism and apophasis the stakes are defined by how 'the practices of unsaying or undoing [could] render anything salient to bodies and materiality, to which women have been traditionally linked in the Western theo-philosophical corpus'.[31] The body of scholarship on apophatic mysticism is already substantial and as such it is a topic for a book, rather than a chapter. The stakes of negative theology remain relevant, though, when turning to other linguistic gestures – or, as Sells puts it, *languages of unsaying* – that take in more mundane contexts: the experience and accommodation or repudiation of the non-normative, the dilemmas of confession, the relation of the human

Henderson, *Apophatic Elements in the Theory and Practice of Psychoanalysis: Pseudo-Dionysius and C. G. Jung* (London: Routledge, 2014), pp. 1–10. In 'Lacan and Bion: Psychoanalysis and the Mystical Language of "Un-Saying"', *Journal of Melanie Klein and Object Relations* 15.2 (1997), 243–64, Michael A. Sells and James Webb discuss the mystic and apophatic qualities of the Lacanian 'real' and Bion's preoccupation with naming and the unknown.

29 Davis, *Mysticism and Space: Space and Spatiality in the Works of Richard Rolle, The Cloud of Unknowing Author, and Julian of Norwich* (Washington, DC: Catholic University of America Press, 2008), p. 112.

30 As Sells has shown: see *Mystical Languages of Unsaying*, pp. 116–205.

31 Sigridur Gudmarsdottir, 'Feminist Theology and the Sensible Unsaying of Mysticism', in *Apophatic Bodies: Negative Theology, Incarnation, and Relationality*, ed. Chris Boesel and Catherine Keller (Bronx, NY: Fordham University Press, 2009), pp. 273–85 (p. 273).

and non-human, the physicality of speech, how all of these are represented in literature and culture and how they contribute to an understanding of discourses on gender and sexuality in the Middle Ages.

A THOUSAND TONGUES

The unspeakable and the ineffable are, perhaps predictably (especially in the case of mysticism, which so often draws its force precisely from what it cannot express), harnessed to the utterances with which medieval discourse speaks, or attempts to speak, of heaven, hell and purgatory. In a very material move for such abstract subject matter, the connection between an overabundance of speech and no speech at all is perhaps most sharply drawn in the trope of the iron voice. In one common trope, hell is not speakable even by a hundred or, as in the case of the thirteenth-century devotional text *Sawles Ward*, even a thousand tongues. The writer of this treatise declares, 'Ich habbe bigunne to tellen of þing þet Ich ne mahte nawt bringe to ende, þah Ich hefde a þusent tungen of stele ant talde aðet ha weren alle forwerede' (I have begun to tell of things I could not bring to any conclusion, even if I had a thousand tongues of steel and spoke until they were all worn out).[32] There is a long tradition of the pains of hell or purgatory being described with this expression, which Robert Hasenfratz traces in the *Aeneid* and a Latin redaction of the *Visio Pauli*.[33] It occurs at several points in Old English literature and continues in later Middle English (and indeed beyond). The many and various pains of hell and purgatory, that are so great that no tongue can tell them, are quite often accompanied by a variation on this expression of inexpressibility.[34] Virgil may have originally adapted it from Homer or some common source, and he seems himself quite taken with the image: not only is it used to describe hell but he also declares his inability to cover all of the subjects of poetry in the same way.[35] Like any good metaphor for unspeakability, it yokes together the

32 'Custody of the Soul' (*Sawles Ward*), in *Medieval English Prose for Women*, ed. and trans. Bella Millett and Jocelyn Wogan-Browne (Oxford: Oxford University Press, 1990), pp. 92–3. See also J. A. W. Bennett and G. V. Smithers, eds, *Early Middle English Verse and Prose*, 2nd edn (Oxford: Oxford University Press, 1974), p. 423, n. 129.

33 See Robert Hasenfratz, 'Eisegan stefne (*Christ and Satan* 36a), the *Visio Pauli*, and ferrea vox (*Aeneid* 6, 626)', *Modern Philology* 86 (1989), 398–410, on the iron voice or tongue and its sources. See also *Jerome's Epitaph on Paula: A Commentary on the Epitaphium Sanctae Paulae*, ed. Andrew Cain (Oxford: Oxford University Press, 2013), p. 99.

34 See Eileen Gardiner, *Visions of Heaven and Hell Before Dante* (New York: Italica, 1989); Gardiner, *Medieval Visions of Heaven and Hell: A Sourcebook* (London: Routledge, 1993), especially pp. xxvi–xxxi.

35 On Virgil's possible sources see Stephen Hinds, *Allusion and Intertext: Dynamics of Appropriation in Roman Poetry* (Cambridge: Cambridge University Press, 1998), pp. 35–9. Virgil describes the pains of hell in *Aeneid* (VI. 625–7) in this way:

> non, mihi si linguae centum sint oraque centum,

worst and the best. Yet when matters approach closer to earth the unspeakable utterance becomes, if anything, even more potent. Unspeakability is to be expected in heaven and hell: it weighs far more heavily on the corporeal and the terrestrial, the human behaviour this book treats. The lower the subject matter, it seems, the higher the stakes.

The medieval unspeakable thus forms a continuum that makes unmentionable sin contiguous with the unsayable divine that is figured as its opposite. Structurally, they may represent opposite ends of an ethical continuum; however, they might equally be seen as occupying the same metaphysical plane in that both are of the world, and yet the logic that underpins their place in our understanding – and in orthodox social and theological orders – insists they are also not of the world, the one being beyond it and the other cast out of it. Barbara Newman's recent work on 'crossover', or the '*sic et non* principle', is helpful here in as much as it reminds us that in medieval texts, 'Sometimes incompatible meanings simply collide.'[36] Where the sacred is always a given, even within the secular, Newman argues, 'Ambivalence itself is a key part of the meaning that must not be exegeted away.'[37] How does the inability to frame the divine in mundane language compare with the refusal to name a practice or behaviour one wishes to marginalise? On the one hand, such moments may both be assessed as flashpoints for the imperfect relation of language to that which it describes, the tension between capture and escape that sustains speech and renders yet more of it necessary.[38] On the other hand, these are also manifestations of a relation between individuals and power structures that are revealed in and take place through language.

While the aphaeresis advocated in neoplatonic thought, abstracting from the lower in order to gain a sense of the higher, implicates (for instance) the mundane in contemplation of the divine, the unspeakable is invested in and

> ferrea uox, omnes scelerum comprendere formas,
> omnia poenarum percurrere nomina possim.
>
> (Nay, had I a hundred tongues, a hundred mouths, and voice of iron, I could not sum up all the forms of crime, or rehearse all the tale of torments.)

R. A. B. Mynors, ed., *P Vergili Maronis Opera* (Oxford: Clarendon, 1969). *Virgil: Eclogues, Georgics, Aeneid I–VI*, Loeb Classical Library, trans. H. Rushton Fairclough and Rev. G. P. Goold (Cambridge, MA: Harvard University Press, 1999), p. 577. (The image also appears in *Georgics*, II. 42–4).

36 Barbara Newman, *Medieval Crossover: Reading the Secular Against the Sacred* (Notre Dame, IN: University of Notre Dame Press, 2013), p. 8.

37 Newman, *Medieval Crossover*, p. 11.

38 Leslie Dunton-Downer makes a similar observation of obscenity and its relation to poetic language, and indeed language in general, since 'Obscene language resides in an unusual poetic space of neither-norness that calls attention, ultimately, to certain (poetic) paradoxes and problems inherent in the language system.' See Dunton-Downer, 'Poetic Language and the Obscene', in *Obscenity: Social Control and Artistic Creation*, ed. Jan M. Ziolkowski (Leiden: Brill, 1998), pp. 19–37 (p. 25).

predicated on the experience of the body. What does it mean that the divine and the unspeakable may be articulated, or not articulated, through the same structure? When the body is a hindrance or a conundrum for the mystic, and to the gestures towards the transcendent, where should this body enter into a theology of unsaying? Catherine Keller detects a certain element of resistance or suspicion when she wonders, 'Is it an accident that just as certain groups marked as bodies, long silenced for their bodily difference, begin to find voice within theological institutions a mysticism of transcendent silence becomes trendy?'[39] Yet the apophatic and the unspeakable do work through the body – an utterance or the record of an utterance requires the mouth that moves, the hand that writes, the ear that receives, the eye that sees. The body is intimately involved in the unspeakable as in order to speak, say, name, there must be something to speak, say or name with; in order not to speak, there has to be the possibility of speaking and a body that does not speak, does not hear. Moreover, this is a body that is inevitably invested in its own corporeality, and that is gendered, differentiated and marked by race, native ability, situation, location. Gudmarsdottir takes up this concern in her contemplation of 'apophatic bodies', asking what possible bodies these might be: 'Would they be free bodies or maybe silenced bodies, nobodies, raped, battered, and mutilated bodies, gendered, transsexual, queer bodies?'[40] For her part, Gudmarsdottir looks to the apophatic mode as one that might 'perhaps help unravel those ideologies that oppress, silence, and batter those bodies, or heap them into a singular idealised body and its abjected other'.[41]

The unspeakable is a mode that queers the apophatic, the divine and transcendent, that recalls and even foregrounds their relation to the flesh. The study of medieval gender and sexuality brings into focus the acknowledgement of 'an economy of the unsayable and the sayable as the basis of every possible language'.[42] One's place in such an economy depends on one's access to language; since subjects brought into relation by a shared language by no means possess the same access to that language, the awareness of who or what is speaking and who or what is spoken becomes a powerful measure of structural inequality. Aristotle insisted that while the possession of voice indicated possession of a soul,[43] language is 'peculiar to man. For while whatever has language has a voice, not everything that has voice has language.'[44]

39 Catherine Keller, 'The Cloud of the Impossible: Embodiment and Apophasis', in Boesel and Keller, *Apophatic Bodies*, pp. 25–44 (p. 26).

40 Gudmarsdottir, 'Sensible Unsaying', p. 275.

41 Gudmarsdottir, 'Sensible Unsaying', p. 275.

42 Franke, *Philosophy of the Unsayable*, p. 21.

43 'Voice is a particular sound made by something with a soul; for nothing which does not have a soul has a voice', Aristotle, *De Anima*, II. 8. 420b5 in *De Anima II–III*, trans. D. W. Hamlyn (Oxford: Clarendon Press, 1993), p. 32.

44 Aristotle, *The History of Animals*, IV. 9. 536b2–3, in *The Complete Works of Aristotle:*

In such a context, language and the ability to use it is that which separates the human from the animal: to suppress an individual's speech is to dehumanise, and to find behaviours or identities unspeakable is to threaten the humanity and justify the exclusion of those who engage with them.[45] In the Middle Ages, when individual self-expression and relations within communities were so thoroughly intertwined with the recognition and confession of sin on the one hand, and the regulatory influence of liturgical and parochial custom on the other, the greater the perceived affiliation with sin and the flesh, the further the societal validation of one's expression and relationships diminished. I argue that the consideration of gender and sexuality – of bodies – is important to the unspeakable not because of the sexual sins categorised as unspeakable but because of the comparative silence on and of non-male, non-heterosexual, non-normative individuals and communities. Medieval (and modern) subjects do not enjoy parity in their access to language, and language reflects who or what is speaking or being spoken – there are those subjects who are less likely to speak for themselves and those whose speech is more likely to be validated. The unspeakable links up the inability to speak with an experience of incoherence or discoherence of the body, with abjection, with a continuum of the internal and external. As a phenomenon it reveals something about how institutions are constructed, and in so doing it is capable of radically deconstructing. The stakes are still relevant at a time when, for instance, same-sex marriage has been brought into law but debates about traditional and conservative values still rage, or when lesbian, gay, bisexual, genderqueer, transgender and non-binary individuals have rarely been so visible and yet this visibility is still accompanied by reactionary rhetoric and hate speech.

THE UNSPEAKABLE: IN THEORY

When speech fails, for whatever reason, the gap it leaves requires another, equally 'unspeakable' mode of expression to bridge it. There is not a template for the study of the unspeakable so much as there is an insistence on the different milieux of the unspeakable and the theoretical positions it 'speaks' to. Its appearance as a concept can be characterised in different ways – as acts, identities, spaces – and involves the coalescing and co-operation of the metaphorical, rhetorical, legal, theological, cultural. Analysing how the unspeakable underpins symbolic orders in the realms of legal and political discourse, as well as theological and penitential, inevitably a sense of binarism emerges – expressed and suppressed speech, included and excluded bodies,

The Revised Oxford Translation, ed. Jonathan Barnes, 2 vols (Princeton, NJ: Princeton University Press, 1984), I (p. 848).

45 For a range of explorations of human, divine and animal voices and silences, see *Voice and Voicelessness in Medieval Europe*, ed. Irit Ruth Kleiman, The New Middle Ages (Basingstoke: Palgrave Macmillan, 2015).

prescribed and proscribed acts – and with equal inevitability dissolves, but not without providing a focus for important questions. What is the medieval unspeakable? How is it gendered? What forms does it take and how can it be read? How do the non-speaking return to discourse? What is the role of the unspeakable as a concept and (differently) as a label? These questions may be extended and transformed further when they are examined through one of the many theoretical lenses that may be introduced – the unspeakable might be explored from the perspective of the postcolonial, the posthuman, the animal[46] – but here my concern is gender. How does unspeakability interact with and influence our understanding of medieval gender and sexuality?

This book has a broad historical remit and its theoretical affiliations are likewise diverse, but they crystallise around the legacy of Foucault and Lacan's work on silence, language and power.[47] If Foucault's fascination with discourse and silence is their making and breaking of institutional power, Lacan's interest is the negotiation of a symbolic order that 'makes' its speakers even as it represents where they must break from this same order. Like Foucault, though perhaps less frequently, Lacan draws on the Middle Ages to ground his statements or throw their concepts into relief – and, like Foucault, with variable resonances for medievalists.[48] He muses that the early years of psychoanalysis might be compared to 'the structure of what was called in the Middle Ages, "the liberal arts"', associating these on the one hand with a lack of 'true formalization' and a concern with 'a body of privileged problems', but on the other hand acknowledging their particular 'humanity'.[49] The Lacanian structural paradigm of the psyche and language develops the idea that language says something other than what is said and that language figures a 'real' that cannot be perfectly captured by either the 'symbolic' or the 'imaginary', but which may be traced by their gaps, dissonances and shortcomings. In the Lacanian orders, where the big Other, or God, is that which cannot be grasped by the symbolic, and yet which underpins the operations of the symbolic, the utterly transcendent indeed becomes the utterly immanent. Foucault's emphasis on the contingency of what is otherwise thought of as central and essential, and on the material traces not the narrative they might fit into, takes up the unspeakable in the architecture of the social and the epistemological, and especially with relation to power.

46 For a fascinating engagement with these theoretical debates in relation to contemporary literature, see Kalpana Rahita Seshadri, *HumAnimal: Race, Law, Language*, post humanities 21 (Minneapolis: University of Minnesota Press, 2012).

47 In particular, Foucault's *History of Sexuality* and Lacan's *Seminar*, Books XI and XX (which respectively deal with, among other topics, the concept of the Lacanian other and the access of women to language and the symbolic order of representation).

48 For an extended discussion of Lacan's reading of medieval texts, see Erin Felicia Labbie, *Lacan's Medievalism* (Minneapolis: University of Minnesota Press, 2006).

49 Lacan, 'Function and Field', in *Écrits*, pp. 83–4.

Among the critics from whom I draw, Agamben in particular looks to Foucault for the development of his extended analysis and elaboration of modern biopower and biopolitics.[50] I also turn to the intersection of feminist theory, philosophy and (erstwhile Lacanian) psychoanalysis represented in the works of Irigaray, Cixous and Kristeva in response to unspoken assumptions and gendered blind-spots that inform the writings of both Agamben and Lacan. Irigaray deploys Hegelian twoness in answer to Lacan's primary signifier, famously focusing on the twoness of lips, a twoness that is not two things added together, not one and the other, and not creating a hole that signifies a lack.[51] Kristeva, meanwhile, finds her model for the resistance of phallocentrism in the *khora*, theorising a chaotic and prelinguistic space from Plato's quasi-maternal receptacle.[52]

The implication of the unspoken, as opposed to simple silence, is that what is unspoken is already known. The unspeakable therefore participates in the intimate and inextricable connection of this dichotomy of spoken and unspoken. By exploring the unspeakable in medieval literature, I want to investigate two key manoeuvres: the strategic refusal to refer to something in speech (such as is the case with, for example, sodomy), and the inability to express something in words (for instance, when attempting to speak of God). In the economy of the partial through which language operates, neither trait equates to a disappearance of the listener's awareness of whatever it is that is deemed 'unspeakable'; on the contrary, each reveals a different effect of the same phenomenon – the missing fragment. While the refusal to refer essentially removes a name or sign from discourse, effecting one of the many Foucauldian silences that 'underlie' it, the inability to refer tends to inspire, conversely, the attempt to appropriate new names or to resort to symbols in order to find a missing link: the 'response of the other' that will confirm one is understood. A discursive hole made by a missing fragment can be filled until it is overflowing with alternative solutions.

SPEAKING OF THE UNSPEAKABLE

The chapters that follow are organised in two parts, which might be broadly characterised as exploring the linguistic and the physical – how the linguistic

50 On Agamben's engagement with biopower, see in particular *Homo Sacer: Sovereign Power and Bare Life*, trans. Daniel Heller-Roazen (Stanford: Stanford University Press, 2001); *Remnants of Auschwitz*, trans. Daniel Heller-Roazen (New York: Zone Books, 2002); *State of Exception*, trans. Kevin Attell (Chicago: University of Chicago Press, 2005).

51 See Luce Irigaray, *This Sex Which Is Not One*, trans. Catherine Porter (Ithaca, NY: Cornell University Press, 1985); Irigaray, *Speculum of the Other Woman*.

52 See Julia Kristeva, *Powers of Horror: An Essay on Abjection*, trans. Leon S. Roudiez (New York: Columbia University Press, 1982).

conditions the physical and how the physical conditions the linguistic. Thematically, Chapters 1 and 2 coalesce around the analysis of sin, suppression of speech, and the dialogic relation of speech and silence, principally in relation to cultural constructs, particularly confession; Chapters 3 and 4, around analysis of political life and law, the non-human and dehumanising, and the dynamic of exile and return, principally in relation to socio-legal structures and the operations of power. The selection of texts reflects the principal themes in and through which the unspeakable works, and works particularly on gender.

Chapter 1 contrasts the open spaces and expression and gender fluidity of the Old English *Mary of Egypt* with *Ancrene Wisse*'s enclosed spaces, suppressed speech and concern with the closed female body. Both texts were copied and translated many times in Latin and the European vernaculars, and both stage confession and worldliness. The issue at stake here is not only sexuality but also the negotiation of individualistic spirituality and social convention. The chapter thus considers the operation of the unspeakable in the penitent–confessor relationship, where unspeakable things reside in the (male) ecclesiastic rather than in the female confessing subject, whether she is a penitent whore or an enclosed recluse. The behaviours of these very different holy women both underscore the limitations imposed on them by gender, location and sensory (and sensual) experience, and at the same time undermine these same limits, producing instead a performance of liminality, synaesthetic expression and queer gender (particularly in the case of Mary and Zosimus). Socially or physically marginalised and continually poised in the middle, the anchoress and her desert saint exemplar end up straying far from their initial settings, in a type of performance that privileges space yet loves boundaries.

From confession, the next chapter moves to familiar ground – the unspeakable sin. Part of the challenge for contemporary medievalists writing about the unspeakable sin is that there has been so much great scholarship on this phenomenon, yet equally it would be unthinkable to leave out this ideal case study for both the rhetorical and interpretative manoeuvres the unspeakable performs and their bearing on a study of medieval gender and sexuality. Taking a cue from such scholars as Larry Scanlon and William Burgwinkle,[53] in Chapter 2 I look at the contradictions and the unnaturalness of the natural, and at the scarcity of women in discussions of sodomy and the unnatural vice (along with Lochrie and Jacqueline Murray). While Chaucer's Pardoner has become one of the usual suspects in this discussion, work on the most infamous (male) sodomite of the Middle Ages still neatly illustrates

53 See Larry Scanlon, 'Speaking the Unspeakable: Sexual Regulation and the Priesthood of Genius', *Romanic Review* 86.2 (1995), 213–42; William E. Burgwinkle, *Sodomy, Masculinity, and Law in Medieval Literature: France and England, 1050–1230* (Cambridge: Cambridge University Press, 2004).

its stakes. By contrast, Gower's artful treatment of the legend of Iphis and Iante is exemplary of that 'twice marginalised', twice unspeakable figure Murray identifies in medieval erotic life – the medieval lesbian. Meanwhile, the *Roman de Silence* responds to and complicates the 'grammar of sex' in Alain de Lille's *De Planctu Naturae* with the contest between Nature, Nurture, Reason and God that plays out in, on and through the body of its protagonist. Lacan's theoretical framework has been used in the past to analyse the 'Pardoner's Tale', while Irigaray's answer to Lacan's seminar on gender offers a counterpoint to Lacanian readings on unspeakability. Where the workings of repression and power upon sexuality may produce silence, it is a silence that breeds whispers, more and more possible 'fits' to fill the pointed pause in discourse, and a focus for a lot of speculation. Here I explore the proliferation of speech on unspeakable, 'unnatural' acts, and how this generative potential is tapped precisely by turning bodies into (unspeakable) words.

The second half of the book examines the role played in law, society and language by what has been excluded. Chapter 3 links two texts about 'wolves' and exile: *Wulf and Eadwacer* and *Bisclavret,* two reflexes of the medieval werewolf narrative that exemplify the semantic flexibility and instability of Old English poetry and the self-conscious semantic hybridity of writers of French in England. *Bisclavret* meditates on externality and animality, the apparent lack of voice; *Wulf and Eadwacer* similarly engages with conceptual, spatial and textual boundaries, with a particular focus on identity. Present both within and outside the prevailing order, the continued manifestation of the strategically unmentionable serves as a constant reminder of the formative exclusion upon which the spoken – the nameable, the representable portion of reality – is founded. Continuing the analysis of boundaries from Chapter 1, I trace the implications of Giorgio Agamben's work on *sacratio* and bare life for the women in these texts, drawing on Kristeva as a counter to Agamben's somewhat genderless, or presumptively gendered, model. While *Bisclavret* focuses on protagonists whose voices, indeed, whose very humanity, are at risk of permanent removal under the sovereign ban, the textual slipperiness of *Wulf and Eadwacer* reveals again the challenge of acknowledging gender amid multiple interpretations and a text that seems to speak with more than one voice.

Chapter 4 returns to Chaucer and Gower, focusing on the 'Tale of Tereus' (of *Confessio Amantis,* book V), otherwise known, as it is in the *Legend of Good Women*, as the story of Philomela. In these narratives, the themes of the previous chapters combine with particular force in the story of the raped, mutilated and silenced protagonist. Sexual violence is conflated with incest and infanticide – two more unspeakable crimes – and enclosure is Tereus's method of ensuring silence. Philomela's lack of voice does not align her with the animal (indeed, neither does Bisclavret's) but unlike Bisclavret she becomes one in regaining her voice. The tale foregrounds once more the physical and material character of the unspeakable, and the chapter considers the implications of gender in 'glossing' medieval tongue cutting, looking both at contexts for symbolic disfigurement and the alternative 'tongues' and literary or artistic prostheses to which it gives rise. Tracing themes of dismemberment, prosthesis and gender switching – in Gower and in other treatments of the legend – it argues that the feminine performances of Procne and Philomela combine not only to restore Philomela's voice but to deprive Tereus of his. In its silent communication of an unspeakable crime, Philomela's embroidered message performs the work her tongue threatens to do before Tereus cuts it out: a form of proto-écriture féminine as expounded by Hélène Cixous, with Philomela's final transformation into a bird speaking to Cixous's metaphor for female speech that steals and flies.[54]

One more point I wish to mention in this introduction is the stance I adopt with regard to the chronology of primary texts. During the period that falls between those that are traditionally and securely Old and Middle, two developments unfolded that have a particular impact on the study of the unspeakable in medieval life. Firstly, confession and its texts and mechanisms were becoming increasingly prominent and systematised in canon law. The period of the Crusades, from the late eleventh century, saw growing concern with the importance of suppressing heretical sects, a concern highlighted in the canons of Lateran III (1179) and IV (1215). The ordination of priests was more strictly limited, princes were urged to suppress heretical activity, sodomy was designated a sin against nature and confession was made compulsory. Secondly, the system of jurisprudence in England underwent the shift from Anglo-Saxon vernacular law codes to the post-Conquest Latinate system of common law. Juridical processes on the Continent were undergoing lasting change with the interest in and revival of Roman law, in particular Justinian's Digest and Code.[55] In England, meanwhile, Henry II's reforms, beginning in the 1160s, sought to clarify the distinctions between the new 'Common Law' and canon law. In the process they provoked the Becket crisis, but they did have the effect of rationalising legal administration, greatly extending the use of juries (as opposed to trial by combat) and providing an orderly system of appeals. Only royal courts could now try criminal cases, but reforms allowed tenants to look to their landlord's superior: the king. The first two chapters here are on themes that are intertwined with the increasingly formalised mechanism of confession and the need to speak, the second on themes related to the individual's access to power and speech. (Nor are the implications of these changes for studies of gender incidental, as Jo Ann McNamara shows in

[54] See Hélène Cixous, 'The Laugh of the Medusa', trans. Keith Cohen and Paula Cohen, *Signs: Journal of Women in Culture and Society* 1.4 (1976), 875–93.

[55] Charles M. Radding and Antonio Chiaralli, *The Corpus Iuris Civilis in the Middle Ages: Manuscripts And Transmission from the Sixth Century to the Juristic Revival* (Leiden: Brill, 2007).

her analysis of how the reshaped ecclesiastical and legal system precipitated a crisis of masculinity even as it seemed to cement male social dominance).[56]

The texts in this book cover the period from the tenth to the fifteenth century, including two Old English texts (*Mary of Egypt*, *Wulf and Eadwacer*), three Middle English texts (Chaucer's *The Canterbury Tales* and *Legend of Good Women*, Gower's *Confessio Amantis*), two texts from the high Middle Ages in England (*Ancrene Wisse*, *Bisclavret*) and other French analogues. To this extent, my methodology also engages another near-inexpressible phenomenon – the process by which Old English is divided (and separated off) from Middle English. This is a topic that has long exercised scholars of medieval texts,[57] but which has gained more attention in recent years from scholars looking to push beyond the existing categories and exclusions. This push is in part geared towards the peculiar lacuna that the traditional markers 'Old' and 'Middle' both create and obscure (and geared as well at the attendant 'gap' in the medievalists' market). While the changes that occur in the language over several centuries – particularly post-Conquest – are inevitably marked by transition and crossover, the canonical 'Old' and 'Middle' do not always reflect the subtler shifts. Scholars have called for a greater degree of connectivity between these bodies of text, exploring more diverse interpretations of the past by means of interdisciplinary or collaborative efforts.[58] The so-called long twelfth century is ground that Christopher Cannon has explored in recent years, as has Elaine Treharne, whose work on the English of post-Conquest England (responding to Cannon's), has broadened the horizons of early and late medievalists even further.[59] This is part of a move that, as Clare Lees argues, encourages Anglo-Saxonists to '[rethink] the before-and-after model of periodization'.[60]

56 See 'The *Herrenfrage*: The Restructuring of the Gender System, 1050–1150', in *Medieval Masculinities: Regarding Men in the Middle Ages*, Medieval Cultures 7, ed. Clare A. Lees, Thelma S. Fenster and Jo Ann McNamara (Minneapolis: University of Minnesota Press, 1994), pp. 3–29.

57 See, for example, Kemp Malone, 'When Did Middle English Begin?', *Language* 6 (1930), 110–17.

58 See, for example, Fred Orton, Ian Wood and Clare A. Lees, *Fragments of History: Rethinking the Ruthwell and Bewcastle Monuments* (Manchester: Manchester University Press, 2007).

59 See Christopher Cannon, 'Between the Old and the Middle of English', *New Medieval Literatures* 7 (2005), 203–21; Cannon, *The Grounds of English Literature* (Oxford: Oxford University Press, 2007); *Re-Writing English in the Twelfth Century*, ed. Mary Swan and Elaine M. Treharne (Cambridge: Cambridge University Press, 2006); Elaine Treharne, *Living Through Conquest: The Politics of Early English, 1020–1220* (Oxford: Oxford University Press, 2012).

60 Clare A. Lees, 'Actually Existing Anglo-Saxon Studies', *New Medieval Literatures* 7 (2005), 223–52 (p. 228). See also Allen J. Frantzen, *Desire for Origins: New Language, Old English, and Teaching the Tradition* (New Brunswick, NJ: Rutgers University Press, 1990).

Bearing all this in mind, I will be looking here at the Old and Middle English traditions, but also what lies between them. The choice of texts is, of course, representative; the whole of a period such as this could not be persuaded into a single book. It also represents what might fairly be called the canon, but with an effort to read the texts in a different way. Medievalists have taken to reimagining temporality, testing different possibilities of understanding a past that is frequently conceived in terms that are alien, static, completed: Carolyn Dinshaw's much-cited dynamic of contingency – 'touching' the past – is now in its second decade.[61] While I orient individual texts in their socio-historical contexts, this is not a strictly chronological approach. Throughout this book I argue for two strategies of articulating the unspeakable – the one emphasising the space of a missing word or fragment, the other addressing the play of overlapping and conflicting utterances that may render a subject uncategorisable or unnameable – which may also be characterised by their relation to chronology. This is a mutable, back-and-forth movement, whereby the latter strategy might be seen as working forwards through time, from the thing that is unspeakable to the proliferation of utterances that emerge in its circumlocution, while the former is inclined to work backwards, looking from the unspeakable or the absent towards what may once have been speakable, was once present.

In striving to recover lost access to speech, there are more lost things to be uncovered, more loose ends and more unanswered questions. Not everything has been written, nor said – there are things that get left out or glossed over, missing pieces, missing persons and ghosts that skulk, unacknowledged, behind texts. In engaging with the unspeakable as a means of analysing the fragmentary relationships between the present and absent, spoken and unspoken, I have also in mind the modern experience of the medieval. Pursuing the strategic silences evoked by Foucault as they occur in the distances and disconnections that so often seem to define this experience, I wish to show instead how the unspeakable may work to negotiate these distances, and provide an account of how the silent and past can be heard to speak to the present.

61 See Dinshaw, *Getting Medieval*, p. 12 and *passim*. For the continuing impact of Dinshaw's metaphors of touch, see the special issue of *Journal of the History of Sexuality* 10.2 (2001), ed. Elizabeth A Castelli; Kathy Cawsey, *Twentieth Century Chaucer Criticism: Reading Audiences* (London: Rouledge, 2016), pp. 123–30.

1

SPEAKING UP AND SHUTTING UP: EXPRESSION AND SUPPRESSION IN THE OLD ENGLISH MARY OF EGYPT AND ANCRENE WISSE

The elderly religious woman – wrinkled, white haired, huddled in a wrap she has borrowed for the occasion – smiles at the visitor whose questions she has been indulging. 'My life at that time was a hard one. Food was so scarce I had to ration myself very severely and I saw no-one. But I was guided by Our Lady.' She grows more candid. 'The real problem was, I was simply filled with desire for fucking.'

The extended interview between St Mary of Egypt and the monk Zosimus does not generally take this form, of course. In making it understood that her former lifestyle was one of unbridled hedonism and licentious behaviour, Mary herself does not put too fine a point on it: she describes her vices and desires as *unasecgendlic* – unspeakable – and she is tormented by her thoughts of *hæmed* – sex, or (to borrow a translation in Mary's own unvarnished style) fucking.[1] Mary's desire is not contained in a sanitised or circumlocutory turn of phrase, though modern treatments of her *vita* sometimes find one.[2] While Mary calls her sins unspeakable, the lesson of her life is that there are occasions when the only thing more important than constraining speech is

1 See Clare A. Lees and Diane Watt, 'Age and Desire in the Old English *Life of St Mary of Egypt*: A Queerer Time and Place?' in *Middle-Aged Women in the Middle Ages*, ed. Sue Niebrzydowski (Cambridge: D. S. Brewer, 2011), pp. 53–68 (p. 59).

2 Mary's thought of *hæmed* most often becomes 'thought of intercourse', as the literal meaning implies (see Bosworth-Toller; *hæmed* also covers marital sex, whereas adultery or fornication may be *woh-hæmed* or *unriht hæmed*). See, for instance, Hugh Magennis, *The Old English Life of St Mary of Egypt* (Exeter: Exeter University Press, 2002), p. 101. Elsewhere, Leslie Donovan translates this concept as passion; see *Women Saints' Lives in Old English Prose*, ed. and trans. Donovan (Cambridge, D. S. Brewer, 1999), pp. 97–120 (p. 114). Benedicta Ward translates the Latin of Paul the Deacon – 'Cogitationes (…) ad fornicationem' – as thoughts of 'harlotry'; Mary's subsequent admission, 'Ignis intus infelix corpus meum nimis succendebat, et totam me per omnia exurebat, et ad desiderium commistionis pertrahebat' (a fire burned fiercely inside my miserable body and consumed my whole being through and through, luring me into a longing for intercourse) goes untranslated by Ward, and here Mary asks only, 'how could I tell you about those?'. See *Vitae Patrum*, *PL* 73, cols 671–90, trans. Ward, in *Harlots of the Desert: A Study of Repentance in Early Monastic Sources* (Kalamazoo, MI: Cistercian Publications, 1987), p. 50 (*PL* 73 at col. 684C; translation here my own).

not constraining it. It is confession that makes her admissions desirable, rather than unspeakable.

This chapter explores the uses of silence, speech and the unspeakable in the Old English version of the life of Mary of Egypt and the guide for anchoresses known as *Ancrene Wisse*. The first is a desert saint whose ascetic, isolated lifestyle is the inspiration and precursor to the second, the anchoritic subject who is figuratively cut off from the world. Speaking of oneself is central to both texts – how is the individual defined in relation to the outside world? How does one speak to and of God, of one's own religious experience? What must be expressed and what suppressed? Each text handles sin, confession and the best practice for holy life – ostensibly for a woman (or women) but also, by selective implication and extension, a man. The comparison between the two texts is not a like-for-like one, but they both deal with the confessing female subject and the unspeakable sins they (may) have committed. The occasion of confession is the focal point in each text, both in terms of narrative and form – their central sequences detail the long and (almost) complete confession to a figure of (male) religious authority. As these reveal, there is both power and danger in silence, just as there is at once safety and vulnerability in confession. Mary of Egypt wrestles with 'unspeakable' sins, but insists that she will leave nothing uncovered in her extended confession to the monk Zosimus. In her yearning for absolution she speaks things even she does not wish to hear; in her free-range wanderings and unschooled wisdom she confounds her confessor, the cloistered, book-fed monk. By contrast, the 'dear sisters' of the anchorhold, to whom the *Wisse*-writer addresses his guide, are encouraged to keep a guard on their mouths and their speech at all times – the influence of post-Lateran IV *summae* is felt keenly. The *Wisse* famously pays much attention to the dangers of seeing, but the emphasis on the dangers of speech is, if anything, even more pronounced. Cursing, swearing and preaching are forbidden; yearning to hear a loved one's speech is a form of madness. The rundown of the seven deadly sins thus includes the many species of oral sin that spring from pride, which should be suppressed, and from lechery, deeds a 'well-mannered mouth' should not describe plainly even with a priest. The act of confession is bolstered both by the completeness of the speech to the confessor – though even here, the author advises his charges to refrain from speaking about certain things – and by the silence with which the anchoress's other activities should be conducted.

The dates of the texts also correspond with different stages in the development of the sacrament of penance: whereas *Ancrene Wisse* is generally accepted to post-date Lateran IV, which set the form of confession in the canon *Omnis utriusque sexus*, the Old English *Mary of Egypt* comes considerably earlier and reflects older, tariffed penances that typically focused on fasting.[3]

[3] For the development of tariffed penance in pre-Conquest England, see Allen J.

Neither account is typical of the way that this rite was generally conducted in the medieval period, where confession was characterised by its openness, both in terms of the uncovering of sins and the (generally public) space in which it took place. While post-medieval confessor–penitent conversations are enclosed in the confessional, the more usual image of confession for the medievalist is likely to be the public setting that John Bossy describes: for 'confession, we need to remember, was a face-to-face encounter between two people who would probably have known each other pretty well; we may also remember that it occurred, normally speaking, once a year, in the not-so-remote presence of a large number of neighbours'.[4] Despite this transparency, the confessor was also held to a silence and secrecy of his own – any confessor who revealed sins divulged in confession would be judged even more harshly than the original sinner. Zosimus, we are to understand, talks about the confession he has heard – not a feature of a Lateran confession – but then again, Zosimus does not function in quite the same way as a usual confessor since he does not presume to absolve Mary. The anchoritic confession, which of course is not heard as such, only described in the abstract, is also atypical in that it is enclosed and (though the anchoress may heed the *Wisse*-author's advice to have a witness to her sacerdotal visits) less likely to have an audience, unlike the very open confessions of common folk. This in itself could theoretically encourage a more complete confession, of course.

The medieval focus on the body of the female subject and insistence on its fleshliness has the effect of bringing to a meditation on the religious or spiritual life a preoccupation with the corporeal and material. The discussion of the unspeakable in this chapter is thus often a materialist one. The texts deal in detail with the corporeal, particularly the regulations of behaviour that literally stop speech, and are informed at a narrative and structural level by the speaker's relation to the space and boundaries in which they find themselves – the texts' respective physical settings have their parallel in the boundaries (or lack of boundaries) on their protagonists' speech.[5] The materialist angle on the unspeakable thus comes through in two ways – the control of the body that is emphasised in each case, particularly the regulation of the

Frantzen, *The Literature of Penance in Anglo-Saxon England* (New Brunswick, NJ: Rutgers University Press, 1983).

4 John Bossy, 'The Social History of Confession in the Age of the Reformation', *Transactions of the Royal Historical Society* 5.25 (1975), pp. 21–38 (p. 24). See also Tentler, *Sin and Confession*, pp. 82–3.

5 On the affinity between language and space in *Ancrene Wisse* in particular, see Cannon, *The Grounds of English Literature*. Cannon observes the materiality embraced in the concept of selfhood in *Ancrene Wisse* and the texts of the *Katherine*-Group that 'placement is so important to the procedures of self-fashioning articulated by the AB texts that they also spend a great deal of time exploring the concept of place as such' (p. 144). See also *Rhetoric of the Anchorhold: Space, Place and Body Within the Discourses of Enclosure*, ed. Liz Herbert McAvoy (Cardiff: University of Wales Press, 2008).

mouth in speech and in other activities, and the contrast between the open and the closed, which equally inflect the space of speech (and, concomitantly, the unspeakable). The extent to which a subject is permitted to stray outside or to remain enclosed within has previously been analysed as a function and reflection of gendered and embodied paradigms.[6] This chapter therefore takes its cue from such studies and relates the role of the gendered body on this play of inner and outer to an exploration of the tensions between speaking out and shutting up, between what is let out and what is kept in.

Confession paradoxically harnesses not only the power of expression but, in loosing the constraints on speech, the power of remaining silent about oneself – indeed, shutting oneself up. Whereas Mary's modus operandi is to speak without inhibition, the (implied female) reader of *Ancrene Wisse* is advised to stop up her speech and speak as little as possible, in order to ensure that God will listen when she breaks her silence. But, the author also admits, silence fosters speech – this is the challenge his anchoresses must address. The two modes of female speech correspond with their respective scenes – Mary wanders the desert, outdoors, unrestricted; the anchoress is committed to the anchorhold and is not to venture out. The boundaries negotiated by the speaking subject in each case are as much linguistic as physical. For Lacan, the problem of adequately representing oneself to another, 'is not a question of knowing whether I speak of myself in a way that conforms to what I am, but rather knowing whether I am the same as that of which I speak [...] I think where I am not, therefore I am where I do not think.'[7] The insufficiency of language shows up in the resistant, residual elements that evade representation – the Lacanian 'real' – which exists as a foreclosed zone, beyond the limits of the symbolic order that governs speech.[8] The Lacanian unconscious being famously structured like language, the attempt to frame the self within linguistic parameters is (necessarily) doomed before it is begun. It is impossible to speak oneself if the locus of speech is always where the subject is not.

6 See *Anchorites, Wombs and Tombs: Intersections of Gender and Enclosure in the Middle Ages*, ed. Liz Herbert McAvoy and Mari Edwards (Cardiff: University of Wales Press, 2005). Cary Howie also discusses the paradoxical effects of the devotion of the *inclusus*, and indeed Mary of Egypt, under the term 'claustrophilia', a phenomenon whose most readily perceived characteristic is the 'particularly intense and necessarily ambivalent erotic relationship with enclosed space, a relationship that hinges upon the metonymic touching between bodies and the spaces that contain and articulate them'; see Howie, *Claustrophilia: The Erotics of Enclosure in Medieval Literature* (Basingstoke: Palgrave Macmillan, 2007), p. 40.

7 Jacques Lacan, 'The Agency of the Letter in the Unconscious or Reason Since Freud', in *Écrits: A Selection*, trans. Alan Sheridan (London and New York: Routledge, 1977), pp. 161–97 (pp. 182–3).

8 Slavoj Žižek in *The Sublime Object of Ideology* (London and New York: Verso, 1989) clarifies the concept of the real as 'that which resists symbolization: the traumatic point which is always missed but none the less always returns, although we try – through a set of different strategies – to neutralize it, to integrate it into the symbolic order' (p. 69).

Though the real is 'that which always returns to the same place', that place is, by definition, out of reach of language.[9]

However, the idea of *locating* language in any capacity joins the physical, the material and the embodied to a system of determination that is otherwise largely abstract. The real, by existing outside boundaries, beyond the perimeters of the symbolic or the linguistic, can be construed as a place, but a place that can never quite be reached. This place that defines and yet (consequently) remains beyond definition may also be figured in spatial terms, as the 'constitutive outside' against which Judith Butler's theory of performative subjectivity functions. This is the 'zone of uninhabitability [that] will constitute the defining limit of the subject's domain; it will constitute that site of dreaded identification against which – and by virtue of which – the domain of the subject will circumscribe its own claim to autonomy and to life'.[10] Where the Freudian psychoanalysis from which Lacan emerges is concerned with displacement and the return of the repressed, the politico-philosophical influences in Butler's thinking on gender are interested in the workings behind the disenfranchisement of certain gendered positions and sexualities.[11] The subject is therefore 'constituted through the force of exclusion and abjection, one which produces a constitutive outside to the subject, an abjected outside, which is, after all, "inside" the subject as its own founding repudiation'.[12] It is part of Butler's project in examining the process and effects of performativity to expose the hegemonic, heteronormative workings that underlie the construction of certain social groups as marginal or other. This is achieved in part through the citation of performative norms, repeated behaviours that come into continual play in the constitution of the subject (and *Ancrene Wisse* certainly emphasises the crucial importance of regulated and carefully planned habits). On the other hand, the younger Mary, in the rebuffs and snubs she suffers at the hands of others in more powerful, stable positions, embodies just such an 'abjected outside' in relation to society at large. There is more at play here, of course, and as Bachelard warns, though inner and outer combine with such seductive clarity in the metaphorics of cultural and psycho-social life, the subjective experience of the apparently mutual exclusion and formation of *inside* and *outside* also forms 'a dialectic of division, the obvious geometry of which blinds us […] It has the sharpness of the dialectics of *yes* and *no*, which

9 Jacques Lacan, *The Four Fundamental Concepts of Psychoanalysis (The Seminar of Jacques Lacan, Book XI)*, ed. Jacques-Alain Miller, trans. Alan Sheridan (New York: W. W. Norton & Co., 1978), p. 49.

10 Judith Butler, *Bodies That Matter: On the Discursive Limits of 'Sex'* (London: Routledge, 1993), p. 3.

11 For Butler, 'The production of the *un*symbolizable, the unspeakable, the illegible is also always a strategy of social abjection'. *Bodies That Matter*, p. 190 (original emphasis).

12 Butler, *Bodies That Matter*, p. 3.

decides everything'.[13] Butler's other endeavour is thus to probe for places from which the abjected might become empowered, asking, 'How might those ostensibly constitutive exclusions be rendered less permanent, more dynamic? How might the excluded return, not as psychosis or the figure of the psychotic within politics, but as that which has been rendered mute, foreclosed from the domain of political signification?'[14]

Two issues are at stake: the attempt to express one's religious devotion and the necessity to suppress one's worldly experience. In Mary's case, the matter to be suppressed is, in theory at least, her own biography and the sins she has committed – but she will not keep them concealed. In the case of the anchoress, the matter is, rather, the quotidian chatter of worldly concerns, in which she is not meant to indulge, whereas her sins (which must pale in comparison with Mary's) are to be expressed forcefully and regularly. In both cases, it is the former engagement with the world that is to be kept shut up. The dilemma is that mundane experience is also necessary to explain the religious devotion exhibited in these texts and furthermore furnishes the only terms that are available to the saint or the anchorite. This worldly life is sinful in the case of the reformed harlot and carefully constructed to be blameless in the case of the anchoress (at least in theory), but the tension between revealing and concealing their connection to the world, speaking and pointedly not speaking of it, is common to both texts, though with very different effects.

The protagonists of the saint's life (almost) represent this dichotomy of speech and silence single-handed – Mary the expressive *al fresco* wanderer, Zosimus silent and contained but given licence to roam – but the author of *Ancrene Wisse* handles this interplay in a more convoluted fashion. In one sense it is the task of the single notional personage of the *ideal* anchoress, who must live in comparative quiet and solitude but who must also rehearse for her confessor the fullest confession of which she is capable, yet it is also the activity of three real anchoresses who will read the guide; moreover, on another level, this negotiation of speaking and silence is carried out by proxy, by the writer of the guide (whose voice is, in one sense, the only one we can hear).[15] The subjective realities of which the subject herself cannot speak (because they are so sinful, because she is being 'written' by amanuensis, or simply because language cannot approach them) are brought into even sharper focus in the accounts of saintly wandering and anchoritic enclosure

[13] Gaston Bachelard, *The Poetics of Space* (Boston, MA: Beacon Press, 1994), p. 211.

[14] Butler, *Bodies That Matter*, p. 189.

[15] However, see Anne Savage's argument that the composition of the *Wisse* was actually undertaken in much closer consultation with the anchoresses, and that they were not merely readers and recipients; she suggests that the guide was 'modelled [...] on their own practice' and written 'not just at their suggestion, but with their help'. Savage, 'The Communal Authorship of *Ancrene Wisse*', in *A Companion to* Ancrene Wisse, ed. Yoko Wada (Cambridge: D. S. Brewer, 2003), pp. 45–56 (pp. 52, 54).

by the attempts of those around them to circumscribe both their speech and their actions (an activity that naturally continues in the critical literature). The contradictory ways in which these figures understand themselves and are understood by the world recall Lacan's question, '"Who is speaking?" [...] For this reply cannot come from the subject if he does not know what he is saying, or even if he is speaking.'[16] In order to respond, the task is to negotiate the impasse of the speaking and the spoken-about, divisible spaces, zones of uninhabitability and the return of the repressed (or the real), to examine how the unspeakable interpolates speech that falls both within and without limits.

I turn first to a subject who refuses both enclosure and silence: the multi-tasking Mary of Egypt. Much reproduced and adapted throughout the Middle Ages, Mary's *vita* is at once a tissue of hagiographical clichés and a work that seems to throw every category into crisis.[17] As Clare Lees and Gillian Overing remark, 'Mary is an excessive figure (few indeed are the penitent, old, nude whores in the Anglo-Saxon corpus), yet she is one whose figurative dimensions do not annihilate meaning [...] so much as produce and multiply it.'[18] The account of the elderly penitent found wandering the desert by the monk Zosimus is a story about storytelling. Its transmission spans most of the period usually designated 'medieval', across most of the Continent and many of the languages of Europe – from sixth-century Greek accounts to early modern vernacular versions from as far west as Iceland. As Mary herself admits, she was a rather popular woman.

THE BODY THAT SPEAKS

The Old English life of the *vita* of Mary of Egypt is found in British Library Cotton Julius E. vii, the manuscript containing Ælfric's *Lives of Saints*, but Mary is not one of Ælfric's saints. The Old English is an anonymous translation of the Latin *Vita Sanctae Mariae Egypticae*, which was in turn

16 Jacques Lacan, 'The Subversion of the Subject and the Dialectic of Desire in the Freudian Unconscious', in *Écrits*, pp. 323–60 (p. 331).

17 Existing studies trace the significance of the legend to issues of gender – see Onnaca Heron, 'The Lioness in the Text: Mary of Egypt as Immasculated Female Saint', *Quidditas* 21 (2000), 23–44; Clare A. Lees and Gillian R. Overing, *Double Agents: Women in Clerical Culture in Anglo-Saxon England* (Philadelphia, PA: University of Pennsylvania Press, 2001); Robin Norris, 'Vitas Matrum: Mary of Egypt as Female Confessor', *Old English Newsletter* Subsidia 33 (2005), 79–109; the body – see Andrew P. Scheil, 'Bodies and Boundaries in the Old English *Life of St. Mary of Egypt*', *Neophilologus* 84.1 (2000), 137–56; queerness – see Emma Campbell, *Medieval Saints' Lives: The Gift, Kinship and Community in Old French Hagiography* (Cambridge: D. S. Brewer, 2008); and middle age – see Lees and Watt, 'Age and Desire in the Old English *Life of St Mary of Egypt*'.

18 Lees and Overing, *Double Agents*, p. 134. See also Colin Chase, 'Source Study as a Trick with Mirrors: Annihilation of Meaning in the Old English "Mary of Egypt"', *Sources of Anglo-Saxon Culture*, ed. Paul E. Szarmach, Studies in Medieval Culture 20 (Kalamazoo, MI: Medieval Institute, 1986), pp. 23–33.

a translation of an earlier Greek life. Though the Old English is extant in only three manuscripts (and only one containing the full text), the Latin and Greek traditions are attested in many more surviving manuscripts.[19] The life's pan-European dimension is made even more apparent by the sheer linguistic scope of the vernacular tradition: there are Romance *Marys* (French, Italian, Portuguese, Spanish), Germanic *Marys* (Dutch, Norse, German) and Celtic *Marys* (Irish and Welsh).[20] The period before the appearance of the *Legenda Aurea* sees a great output of vernacular translations and adaptations of the legend, and this is not unconnected to the contemporaneous rise of the cult of Mary Magdalene, whose own legend develops in part out of that of Mary of Egypt.

Despite the fact that it was inserted into the same manuscript as Ælfric's *Lives of Saints*, Ælfric was in all probability not the author of the Old English version. Hugh Magennis insists that the original omission was not an oversight – indeed, the wide dissemination and popular traction of the life makes this unlikely – and that Ælfric may have considered this particular life to be too morally ambiguous to include. As the most recent editor of the Old English text, Magennis finds Mary a 'challenging figure', particularly for Ælfric.[21] She fails to satisfy the 'image of the female saint' that Ælfric endorses, and she does so on several counts, being neither virginal, nor aristocratic, nor educated.[22]

19 For a discussion of the literary character of the Greek and Latin lives, see Jane Stevenson, 'The Holy Sinner: The Life of Mary of Egypt', in *The Legend of Mary of Egypt in Medieval Insular Hagiography*, ed. Erich Poppe and Bianca Ross (Dublin and Portland, Oregon: Four Courts Press, 1996), pp. 19–50.

20 See *The Legend of Mary of Egypt*, ed. Poppe and Ross, for studies treating individual reflexes of the legend in the Old and Middle English, Anglo-Latin, Anglo-Norman, Middle Welsh, Middle Scots and Old Norse traditions. Konrad Kunze explores the German tradition in *Studien zur Legende der heiligen Maria Aegiptiaca im deutschen Sprachgebiet* (Berlin: Schmidt, 1969). The southern European tradition is addressed in *La Vie de Ste. Marie Egyptienne: Versions en Ancien et Moyen Français*, ed. Peter F. Dembowski (Geneva: Droz, 1977); *The Life of Saint Mary of Egypt: An Edition and Study of the Medieval French and Spanish Verse Redactions*, ed. Michèle Schiavone de Cruz-Sáenz (Barcelona: Puvill, 1979); and *Saint Mary of Egypt: Three Medieval Lives in Verse*, ed. Ronald E. Pepin and Hugh Fleiss (Kalamazoo, MI: Cistercian Publications, 2005), which translates Latin and Spanish versions.

21 Magennis, *Mary of Egypt*, p. 6. See also Magennis, 'St Mary of Egypt and Ælfric: Unlikely Bedfellows in Cotton Julius E. vii?', in Poppe and Ross, *The Legend of Mary of Egypt*, pp. 99–112. Magennis argues not only that Cotton Julius E. vii 'cannot be viewed [...] as having been compiled under the direct influence of Ælfric himself or his closer associates' but that 'it is difficult to see how he and like-minded churchmen would not have found this work spiritually "incorrect"' (p. 102). He also cites the text's eremitic (rather than cenobitic) emphasis and the suggestion of female infringement of male spiritual authority as motivators for Ælfric's excluding Mary.

22 Magennis, *Mary of Egypt*, p. 22. Mary Clayton also observes that 'there is a clear avoidance of eremitic saints in Ælfric: he seems to have deliberately refrained from presenting the life of the contemplative hermit as an ideal. We find in his work no

However, while Ælfric might be above mentioning Mary, later contributors to the Cotton Julius manuscript were keen to bring her in, regardless of how this might affect the governing ideology of the original selection.[23]

The Egyptian's life was extremely well known throughout the medieval period from around the ninth century, when the Latin *vita* (from which many subsequent translations were taken) was written. The Old English text is headed by the rubric *De Transitu Mariae Aegypticae*, and the idea of transit is appealingly apt for a text that makes its way across a continent and down the ages. This wandering narrative is the story of a wandering, wayward woman. Mary is one of that group of saints sometimes called the 'holy harlots' (along with saints such as Pelagia and, naturally, Mary Magdalene). A whore, a convert, a repentant sinner, a desert hermit and a miracle-worker, she embodies several paradigms during the course of her narrative. Robin Norris additionally analyses Mary's *Life* alongside those of confessor-saints, since she dies of natural causes, has a devoted acolyte and is granted divine foreknowledge of her death.[24]

Her life is described through the eyes of a pious but proud monk called Zosimus, who, tempted by the belief that he is near spiritual perfection, prays for guidance. An angel promises him a revelation if he travels to a monastery near the Jordan; though Zosimus appears to be under the impression that he will finally encounter a monk who can expand on his learning, it is Mary who turns out to be this vision.[25] On a Lenten sojourn in the desert, far away from the confines of the monastery, Zosimus goes many days without

Antony, Paul the Hermit, Mary of Egypt, Hilary, Paphnutius, Guthlac, to name only a few of those of whom he undoubtedly knew. Apostles, martyrs, and confessors are the groups of saints to which he devotes his energies: teachers and those who gave up their lives for the faith are, therefore, the saints whom he considered important': Clayton, 'Hermits and the Contemplative Life in Anglo-Saxon England', in *Old English Prose Saints' Lives and Their Contexts*, ed. Paul E. Szarmach (Albany, NY: State University of New York Press, 1996), pp. 147–76 (p. 162). Magennis notes that even though Ælfric recounts St Cuthbert's period on Farne Island (as he 'could hardly omit so famous an episode'), he plays this down to the extent that he dispenses with Bede's explanation for Cuthbert's seclusion – that he wished to increase his devotion through an eremitical lifestyle: Magennis, 'Unlikely Bedfellows', pp. 105–6.

23 'Its inclusion', observes Magennis, 'reflects the willingness of the compilers of the manuscript pragmatically to adapt and appropriate inherited material to their own purposes, despite Ælfric's evident desire that the integrity of his hagiographical collection should be maintained.' Magennis, 'Unlikely Bedfellows', p. 21.

24 See Norris, 'Vitas Matrum' (*passim*).

25 It is worth noting that later Middle English versions of Mary's life make less use of Zosimus's story as a framing device for Mary's own; in the *Gilte Legende* both Mary and Zosimus have been introduced within the first eight lines, while in the *South English Legendary* Zosimus does not even appear until 121 lines in. See *Gilte Legende*, EETS o.s. 327, vol. 1, ed. R. F. S. Hamer and Vida Russell (Oxford: Oxford University Press, 2006), pp. 254–7; *The South English Legendary*, EETS o.s. 235, ed. Charlotte d'Evelyn and Anna J. Mill (Oxford: Oxford University Press, 1956), pp. 136–48.

receiving his revelation, before glimpsing a figure (whether man or woman, he cannot tell) in the distance. Hurrying to catch up with what he realises is a white-haired, naked and sun-blackened woman, he pursues her until she eventually speaks to him. She appears to know his name already, but tells him that, unless he gives her something with which to cover her nakedness, she cannot turn and face him. Giving her his travelling cloak, he waits for her to cover the parts that 'mæst neod wæs to beheligenne' (there was most need to conceal, l. 270), whereupon both prostrate themselves on the ground.[26] Some time later, Zosimus begs her to teach him of the divine grace he is convinced she possesses, and to bless him; she first enquires how the Christian Church is faring, and then begins to pray. Zosimus cannot make out her words, but he swears that he sees her levitate as she prays (l. 332). At last, she tells him her story.

Born in Egypt, she left her parents' home at the age of twelve, and headed to Alexandria, where she soon descended into a life of promiscuity and amorality. Although she is at pains to stress to Zosimus that she never sought or accepted payment for her sexual sins, she is so ashamed that she is loathe to continue relating them – 'þas mine word ægðer gewemmað ge þe ge þas lyfte' (these words of mine defile both you and the air itself, ll. 406–7). Bargaining her way on board a ship bound for Jerusalem – a seafaring escort and inverse pilgrim – she sails for the Holy Land. While en route, her sins are so many and so various that she declares, 'Nis nan asecgendlic oððe unasecgendlic fracodlicnysse hiwung þæs ic ne sih tihtende and lærende, and fruma gefremed'(There is no form of obscenity, speakable or unspeakable, of a kind that I did not incite and teach, after becoming its instigator, ll. 432–4). Their unspeakability does not prevent her from telling Zosimus all about them. However, despite her lust for sensual pleasures, she undergoes a dramatic epiphany when she attempts to enter the Church of the Holy Sepulchre and finds herself obstructed by an unseen force. Struck with the realisation that her sins have blocked her passage, she prays to an image of the Virgin Mary for admission to the church. The next time she tries the door, she goes through it. When she again prays to Mary for guidance towards salvation, an unseen voice tells her to cross the Jordan. She journeys towards the river and her eventual desert dwelling, buying along the way three loaves, which are to sustain her for the next seventeen years. By the time she meets Zosimus, she has been living in the desert, mostly on plants, for forty-seven years.

Cast out of the Church, excluded from Ælfric's calendar of saints, yet imposing on these religious enclosures anyway, Mary is a decidedly liminal character – though in a markedly different way – repeatedly cast in a suspension between extremes. Her secular passions are conditioned by her

26 *Mary of Egypt*, ed. and trans. Magennis. Subsequent references will be given in parentheses, by line number.

spiritual fervour, her frail old age juxtaposed by the astonishing vigour she displays as she flees from Zosimus. She lives on – or is just barely sustained by – a meagre ration of lentils and breadcrumbs, and makes her home in the wilderness, not in the world and yet not quite out of it, subsisting so austerely that she hovers near death. When she first speaks, the utterance comes simply from 'se lichama' (the body, l. 250); hovering between heaven and earth (literally as well as figuratively at ll. 327–32), she even drifts over the boundary between the territories of male and female:

> þa geseah he him on þa swiðran healfe þær he on gebedum stod swa swa he [*missing text*] on mennisce gelicnysse on lichaman hine æteowan [...] Ða eac witodlice se ende his gebedes wæs gefylled, he þa his eagan bewende and þær soðlice man geseah westweardes on þæt westen efstan, and witodlice þæt wæs wifman þæt þær gesewen wæs. Swiðe sweartes lichamen heo wæs for þære sunnan hæto, and þa loccas hire heafdes wæron swa hwite swa wull and þa na siddran þonne oþ þone swuran.
>
> he noticed then to his right, as he stood at his prayers, as though he [...] appearing in human physical form [...] And when the end of his prayer had been completed, he then turned his eyes and really saw there a human being hastening westwards in the desert, and it was actually a woman that appeared there. She was extremely black in her body because of the sun's heat, and the hair of her head was as white as wool and no longer than down to her neck (ll. 205–18).

This lack of distinction – going from *mennisce* to *wifman*, human (or even mannish) to woman, in a few lines – is not an isolated episode but a theme that informs the rest of the text. Lees and Overing remark that 'the narrative is at pains to keep Mary's meaning ambiguous; as Zosimus draws closer to her, it is a body [...] that speaks'.[27] As Scheil insists, 'Mary is clearly not an unproblematic representation of sainthood. Her body refuses to remain under a stable representational rubric. A danger, linked to the ambiguity of her identity, lurks beneath the surface of the narrative, pulling the reader along in fascination.'[28] If hers is a body that speaks, it is also a body that speaks in multiple registers.

The issue of gender representation appears at first to be in familiar territory: the monastic framing device lends the character of Zosimus a measure of control over the narrative, reporting, editing and mediating the story of Mary's life. Attention is drawn to Zosimus's authority as the male clerical figure, to whom Mary frequently defers. Apart from declaring herself unworthy company for a holy man to be keeping, even running away from Zosimus, Mary begs Zosimus to bless her, pray for her, give her the sacraments and finally to bury her. Indeed, in telling her tale she is also making an

27 Lees and Overing, *Double Agents*, p. 141.

28 Scheil, 'Bodies and Boundaries', p. 142.

extended confession. Yet Mary's petitions and humility are far from conveying the full extent of her relationship with Zosimus. The initial, conventional stance on conceptions of gender is gradually repositioned and in some ways subverted. This is not simply the wretched sinner and her father confessor; for, in his own turn, Zosimus is looking for someone to guide *him*.

At the outset of the narrative, Zosimus's spiritual authority and learning are again evident in the regard with which he himself holds them. Indeed, he muses aloud, 'Hwæðer ænig munuc on eorðan sy þæt me mage aht niwes getæcan' (Can it be that there is any monk on earth who can teach me anything new? ll. 62–3). Going forth in search of his guide, and expecting another monk, Zosimus instead encounters Mary. Here, the gender roles begin to shift, as the reverence and zeal for learning that Zosimus was preparing to render to his imaginary holy man is instead bestowed upon a holy woman (a holy harlot, no less). From their first meeting, throwing themselves on their faces, each seemingly in a bid to out-supplicate the other, Zosimus and Mary are both eager to express (and perform) their willingness to learn and atone: the one for sins of the flesh, the other for the sin of pride. Later, just as Mary asks for Zosimus's blessings and rites, he, too, requests her blessing and intercession – significantly, he calls her 'gastlice modor' (spiritual mother, l. 289). Before he came into the wilderness, he was longing to encounter 'sumne fæder on þam westene' (some father in the desert, ll. 193–4), yet in newfound humility, he is able to discern a desert mother in 'his' place.

Accordingly, Zosimus complies humbly with Mary's instructions to him to return the next year with the sacraments. When she tells him not to speak of their meeting with anyone while she is still alive, he likewise obeys. Following Mary's account of her life, the remainder of the narrative concerns Zosimus's subsequent visits to the desert, at the same time each year, each time under instructions to find Mary at the same place he first saw her. On his second visit, he delivers to her the sacraments of bread and wine; on his third (and last), he finds her body. Following a mysterious written directive, also containing her epitaph (along with her name, which she had never told him), he prays for her and buries her. In the shared spiritual authority of these two 'ghostly fathers', there is a mutual understanding. In the symbiosis that flowers in the desert – between pious and penitent, cenobitic and eremitic, learned and unlettered, cloistered and outcast – Mary and Zosimus are constantly occupying the same spaces. They are both repenting, both advising: the territories that might have found a natural allotment in accordance with their respective professions and lifestyles are, instead, overlapping – a common ground.

The desert becomes a space where any seeking unambiguous models of gender are persistently thwarted.[29] Here, not only does a presumptively

[29] Irigaray also looks at place specifically in terms of sexual difference, arguing that there is a parallel between the two and drawing out the strands of their engagement: 'the masculine', she affirms, 'is attracted to the maternal-feminine as place. But what place

masculine authorising influence end up divided between the male and female protagonists, but the way in which gender is performed and perceived is altered over the course of the narrative. Both Mary and Zosimus are searching for something in the desert, something or someone who will embody their desire. While Zosimus has his whimsical holy 'man', Mary – though hers is a quest for salvation in the wider sense – exhibits a particular veneration for the Virgin Mary, the antithesis of her own former self and the catalyst for her conversion. It is the Church of the Virgin that Mary wishes to enter; her promise to follow 'swa hwider swa þu me to mundbyrdnysse geredst' (wherever you guide me as my advocate, ll. 519–20), is seen out by her continuing devotion. While Zosimus calls Mary his ghostly mother, Mary describes the Virgin as her 'lættewestran' or guide. Desire is also crucial to the gendering of external influences. Zosimus, desiring a male counsellor, stumbles across a woman (indeed, a naked woman), but is initially able to 'see' a masculine figure; Mary, whose object of desire is the very personification of feminine sanctity, finds the role of her Marian guide supplied by a man.

Mary's 'mennisce' appearance and the spiritual authority she assumes at various points indicate a joint occupancy of the masculine space in the narrative; in the same way, the archetypally feminine roles and space are not the exclusive domain of the woman in the story. The combining and intermingling in the desert of spheres usually kept apart is seen again in the peculiar temperaments of Mary and Zosimus. Both exhibit behaviours and predispositions that complicate established medieval models of gender, particularly the theory of humours, which prevailed from Hippocrates and Galen onwards.[30] The four humours were thought to affect, indeed, *effect* the difference between men and women: while men were hot and dry, their bodies 'closed', women were cold and moist – the leaky vessel, lactating, menstruating, exuding in all directions. Yet, although Mary relates how she weeps copiously for her past wantonness and bodily excesses, by the time of her meeting with Zosimus not only has she been sexually continent for the past forty-seven years, she has given up all her vices and all but ceased to eat; and it is not she who weeps now.[31] Instead, the tears and groaning are left to Zosimus. The gift of

does the masculine offer to attract the feminine? His soul? His relation to the divine? Can the feminine be inscribed or situated there?' Irigaray, *An Ethics of Sexual Difference*, trans. Carolyn Burke and Gillian C. Gill (London: Continuum, 1993), p. 35.

30 For an overview of Anglo-Saxon medical theory, see M. L. Cameron, 'The Sources of Medical Knowledge in Anglo-Saxon England', *Anglo-Saxon England* 11 (1983), pp. 135–55. Cameron notes the presence of 'a mass of tractates on blood-letting, minor accounts of the four humours, prognostics of life and death, dietarics and so on' in circulation by the middle of the eighth century (p. 142); he concludes that Anglo-Saxon medicine 'in most respects borrowed directly from the Classical Greek and Latin background' and 'was based on the entirely erroneous theory of the four humours' (p. 152).

31 Stevenson surveys the attitudes of patristic as well as medical writers and their 'strongly

tears, in as much as tears symbolise grace, tends not to be gender-specific, but Zosimus becomes almost hysterical in his readiness to lament and sob. From his weeping cry upon first meeting her ('hluddre clypunga wepende', l. 235), to the pouring tears he sheds as he buries Mary's body ('forðagotenum tearum', l. 941), Zosimus is continually crying. (Norris points out that 'Zosimus begins crying before he even meets Mary').[32] Indeed, his sorrow on occasion reaches quite spectacular depths; when he returns the third year and, after a long search, still cannot find Mary, he is so distraught that he cries enough to soak himself with tears ('he hine sylfne mid tearum ofergeotan', l. 876). In his nervous anticipation on first meeting Mary, Zosimus is also said to be covered in beads of sweat (l. 287). However, although Zosimus seems to be always speaking 'mid tearum' (both in the sense of articulating in spite of them and in the sense that his tears convey what he is *unable* to articulate), his tears do not lose their meaning. They are, in fact, even more significant at the end of the narrative than at any point before.

When Zosimus finally finds Mary's lifeless body, he weeps once more and mourns her passing, and wishes to lay her to rest with all rites and dignity. In this task he is aided, in a curious touch, by a passing lion or, perhaps, lioness – the Old English refers to the beast in both genders; even its fauna is affected by the pervading gender ambiguity in the desert.[33] (Howie notes a similar moment of gender transfer or ambiguity in the Old French verse life, where Mary's corpse is 'at once feminine and masculine in its nudity, "tote nue" [...] and "tot nu".')[34] Rather than a quirky detail – exit, interred by a lion – this is the last of a series of features associated with *imitatio Christi*.

positive associations with dryness', noting that 'The idea that women's bodies were softer, wetter and more porous than men's, and therefore less good, is a product of medical and physiological thinking, and Christian ascetic thought merely reflects and develops this [...] In this purely physiological sense [that fasting induces amenorrhoea], the female ascetic approached the masculine, or even the super-masculine, by virtue of her dryness.' Stevenson, 'Holy Sinner', pp. 38–9.

32 Norris, 'Vitas Matrum', p. 87.

33 In the Middle English versions, this detail is absent and the lion is consistently masculine. Onnaca Heron looks in detail at the contrast between the Greek and especially the Latin version of the text in her article 'The Lioness in the Text' (pp. 35–8). Examining the significance of the spindle Mary cast aside (before embarking on her career of harlotry) when compared with the small stick with which Zosimus is unable to dig her grave, Heron argues that 'in picking up the spindle-like stick, Zosimus seems to switch gender roles by adopting the feminine symbol which Mary had discarded before her departure from Alexandria [...] Just as the lion seems to change genders by being transformed into a lioness, Zosimus here seems to have been transformed into a womanly man by grasping the womanly' tool for weaving' (pp. 38–9). However, where Heron views the presence of both grammatical genders in the passage concerning the lion(ess) as indicative of a seemingly sequential change from masculine to feminine on the part of both the animal and Zosimus, I would argue that it is, rather, symptomatic of the gender fluidity suggested by Scheil, and Lees and Overing (see works cited above).

34 Howie, *Claustrophilia*, p. 49.

The miraculous levitation Zosimus observes on their first meeting is only the start of Mary's more extraordinary performances. The tale of her seventeen-year survival on nothing but two and a half loaves of dried-up bread (l. 600) is obviously reminiscent of the story of the loaves and the fishes,[35] while at her last (living) meeting with Zosimus he beholds her, Christ-like, walking across the Jordan 'onuppan þa hnescan yða [...] swa swa on drigum' (on top of the soft waves [...] as though on dry land, ll. 807–8).[36] Though the correlation between Zosimus and Mary's beloved *lættewestran* is to some extent apparent in the monk's discipline, chastity and devotion, this series of moves effecting a sympathy between Mary and Christ achieves, by extension, a similar connection between Zosimus and the Virgin Mary. Having washed her feet with his tears (Magdalene-like) at their last parting, when he weeps over Mary's body he embodies another famous image: that of the grieving Virgin after the crucifixion.

Zosimus's crying also draws attention to the performative distinction between himself and Mary. His reiterative act is almost a default position, indeed, it reflects his prevailing ideology – at least as it is as his story begins. The vision he craves when he goes into the desert is the peak of his yearning to *see*. From the start, Zosimus is introduced as one who was blessed with *gastlic gesihþ*, divine sight (ll. 47–8). Enlightenment, being made to see, is the spiritual goal of the brothers at the Jordan monastery: when they set out each year for their time in the desert, they mark their passage through the monastery gates with the singing of the first line of Psalm 26 – 'Dominus illuminatio mea', the Lord is my light. It is his hunger for illumination, and his confidence in the power of sight, that causes Zosimus to run after a fleeting suspicion of a human presence, despite his fears that it is, in fact, 'sumes gastes', a ghost, that he sees. He is also in violation of the code by which the monks conduct their solitary journeys, which dictates he should turn away and pursue a different course if he comes across another person (ll. 167–71). Yet he pays no heed to either of these obstacles, instead 'georne behealdende' (gazing intently) at his vision, 'þære gewilnedan swetnysse þære wuldorfæstan gesihðe' (the longed-for loveliness of that glorious sight, ll. 219–21) overriding a more logical response. Zosimus's impulses expose a performative identity wherein his desire is channelled through his eyes – looking, searching, weeping.

The strictures of monastic rule are inclined to emphasise the pursuit of enlightened vision over most other sensory experience, particularly the oral. Though Zosimus does reserve one pleasure – the singing of psalms – the monks shun 'unnytte spræce' (pointless speech, l. 108), or anything that might distract them from the 'godcundan gespræcu' (divine discourses, l. 114). They consume only bread and water while in the monastery, and only beans, lentils

[35] Matt. 14.19, Mark 6.41, Luke 9.16, John 6.11.

[36] Matt. 14.25–31, Mark 6.48–51, John 6.19.

or palm-fruits in the desert. The text claims they do not even know the names for gold and silver, and even their exploits in the desert are to be kept secret from one another. All this diligent oral regulation does not, however, have any impact upon Mary; her philosophy and her performance are the opposite of Zosimus's. Though the boundaries of sex do not settle within the text, Mary's is arguably a particularly feminine type of performance. While Zosimus attempts to rise above speech (in keeping with his wish to subject the flesh to the spirit, ll. 34–5), Mary absolutely insists upon speaking, even when she is convinced she cannot express what is in her mind.

The story of Mary's life and way of living, up to the point where she meets Zosimus, accounts for over three hundred lines of text, roughly one-third of the whole *vita*. All of this is written as reported speech, a long autobiographical monologue, through which is also woven a disquisition on sin and forgiveness. Although the narrative is also concerned with Zosimus's spiritual development, charting his experiences in the monastery and relating his three journeys to the desert, the outstanding feature of the text is Mary's own speech (of which there is a good deal more than three hundred lines). Mary vocalises even what she is afraid will offend or frighten, indeed 'pollute' the very air; she is determined to speak the unspeakable. The text hints at the ways in which Zosimus's exacting linguistic protocol operates around certain forbidden topics, but though there is even more in Mary's lifestyle that might be deemed unmentionable, she does not place boundaries on her speech. Virginia Burrus declares that Mary 'will not suffer enclosure. She is as vast – and as uncompromisingly elemental in her passions – as the desert itself', and takes note of the provocative quality of mentioning these unmentionables ('What reader does not at this point strain to imagine the unspeakable?').[37] Despite Mary's consistent rhetorical emphasis on her full disclosure of sins she indulged, incited and taught others en route to Alexandria, she also alludes to the impure (*fullic*) acts she committed once in Jerusalem that were 'even worse' (l. 447). Whereas she specifies her loss of maidenhood and her desires for intercourse (or fucking), even for Mary, some sins seem to remain unspoken – though in the context of sexual sin, we might not be at such a strain to imagine which is 'unspeakable'. (Of course, if in her mention of unspeakable sins Mary is admitting to sodomy, the medieval discourse on the unspeakable, unnatural and sodomitical still presents many alternatives as to which act this might be. Chapter 2 takes up the *unspeakable sin*).[38]

37 Virginia Burrus, *The Sex Lives of Saints: An Erotics of Ancient Hagiography* (Philadelphia, PA: University of Pennsylvania Press, 2004), pp. 147, 151.

38 Again, the queer perspective of Lees and Watt is an interesting one to consider here, as in Mary's veneration of the Virgin (and Zosimus's for the guide he imagines), 'relationships of desire and identification are same-sex [...] and queer' (Lees and Watt, 'Age and Desire in the Old English *Life of St Mary of Egypt*', p. 59); Mary's admission does not necessarily tie her to the sailors.

For most of her narrative, though, Mary echoes the mission statement of the anonymous author of the Old English *Life*. Taking his cue from the words of the angel Raphael to the prophet Tobit – advising the latter that it is reprehensible to keep quiet about the glorious work of God (ll. 13–14) – the author swears he will not 'forsuwige þa halga geræcednyssa' (conceal this holy story in silence, ll. 14–15). There is a discernible shift from the visual to the oral taking place throughout the narrative; it is significant here that the anonymous writer's insistence on 'telling' – from *ræccan*, or reckoning – juxtaposes the story of Tobit losing his eyes. Accordingly, on each of the three occasions on which Zosimus seeks out Mary, while he tries hard at first to *see* her, it is only when he begins to vocalise a prayer or a cry that he receives his desire (ll. 205–14; 785–93; 867–80). Although Mary implores him not to reveal anything about their meeting while she is still alive (in addition to the customary monastic reticence concerning the Lentern trips), Zosimus's attitudes to speech have shifted by the time he returns to the monastery after their first meeting. Where before he did not appear to have any trouble suppressing his speech, and keeping quiet about those things that were not to be discussed, he now desires speech: though he holds his peace, he lets slip small things ('læstra þinga', l. 759), and his impatience to revisit the object of his desire manifests itself in impotent sighs ('mænigfealdum sworettungum', ll. 762–3). In spite of Mary declaring her story to be unspeakable, unrepeatable, the knowledge of it precipitates a significant shift in Zosimus's thinking and performance.

The supremacy of speech and orality is highlighted, too, by her claim that she never learned to read or write, despite (as Zosimus points out) having somehow come by a thorough knowledge of scriptures (ll. 686–98). Her explanation for this innate biblical comprehension is – mind-bendingly – framed by another untaught biblical quotation. The word of God, she replies, is a living thing and sharp in its potency ('cucu and scearp', l. 697), straight from Hebrews 4.12. Leaving for another discussion the issue of the extent or even existence of Mary's education – who wrote her epitaph and the message to Zosimus, if not her? – the citation from Hebrews is an image that conjures not only the Word but also Mary herself. Interaction with tangible, visible texts does not register with her; she channels the living Word, bypassing any kind of intermediary stages and inverting the usual order of spiritual learning. Where Zosimus and his fellow monks have devoted themselves to reading, learning, taking *in* works of scripture, Mary articulates, expresses, speaks them *out*. The change this works in Zosimus – reintroducing the oral into his closed, largely silent form of devotion – is echoed in the narrative's ending. Upon his return to the monastery, Zosimus dispenses with the tradition that every brother keeps what he endures in the desert, 'mid him sylfum', inside himself (l. 175), and instead fulfils his promise to reveal Mary's story after her death:

> Sona swa he to þam mynstre becom, þa rehte he heom eallum of frymðe þa wisan, and naht ne bediglode ealra þæra þinga þe he geseah oððe gehyrde, þæt hi ealle Godes mærða wurðodon, and mærsodon þære eadigan forðfore dæg.

> As soon as he arrived at the monastery he related the matter to them all from the beginning, and concealed nothing of all the things that he had seen or heard, so that they all exalted the glories of God and celebrated the day of the passing of the saint. (ll. 950–4)

Like the author of the life of Mary, and Mary herself, Zosimus has been converted to the principle of disclosure – he no longer censors his speech or declines to report his spiritual experience, following the saint in relating what was hitherto unspeakable. Moreover, the brethren appear to follow his lead; their celebration of Mary's life and story heralds a change in the practices of the monastery. Although it is not made explicit what these changes are, the need to correct them had been foreseen by Mary (ll. 743–6; 954–6); her own vocal holiness being so much at odds with the monastery's hush, it is very tempting to reason that a space for unrepressed speech would meet with her approval.

This point on Mary's impact on the monastery is significant. Like an anchorite, Mary remains outside a church even when she is affecting what goes on within it. She is also singled out from the *Lives of Saints* even when she is included within it.[39] Magennis reasons that Ælfric himself did not include this life partly because he was more interested in cenobitic models of community and moderation. I would like to suggest, however, that while Mary could not be accused of doing anything by halves, she does draw together the cenobitic community and increase the communication between brethren when she encourages Zosimus to go back, not conceal what he has seen and heard. It is not strictly true that she is indifferent to or against the ideal of community and the interaction between the monastery and what lies beyond it. Both within and apparently without Ælfric's compendium, Mary is another sort of constitutive outside, defining the *Lives of Saints* by what she is not. For Ælfric she may have been an awkward fit. For his copyists and early readers, she was conspicuous by her absence, a silence asking to be broken.

THE BODY THAT SHUTS

Zosimus's monastery becomes a space where experience shall no longer be concealed, and Mary's example is taken up within its walls as well as beyond them. Day-to-day monastic discipline is combined with that almost purgative aspect of the desert regimen that compels that the religious experience be expressed in words. In a text in which speech is less an abstract entity but

[39] Indeed, her *vita* is firmly 'enclosed' within British Library MS Cotton E vii, where the story of Mary the Egyptian is found at ff. 122v–136r, in the middle of its 241 folios.

rather a physical pollutant that might even contaminate the air, the emptying of speech from the body is in this way configured as one more way in which the brethren may perform their asceticism. For all the lavish corporeality of Mary's past, her custom in the desert mirrors, indeed exemplifies, the ideal of the brethren at the monastery, being (all but) 'on lichamen dead and on gaste libbende' (dead in body and living in spirit, ll. 111–12). Unsurprisingly, her already popular life was particularly favoured by other aspiring ascetics and recluses. For the recluse especially, the example of this desert mother might be appropriated not as a model of penitence but as the ideal of the secluded life and the rejection of the world. Stevenson notes that it was used as a model for at least one female recluse in eleventh-century England; however, it is at the expense of Mary's past life in the 'drastically expurgated and carefully-slanted account' that came to be read in Eva of Wilton's solitude.[40] From a 'harlot of the desert' Mary becomes, rather, an icon of endurance when the audience for her *vita* is not male and monastic but female and enclosed. While the institution of the anchoritic life has its origins in the lives of the 'desert saints' – Anthony, Paul, Mary of Egypt and their ilk – the life of an English recluse was not that of a Mary or a Thaïs.[41] Not roaming but confined, not a spiritual guide but prohibited from teaching, not outspoken but at times barely speaking at all, the handling of women's speech in this tradition is very different, as the guide known as *Ancrene Wisse* makes clear.

Ancrene Wisse was written at the request of three sisters resident in an anchorhold, by a cleric who may have been their confessor. It exists in seventeen manuscripts in Middle English, French and Latin, dating from the thirteenth to sixteenth centuries, and it is generally accepted that the lost original version was composed some time after 1215 and most likely between 1221 and 1250.[42] On the basis of internal and linguistic evidence, the anchorhold has been

[40] Stevenson, 'Holy Sinner', p. 45.

[41] The classic studies of anchoritic life and English recluses are still R. M. Clay, *The Hermits and Anchorites of England* (London: Methuen, 1914) and Ann K. Warren, *Anchorites and their Patrons in Medieval England* (Berkeley: University of California Press, 1985).

[42] There are seven extant English versions, four in French and four in Latin. For the textual transmission, see E. J. Dobson, 'The Date and Composition of *Ancrene Wisse*', *Proceedings of the British Academy*, 52 (1966), pp. 181–208; E. J. Dobson, *The Origins of* Ancrene Wisse (Oxford: Clarendon, 1976); Bella Millett, ed., 'Textual Introduction', *Ancrene Wisse: A Corrected Edition of the Text in Cambridge, Corpus Christi College, MS 402 with Variants from other Manuscripts*, 2 vols, EETS o.s. 325, 326 (Oxford: Oxford University Press, 2005, 2008), vol. 1, pp. xi–xlv. For a discussion of the original language of the *Wisse*, see Yoko Wada's introduction, *'Temptations' from Ancrene Wisse* (Osaka: Kansai University Press, and Cambridge: D. S. Brewer, 1994), pp. xxiv–v. For the purposes of this chapter I will be referring to Bella Millett's edition of the Corpus MS, the most recent edition of any *Ancrene Wisse* manuscript. I also quote Millett's excellent translation. See *Ancrene Wisse: A Corrected Edition of the Text in Cambridge, Corpus Christi College, MS 402 with Variants from other Manuscripts*, ed. and trans. Bella Millett, 2 vols, EETS o.s. 325 (Oxford: Oxford University Press, 2005); Ancrene

localised to the West Midlands, probably near to the Welsh border; the author was a cleric, very well read, most likely from the Dominican order.[43] Though written originally for an extremely small and sequestered group that seems the very definition of a niche audience, the work became much more popular and was translated and adapted for male readers and lay audiences. Indeed, it was sufficiently influential within the lifetime of its original author for him to make revisions that addressed a network of anchoresses that now numbered twenty or more. The work is associated with two other separate series of texts: the *Katherine* Group, which comprises the lives of three saints (Juliana, Margaret and, of course, Katherine), plus two tracts on the guarding of the soul and virginity respectively, and the *Wooing* Group, a set of four religious works in alliterative prose and verse.[44] The connection between *Ancrene Wisse* and the *Katherine* Group, with which it shares a loose theme and a narrow dialect (known, since its identification by Tolkien, as the AB language), has ensured a long academic interest in the language of the guide.[45] The origins of this sophisticated nexus of works have been a tantalising prospect for scholars since the seventeenth century, but particularly since James Morton, in his 1853 edition, declared it was composed first in English and not Latin.[46] E. J.

Wisse: *A Guide for Anchoresses*, ed. and trans. Bella Millett (Exeter: Exeter University Press, 2009). References will be given in parentheses, by book and page number.

43 Yoko Wada provides a concise and lucid summary of *Ancrene Wisse* scholarship on the manuscript tradition and questions of dating, authorship and provenance in 'What is *Ancrene Wisse*?', in *A Companion to* Ancrene Wisse, ed. Yoko Wada (Cambridge: D. S. Brewer, 2003), pp. 1–28.

44 See Geoffrey Shepherd, introduction to *Ancrene Wisse: Parts Six and Seven* (Exeter: Exeter University Press, 1985), for a table showing agreement in content between six MSS (p. xiv).

45 J. R. R. Tolkien characterised the language of the *Ancrene Wisse* as 'self-consistent and unadulterated. It is a unity. It is either a faithful transcript of some actual dialect of nearly unmixed descent, or a "standard" language based on one.' He also made the argument more forcefully than previous scholars that the language of *Ancrene Wisse* (A) was 'identical, down to the minute and therefore significant details, with the language of MS Bodley 34'. See '*Ancrene Wisse* and *Hali Meiðhad*', *Essays and Studies* 14 (1929), 104–26 (pp. 106–7). For major studies of the AB language since Tolkien see Þe Liflade ant te Passiun of Seinte Iuliene, ed. S. R. T. O. d'Ardenne, EETS o.s. 248 (Oxford: Oxford University Press, 1961); and Arne Zettersten, *Studies in the Dialect and Vocabulary of the 'Ancrene Riwle'* (Lund: C. W. K. Gleerup, 1965). D'Ardenne localised the AB language to the West Midlands, while Zettersten analysed the dialect's diachronic and synchronic development. The lexicon of *Ancrene Wisse* and the AB texts is still under construction in linguistic analysis and combines English, French, Latin, Welsh and Scandinavian elements; see for example Andrew Breeze, 'Welsh *Baban* "Baby" and *Ancrene Wisse*', *Notes and Queries* 40.1 (1993), 12–13; Carole Hough, 'Two Puns in *Ancrene Wisse*', *Notes and Queries* 54.2 (2007), 122–3.

46 *The Ancren Riwle; a Treatise on the Rules and Duties of Monastic Life, Edited and Translated from a Semi-Saxon MS. of the Thirteenth Century*, ed. James Morton (London: Camden Society, 1853).

Dobson traced the *Wisse*'s lineage and argued the case for Brian of Lingen, a secular canon of Wigmore, as having been the author; while this research had its flaws and the attribution is no longer accepted, *Origins of Ancrene Wisse* still attests the investigative depth and imaginative leaps demanded by such a search.[47] The historical silence of the anchoresses themselves has not been broken; the *Wisse* itself is nonetheless beguilingly eloquent about what these women may have been like.

The guide is structured in eight parts (or *dalen*), which represent a formal interpretation of the containment the work describes, being composed of two segments (I and VIII) that address behaviour and daily habits, or 'outer rule', which bookend and enclose a further six sections that treat the 'inner rule'.[48] The outer rule, the author specifies, should be the handmaid to the inner rule, and should be read by the anchoress to her own handmaid on a regular basis. In the anchorhold, the boundary with the external is regulated rigorously in order to bring regulation to the internal self. As such, the *Wisse* is 'an uncommonly worldly book' – not only a guide in which the external rule is handmaiden to the internal, but one in which the anchoress learns to reconfigure her knowledge and memory of the secular and external as experience that may be devotional and internalised.[49] The anchoress *needs* precisely the sense of vibrant, noisy, scruffy life outside her anchorhold that the *Wisse* continually evokes, in order to endlessly create her own enclosure on its inside; an 'abjected outside' that lives in the subject in the form of 'its own founding repudiation'.[50] Thus, while the anchoress is kept within four walls, endlessly negotiating the outside world that is her frame – literally her frame – of reference, she is also situated on the exterior, dwelling (though she may look on the mass through her squint) on the outside of a church.

47 See Dobson, *The Origins of* Ancrene Wisse. Dobson misidentifed the anchorhold at Deerfold as the home of a group of sisters, rather than (as it was in fact) brothers. The correction of *sororibus* to *fratribus* and its implications for Dobson's identification comes in Sally Thompson, *Women Religious: The Founding of English Nunneries after the Norman Conquest* (Oxford: Clarendon Press, 1991). See also Bella Millett, 'The Origins of the *Ancrene Wisse*: New Answers, New Questions', *Medium Ævum* 61.2 (1992), 206–28, which re-examines Dobson's identification of the author with the Victorine order, proposing Dominican authorship instead.

48 On the form of *Ancrene Wisse*, Janet Grayson shows that 'This is no incidental distinction by which the ordinary duties of everyday life are separated from contemplative withdrawal [...] Nor is the linear division of the two Rules ever static.' Grayson, *Structure and Imagery in* Ancrene Wisse (Hanover, NH: University Press of New England, 1974), p. 10. Grayson also notes that the writer borrows this structure from Aelred (p. 4).

49 Linda Georgianna, *The Solitary Self: Individuality in the* Ancrene Wisse (Cambridge: MA, Harvard University Press, 1981), p. 32; see also pp. 32–78.

50 Butler, *Bodies That Matter*, p. 3

Of the 'inner rule', the majority is given over to a discussion of temptation, confession and penance, a sort of penitential within the guide.[51] This central passage is notable for its extended treatment of the seven deadly sins, where the desert is not the Egyptian's zone of solitude and contemplation – or even of uninhabitability – but a waste swarming with venomous and vicious animals, a taxonomy of zoomorphic vice in which each sin-animal ceaselessly produces offspring of equal repugnance.[52] Like the text as a whole, this section is also a meditation on the boundaries of inner and outer, and adds another dimension to the series of concentric spaces the *Wisse*-author evokes when he moves from the book to the body, from the body to the mouth, from the mouth to sin and, in the parade of sin-animals, sins inside sins.[53] In this chapter I will be looking chiefly at the second and fifth books, which deal with the control of the senses (including speech) and the conditions of confession respectively; in these two books the author expounds the extraordinary power of speech and of the refusal to speak.

Like the life of Mary of Egypt, the text of *Ancrene Wisse* was transmitted through several languages and dialects from a single source, but unlike Ælfric's *Lives of Saints* there is editorial alteration and adaptation present in the work even in its earliest stages, when it was probably reworked by its original author. Bella Millett has characterised the transmission of *Ancrene Wisse* as a textual history that reveals 'the effects of *mouvance*', the text having been 'modified and modernized as it travelled through space and time'.[54] The text's language and meandering textual tradition, its multi-lingual borrowings,

51 For the argument that the 'shrift book' section may not have been intended for anchoresses, see Gerard Sitwell, 'Introduction', *The Ancrene Riwle*, trans. M. B. Salu (London: Burns and Oates, 1955), pp. vii–xxiii (pp. xviii–xix). Linda Georgianna takes issue with this, emphasising that '[Sitwell's] explanation of the discrepancy – that these sections were not written with the anchoresses in mind at all – seriously undermines the unity of the work, a subject on which the *Wisse* author is particularly insistent. He takes every opportunity to point out how carefully he has put his book together'; see Georgianna, *The Solitary Self*, p. 79.

52 Wada notes that '[t]he treatment of each Sin as an animal is by far the earliest in English literature'; see *'Temptations' from Ancrene Wisse*, ed. and trans. Yoko Wada (Osaka: Kansai University Press, and Cambridge: D. S. Brewer, 1994), p. xxi.

53 For studies on the formal and spiritual significance of the *Wisse*-author's insistence on the physicality and materiality of the anchoress's devotion, see Jocelyn Wogan-Browne [Price], '"Inner" and "Outer": Conceptualizing the Body in *Ancrene Wisse* and Aelred's *De Institutione Inclusarum*', in *Medieval English Religious and Ethical Literature: Essays in Honour of G. H. Russell*, ed. Gregory Kratzman and James Simpson (Cambridge: Cambridge University Press, 1986), pp. 192–208; Elizabeth Robertson, 'The Rule of the Body: The Feminine Spirituality of the *Ancrene Wisse*', in *Seeking the Woman in Late Medieval and Renaissance Writings: Essays in Feminist Contextual Criticism*, ed. Sheila Fisher and Janet E. Halley (Knoxville, TN: University of Tennessee Press, 1989), pp. 109–34; Catherine Innes-Parker, 'Fragmentation and Reconstruction: Images of the Female Body in *Ancrene Wisse* and the *Katherine* Group', *Comitatus* 26.1 (1995), 27–52.

54 Bella Millett, '*Mouvance* and the Medieval Author: Re-editing *Ancrene Wisse*', in

even puns, seem almost to echo the way in which the instability of language is repeatedly evoked by its author. He makes a point of telling his readers to reflect at length and very carefully on certain words he uses in his guidance when he advises, 'eauerihwer-se Ich ga swiðere uorð, leaueð þer lengest, for þer Ich feðeri on a word tene oðer tweolue' (wherever I move on more rapidly is where you should pause the longest, since there I am compressing ten or twelve words into one, IV. 76). This is his qualification on the already lengthy section listing the 'cubs' of the lion of pride, which itself falls in what is by far the longest of *Ancrene Wisse*'s eight sections. Although he is only supplying the names, it is not at all to be supposed that there is no more to be said of them: where he is brief his words may be weighty, and in fact, the less is said, the more import there may be. The words that are to be inferred, and their capacity to accrue interpretations and meanings, are turned to the *Wisse*-writer's advantage; by the same manoeuvre, the impracticality or even impossibility of ever expressing oneself fully may be best expressed by the words the author cannot find space, time or, on occasion, the daring to write. Though the pensive reflection he encourages of his dear sisters, as they meditate on all his possible meanings both expressed and unexpressed, is to be considered no less valid for it, the author also concludes, with wry pragmatism, 'ȝef Iche schulde writen al, hwenne come Ich to ende?' (if I were to write everything, when would I come to an end?, IV. 78).

If the *Wisse*-author's writing must be limited, an anchoress's speech is all the more so. On the one hand, silence is so pervasive it can be analysed as an alternative linguistic code.[55] As Anne Savage points out, the whole text is designed so that the anchoresses may be kept as silent as possible.[56] On the other hand, the difficulty with silence is that it causes the silent subject to long for speech – it is 'wordes fostrilt', as the *Wisse*-author renders Gregory's maxim. The physical action of speech and its dependence on the sensuous movement of tongue, lips, throat and breath becomes an almost erotic

Late-Medieval Religious Texts and their Transmission: Essays in Honour of A. I. Doyle, ed. A. J. Minnis (Cambridge: D. S. Brewer, 1994), pp. 9–20 (p. 13).

55 See Risto Hiltunen, 'Telling the Anchorite Code: *Ancrene Wisse* on Language', in *Discourse Perspectives on English: Medieval to Modern*, ed. Risto Hiltunen and Janne Skaffari (Amsterdam: John Benjamins, 2003), pp. 57–86. Hiltunen argues that silence may have a 'communicative aspect' when it is the response to speech (p. 69) and compares the 'anchoritic code' with the use of silence among Quakers. Hiltunen also casts the *Wisse*-author as the originator of a code of speech and of silence, a linguistic prescription: 'The author of the text is concerned above all with how the three sisters who formed the original audience of the book should behave as anchoresses in terms of speech. In a sense he is thus providing a linguistic code for them. The purpose of the code is to establish a set of routines that cater, if possible, for all social contingencies where the sisters might need to speak' (p. 73).

56 Savage, 'The Communal Authorship of *Ancrene Wisse*', in *A Companion to* Ancrene Wisse, ed. Wada, pp. 45–57.

combination and as much to be suppressed as the eroticism of Mary of Egypt. And once tempted into speech, one word may easily become many. As with food, too much speech is inherently sinful since it is without moderation. Even the pious intention to speak 'lutel ant wel isette wordes' (a few well-chosen words, II. 31) can be thwarted by the failings of flesh, for 'þe tunge is slubbri for ha wadeð i wete, ant slit lihtliche forð from lut word into monie' (the tongue is slippery because it wades in water, and glides on easily from a few words into many, II. 31).

The comfort and security of the internal life are often dependent on the regulation of the external life, and extreme care when externalising thoughts and speech. Speech receives a lot of attention in *Ancrene Wisse* (for all that the sections on sight are so well-known). Many of the sins and sub-species of sin described in part IV are sins of the tongue (about which more in Chapter 4 of this book), and the onus is on the anchoress not only to ensure she does not commit any herself but to prevent her maids uttering scandalous words, or suffering anyone outside the anchorhold to be connected with her in any unseemly fashion. The anchoress's responsibility for speech extends to all around her. No more must be said of an anchoress than of a dead person – though plenty is said of the dead, of course. A man who offers friendship that might be feigned is especially to be feared, and again the advice of the *Wisse*-author is simply, 'ne 3eoue 3e to swuch mon nan in3ong to speokene' (do not give a man of this sort any opening to speak, II. 39). Even the devil may be prevented from speaking, but in this case it is through speech, not silence (as every sin that is confessed is an entry he must remove from the roll he will read on Judgement Day). The ideal penitent would dumbfound the devil and disable him from speaking at all.

The speech of the anchoress is thus so uneasy, the text of *Ancrene Wisse* so slippery and its expressions so loaded with double meanings and implicit meanings – hinted at but redacted so as not to be discerned by those readers who did not already make the imaginative leap for themselves – that it is tempting to conclude that its message is simply: avoid speaking wherever possible. In many situations this is the case – the anchorite is to speak as little as possible to any who come to her window, who live with her, who ask her questions. She is not even supposed to make vows (Preface, p. 3). While proliferation may be desirable when the anchoress is instructed to dwell on and expand her instructor's terse phrases, allowing them to multiply in her head, once her tongue starts to articulate these words their plurality and quantity become dangerous to her. Nevertheless, for all the *Wisse*-author insists that silence is golden, this would be a gross oversimplification of the text as a whole, since its crucial section concerns that most necessarily vocal and overdetermined speech act, confession. In confession, the anchoress should loose her tongue and, far from being a silent Madonna, talk at what we can only assume is considerable length.

Ancrene Wisse's model of feminine silence (as well as virtue and virginity) is naturally the Virgin Mary, who is known to speak only four times in the course of the Bible. For the anchoress, speech is to be carefully timed, conscientiously stored up and strategically used – 'For hwa-se is muche stille, ant halt silence longe, ha mei hopien sikerliche þet, hwen ha spekeð toward Godd, þet he hire ihere' (For anyone who is often quiet, and keeps silence for long periods, can certainly hope that when she speaks to God, he will listen to her, II. 32). Everyday speech is therefore kept rare so as not to distract from or dilute the confessional speech: both speech and speechlessness wield considerable power.

In everyday living, a recluse 'folhið ure Leafdi, ant nawt te cakele Eue [...] Nabbe ha nawt henne cunde' (follow[s] our Lady, and not the chattering Eve [...] She should not have the nature of a hen, II. 27). To confound sin and the devil, however, the reverse becomes true, for – as the *Wisse*-author stresses frequently – confession is the most potent weapon against sin. In the oral imagery of the central sections, whereas hope is sweet spice to be savoured in the mouth, sin is a toxin to be expelled as soon as possible; the author counsels his readers to '[c]ulche hit i schrift ut utterliche' (vomit it out openly in confession, IV. 79). To expel sin orally is to purge the soul; to reveal one's sin is to cut off the enemy's head, like Judith slaying Holofernes, and force the devil who writes up the roll of one's sins to scrape off the words again and cause him more work and frustration (V. 130). This devil who might be forced to erase or retract what he has been at pains to record is, peculiarly, in an inversion of the author's predicament, in that both grapple with the impossibility of completion. Against this, the author tries to provide guidance for every eventuality (including circumstances he trusts his anchoresses will not experience), even scripting responses where he feels it necessary; and whereas in other circumstances his readers are counselled in silence, here they follow the example of their guide – in confession, an anchoress should say everything.

The conditions and qualities of the ideal confession are listed at the start of part V: it should be 'wreiful, bitter mid sorhe, ihal, naket, ofte imaket, hihful, eadmod, scheomeful, [dredful ant] hopeful, wis, soð, ant willes, ahne ant studeuest, biþoht biuore longe' (accusatory, bitter with regret, complete, naked, frequently made, prompt, humble, shameful, fearful, and hopeful, discreet, truthful, and voluntary, one's own, resolute, and well thought out beforehand, V. 115).[57] Confession may be purgative, but, as Georgianna

[57] For a detailed treatment of the *Wisse*-author's moral philosophy and the development of *Ancrene Wisse*'s views on confession out of contemporary theology and practice, see Georgianna, *The Solitary Self*, pp. 79–119. Georgianna addresses the *Wisse*-author's 'complicated attitude toward the sacrament of confession', arguing that 'of the four aspects of the sacrament usually discussed – contrition, confession, absolution, and satisfaction – the author is almost exclusively interested in the first two. More

observes, it is 'not a spontaneous pouring forth, as the image of vomiting might suggest [...] rather it is an act carefully arranged'.[58] The arrangements demand not only care but the negotiation of considerable contradictions: confession should be thought out in advance, yet must be hasty; it must be truthful, yet discreet. One of the most challenging of these *conditiones* is the instruction that confession conceal nothing, but should rather be *nuda* or naked: as the author admits, knowing how, when and of what to speak and not speak is a delicate balancing act. Still, no more should emerge from the anchoress's mouth than is needful; her expression should, like Zosimus's cloak, cover up what there is most need to conceal. The limits of speech are thus seen when the anchoress is vocal – not when her mouth is shut but when it is permitted to open.

Since the 'naket' confession builds on the 'ihal' (whole) confession, the difficulty arises with the traditional reluctance of confessors to encourage even oral rehearsal of certain sins. Confession must be naked:

> ȝef þu heatest ti sunne, hwi spekest tu menskeliche þrof? Hwi hudest tu his fulðe? Spec hit scheome schendfulliche ant tuk hit al to wundre, alswa as þu wel wult schende þen schucke. 'Sire,' ha seið, þe wummon, 'Ich habbe ihaued leofman', oðer 'Ich habbe ibeon', ha seið, 'fol of me seoluen.' Þis nis nawt naket schrift. Biclute þu hit nawt. Do awei þe totagges! Vnwrih þe ant sei, 'Sire, Godes are! Ich am a ful stod-meare, a stinkinde hore!' ȝef þi fa a ful nome ant cleope þi sunne fule. Make hit i schrift steort-naket: þet is, ne hel þu nawiht of al þet lið þer-abuten.

> If you hate your sin, why do you talk so politely about it? Why do you hide its filthiness? Insult it shamefully and abuse it, if you are really willing to shame the devil. 'Father,' a woman will say, 'I have had a lover', or 'I have made a fool of myself.' This is not naked confession. Don't wrap it up. Get rid of the trimmings! Lay yourself bare and say, 'Father, God have mercy! I am a filthy stud-mare, a stinking whore!' Give your enemy a bad name, and describe your sin crudely. Strip it stark-naked in confession: that is, do not conceal anything about all the circumstances. (V. 120)

... but not too naked:

specifically, he concentrates upon the interdependence of contrition and confession as the internal and external aspects of the sacrament' (p. 119). Major influences on the *Wisse*-author's guide to confession are covered in Bella Millett's article '*Ancrene Wisse* and the Conditions of Confession', *English Studies* 80.3 (1999), 193–215; Millett argues that these are 'less provincial, more in touch with the mainstream European tradition of pastoral teaching and preaching, than has sometimes been assumed' ('Conditions of Confession', p. 215). On the sixteen conditions, their roots in Thomas Aquinas and their development through the Middle Ages, see Tentler, *Sin and Confession*, pp. 106–9, 106 n. 3.

58 Georgianna, *The Solitary Self*, p. 111.

> (Þah to fule me mei seggen. Me ne þearf nawt nempnin þet fule dede bi his ahne fule nome, ne þe schendfule limes bi hire ahne nome. Inoh is to seggen swa þet te hali schrift-feader witerliche understonde hweat tu wulle meanen).

> (Though it is possible to speak too crudely. There is no need to call that filthy act by its own filthy name, or the shameful parts of the body by their actual names. It is enough to put it so that the holy confessor understands clearly what you mean to say). (V. 120)

The injunction to stop short of actually naming 'the filthy act' by its proper name is an insertion made at a later stage in the evolution of *Ancrene Wisse*, and comes virtually direct from Peter of Poitiers.[59] It chimes with the author's previous reticence about sexual sins, so it is perhaps curious that he chooses the sin of lust to illustrate the condition of naked confession. The special conditions of confession make almost all things permissible: uncovering oneself is therefore good (and even exemplary) in confession even when it is not in other circumstances. (The verb *unwrihen*, used of the penitent who lays herself bare in confession, has been used earlier in the *Wisse* in the analogy of the uncovered pit, which causes others to fall, II. 23). Yet, as the proviso against naming sins and body parts too baldly would seem to suggest, even in confession a few unguarded, uncovered words may become another 'pit'.

There are certain forbidden utterances that are distinguished quite simply, for example the prohibition against speaking of any co-sinners by their own names, and the strict counsel against vowing, lest the vow be broken.[60] Others are fraught with complexity, and the unknown quantity is the knowledge the penitent already possesses – or even possessed by the confessor himself. The likelihood of the priest being tempted, too, must be considered carefully. Whereas the author assures the reader that common sins may be confessed to any priest, if her confession involves any fleshly longing, she must be 'ful trusti [...] o þe preostes godlec þet ha allunge schaweð' (very confident of the virtue of the priest to whom she reveals this fully, V. 130). If it should happen that the anchoress has not her regular confession at a point when she may be *in extremis*, caution can be relaxed to an extent; for this circumstance the author scripts a safe confession, advising that the recluse admit only to a non-specific 'flesches fondunge' (sexual temptation, V. 130), which has drawn her thoughts and tempts her to consent to such a distraction. The dangers of confessing more nakedly than this to an unfamiliar priest are especially great when the substitute is also a young priest.

For the confessor, the decision to (un)cover certain words is still more weighty. The *Wisse*-author stops short of naming certain sins, but instead

59 See Millett, *Ancrene Wisse* vol. II, p. 216.

60 On this point, see Zina Peterson, 'Institution and Individual in Conflict: The Early Middle English *Ancrene Wisse* and the Authority of Speech Acts', *Journal of Historical Pragmatics* 6 (2005), 69–86.

leaves the reader to infer their gravity from their unspeakability.[61] He condemns '[h]ondlunge oðer ei felunge bitweone mon ant ancre' (fondling or any kind of touching between a man and an anchoress) as a sin so vile 'þet nis na neod to speoken ne writen þer-to3eines' (that there is no need to speak or write against it, II. 46). He declares he would rather see his charges hanging from the gallows than see them kiss a man – he is 'stille of þet mare' (say[ing] nothing about more than that, II. 46). Robert Mills suggests of this determined reluctance to name names that there may be another 'unspeakable' (sodomitical) sin lurking in the anchorhold, drawing particular attention to the unnameable offspring of the scorpion of lechery in part IV,[62] where 'the author's circumspection regarding the precise nature of the sin calls sodomy into being in the context of a refusal to incite it'.[63] The particular variety of sodomy in this context might be masturbation (as alluded to in the section on

61 Siegfried Wenzel, 'The Sources of Chaucer's Seven Deadly Sins', *Traditio* 30 (1974), 351–78, relates the Parson's summative sermon to Peraldus's early thirteenth-century *Summa de vitiis*; *Ancrene Wisse*'s sixteen-point list, on the other hand, reflects an earlier tradition that did not have an established order or number of *conditiones*, but which in the early thirteenth century was growing rapidly. See Millett, 'Conditions of Confession', pp. 196–203.

62 'Ich ne dear nempnin þe uncundeliche cundles of þis deofles scorpiun, attri iteilet; ah sari mei ha beon þe, bute fere oðer wið, haueð swa ifaed cundel of hire galnesse, þet Ich ne mei speoken of for scheome, ne ne dear for drede, leste sum leorni mare uuel þen ha con ant beo þrof itemptet. [...] 3e þe of swucches nute nawt, ne þurue 3e nawt wundrin ow ne þenchen hwet Ich meane, ah 3eldeð graces Godd þet 3e swuch uncleannesse nabbað ifondet, ant habbeð reowðe of ham þe i swuch beoð ifallen.'
(I do not dare to mention by name the unnatural young of this devil's scorpion with its poisonous tail; but that woman may be sorry who, with or without a partner, has nurtured like this the young of her lechery, which I cannot discuss for shame, and dare not for fear, in case someone might learn more wickedness than she knows already and be tempted by it [...] Those of you who know nothing about such things need not wonder or speculate on what I mean, but should give thanks to God that you have not experimented with such filthy practices, and feel sorry for those who have fallen into them; IV. 79).
On this zoomorphic sin more generally, see Lucinder Rumsey, 'The Scorpion of Lechery and *Ancrene Wisse*', *Medium Ævum* 61.1 (1992), 48–58.

63 Robert Mills, 'Gender, Sodomy, Friendship, and the Medieval Anchorhold', *Journal of Medieval Religious Cultures* 36.1 (2010), 1–27 (p. 13). On the subject of this spectre of sodomy, Mills also draws parallels between *Ancrene Wisse* and Aelred of Reivaulx's earlier *De institutione inclusarum*, a text the *Wisse*-author knew. Not only does this text figure women's conversation with one another as a potentially dangerous activity – as 'lusty tales generate lusty fantasy' (p. 14) when female outsiders come and speak to the anchoress – but '[w]hat is more, the fourteenth century [Middle English] version contains a chapter referring to despicable sex acts performed outside the company of men' (p. 15). Here again, 'the rhetoric of the unspeakable, and the emphasis on the origins of the sin in a mode of lust performed "wit-oute a man," may also contain sodomitic undertones' as well as the suggestion of autoerotic activity (p. 15). What the *Wisse*-author deems unspeakable is articulated more clearly, if still not explicitly, in the later analogue.

nuda confession, which guides the penitent through the admission that she 'handled' herself) or same-sex relations. Thirteenth-century *summae* tend to worry about masturbation and ways of extracting its confession: Thomas of Chobham, Raymond of Peñaforte, Robert of Flamborough and, particularly, Jean Gerson are all exercised by this problem.[64] It may be that this is a contemporary fixation and one that the author of the *Wisse* was therefore alive to, or perhaps this is a more insidious type of sexual sin for an anchorhold simply because it does not even require another person to be present.[65] Certainly there is an explicitly articulated fear of mentioning sexual sins, even when they are implicitly articulated, and most of all when they are more elaborate than fornication, adultery, seduction or incest. Even in the tour of the devil's court in part IV, where the activities of other sinners are described in detail, all that is said of lechers is that they 'secheð hu ha mahen meast vilainie wurchen' (seek out ways of behaving as badly as possible, IV. 82–3). There are other sins that do not need to be named – the species of gluttony, for example (IV. 78) – but these are not inherently unspeakable; rather, the author is not afraid that his charges will indulge them. Such is the danger of lechery that, though she eats every day, even the redolent description of the drunk, grease-stained glutton's excesses cannot tempt the anchoress as much as one mention of erotic sin.

Despite this, the guide to circumstances of sin in part V, which are the 'trimmings' or disguises of otherwise naked sin, species of lust appear in the illustrative exemplar so often (the imaginary penitent may confess to kissing or 'handling' herself, or a monk, a priest, a clerk or a woman, through her wantonness or weakness) that the author's previous concern about tempting his readers seems almost forgotten (V. 120–1). In the hypothetical seduction that plays out through the relation of circumstances of sin, there is a keen awareness that the possibility of sexual sin exists even in the domicile of one who should be cut off from the rest of the community. There is also a contradiction here between the dangers of what should not be said and the instruction to call sins by blunt names – how foul, one might wonder, is foul enough? The instruction regarding the lexis for confession starts off as having as its goal the hatred of one's sin, by means of naming it foul names; yet the message to 'hate the sin and not the sinner' is quickly inverted in the practice the author advocates: it is, in fact, the anchoress herself (and, in the example provided, only the anchoress)

64 See Tentler, *Sin and Confession*, pp. 91–3; Bossy, 'The Social History of Confession in the Age of the Reformation', pp. 35–8; Lochrie, *Covert Operations*, pp. 34–6.

65 James Brundage notes that 'Masturbation had no legal consequences, was dealt with in confession, not the courts, and hence did not concern the canonists of this generation. Moral writers, however, continued to denounce it as a serious sin. Thomas of Chobham devoted no less than four chapters of his *Summa* to nocturnal emission.' Brundage, *Law, Sex and Christian Society in Medieval Europe* (Chicago: University of Chicago Press, 1991), pp. 400–1.

who is the one being named foully.[66] She is a whore, stinking and filthy; yet the sin is still not named even in a 'naked' confession. Robertson characterises the *Wisse*-author's realism as stemming from a pervading misogyny, in which '[t]his apparently gender-neutral text [...] is governed by its male author's view of women as daughters of Eve, inescapably rooted in their bodies' – and perhaps, too, the materiality of the speaker's body may be more readily conceptualised and identified than the sin of which one must not speak.[67]

The unspeakable in the anchorhold returns to the material, its opposite in some ways, when the necessity to avoid a description leaves the speech with nowhere to alight. The way to naked confession is still unclear, since the wickedness of the sin is articulated but not the sin itself. The assumption that an anchoress is always a (sinful, fleshly) woman first – this is her greatest challenge in the devotional life – here seems to imply that flesh may stand in for the sin, that the anchoress may be the same as her sin. The implications of male authorship must also be taken into account in any consideration of the constructions of the female anchoritic voice, as Robertson points out. These women, she says, 'are taught to control their bodies [...] to be silent and repress anger, and, most of all, to control their senses', so that a cackling Eve may be made into a 'passive, silent Mary rather than into an active, abstract thinker'.[68] Again, the control of the female body is figured in and by the silencing of the female voice, yet the author's articulation of spiritual matters to his charges also depends on his and their recognition of the excesses of the corporeal and material, which are so often alluded to in the *Wisse* as to be constantly on the mind of any anchoress who does as he directs and reads aloud from this text to her maids on a regular basis. All of the boundaries placed on the female anchoritic body proceed from a body outside of hers, wielding the pen and mouthing the words. The practice of proper confession, however, also emphasises that knowledge – what to say, what not to say; what to cover, what to uncover – is of paramount importance, not only to the confessor but to the penitent. It is also keenly felt by the writer, who is sensitive to the time it takes and the impossibility of saying all in any case, and would rather start for Rome than redo his work. If I told all, where would I stop indeed?

[66] In the French version (Trinity MS R 14.7) the insults are gendered both male and female (pp. 71–2), as would seem appropriate for the mixed audience to which it was addressed. In the English and Latin versions they are only gendered female; in Pepys (p. 135) and Nero (p. 143) there is an additional plea for the confessor's mercy, as well as God's. See W. H. Tretheway, ed., *The French Text of the Ancrene Riwle: edited from Trinity College, Cambridge, MS R. 147*, EETS o.s. 240 (Oxford: Oxford University Press, 1958); Arne Zettersten, ed., *The English Text of the Ancrene Riwle: edited from Magdalene College, Cambridge, MS Pepys 2498*, EETS o.s. 274 (London: Oxford University Press, 1976); Mabel Day, ed., *The English Text of the Ancrene Riwle: edited from BM, MS Cotton Nero A. xiv*, EETS o.s. 225 (London: Oxford University Press, 1952).

[67] Robertson, 'Rule of the Body', p. 109.

[68] Robertson, 'Rule of the Body', p. 130.

A MOUTHFUL

There is an oral fixation in both of these texts. Mary, even in her desert wisdom, still remembers with longing her former appetites: her desire is expressed through the actions of her mouth. She speaks (and at considerable length); she offers Zosimus the kiss of peace; she consumes the holy sacraments. Her miraculous meals of lentils and everlasting loaves prove her sanctity, but her memories of food speak to her corporeality. Indeed, she tells Zosimus that the things she missed most about her former life in Egypt were eating flesh and fish, drinking (and becoming drunk on) wine, and singing lewd songs (ll. 616–29). The wine in particular is still in her desires after all this time (l. 623). The anchoress, meanwhile, may have a greater range in her diet but its consumption is stage-managed in considerable detail, even though the writer is confident his charges know the dangers of gluttony. The guidelines on when, what and with whom to eat are very specific, and communion is to be taken no more than fifteen times a year. Yet as Carolyn Walker Bynum has comprehensively shown, 'eating, feeding and not eating enabled [women] to control their bodies and their world'.[69] Moreover, fasting does not eliminate the element of the physical from the holy contemplative life – rather it accentuates it.[70]

Not one to speak with her mouth full, the anchoress should always observe silence at mealtimes (II. 29). Another image that unites the two preoccupations of part II – speech and food – is the translation of utterance into sustenance that produces the axiom, 'Muche fol were þe mahte to his bihoue hweðer-se he walde grinden greot oþer hweate, ȝef he grunde þe greot ant lette þe hweate' (Anyone who had the choice of grinding sand or wheat for his own benefit would be an idiot if he ground the sand and left the wheat, II. 29). Speaking, eating and listening are conflated in the analogy as it continues with the advice for the anchoress to grind nothing but 'sawle fode' with her jaws and drink in nothing with her ears that will not benefit her soul. The anchoress should on no account 'wearien ne swerien' (curse or swear), though she may add the occasional *witerliche* or *sikerliche* to her speech (II. 29). Naturally, she is not to preach or counsel (II. 29).[71] The need for the avoidance of sinful

69 Carolyn Walker Bynum, *Holy Feast and Holy Fast: The Religious Significance of Food to Medieval Women* (Berkeley, CA: University of California Press, 1987), p. 189.

70 Bynum, *Holy Feast and Holy Fast*, p. 250.

71 Though the 'uttre riwle' of the *Wisse* is always only a guide (see VIII. 161), the prohibitions against communication and preaching do not prevent Julian of Norwich writing her famous *Shewings* from the anchorhold, for instance, although they condition the character she ascribes to her visions and her motivations for writing them down at all. Julian also exemplifies the anchoritic directives to remain silent (as she does for many years after she experiences the visions) so that when she does speak, her words should be all the more powerful. See also E. A. Jones, 'Anchoritic Aspects of Julian of Norwich', in *A Companion to Julian of Norwich*, ed. Liz Herbert McAvoy (Cambridge: D. S. Brewer, 2008), pp. 75–87.

speech prompts the author to include scripted speech for certain situations. If anyone asks to which order his anchoresses belong, they should answer that they are of the order of St James. Should a man show too much interest in the anchoress's sleeping arrangements, the author's advice is 'ondswerieð lihtliche, "Sire, þer-of wel mai duhen", and haldeð ow stille' (answer lightly, 'Sir, there's no need for concern about that', and say nothing further, II. 26).[72] On hearing the knock of a visitor, the anchoress performs another ritual of oral safeguarding, first sending her maid to ascertain whether or not it is vital for her to attend to them, and then if she must emerge, making the sign of the cross 'ful ȝeorne muð, ehnen, ant earen, ant te breoste mid al' (assiduously over mouth, eyes, and ears, and your breast as well) before coming forth 'mid Godes dred' (II. 27).

The uses of the mouth – primarily speaking and eating but also kissing – are consistently linked in the discussion of the control of the senses. Alexandra Barratt notes of part II that 'it is the concept of "the sins of the mouth" that functions as its submerged but articulating idea', as it underpins not only the sections on speech but on taste and smell as well.[73] The image of virtue as food occurs regularly, as does the concomitant image of wickedness as filth in the mouth; the idea of the taste of speech transforms the control of the senses into a synaesthetic experience that further emphasises the corporeality of what might elsewhere be ephemeral utterance. The sin of anger, for example, also includes contentious speech, words that are 'fule, stinkinde, scheomelese, ant schentfule, sumchearre mid great sware, monie ant prude wordes, wið warinesses ant bileasunges' (foul, stinking, shameless, and shameful, sometimes with excessive swearing, much arrogant talk, with imprecations and lies, IV. 75). After such utterances, the writer adds, the speakers 'gað wið swuch muð seoððen, ear schrift ham habbe iweschen' (go with their mouths in this state, before confession has washed them), to pray or sing, not considering that their vocalisations 'stinkeð fulre [...] þen ei rotet dogge' (stink more vilely [...] than any rotting dog, IV. 76). The corporeality of vocalisation is thus aligned to a material understanding of abstract sin and punishment.

What is the significance of this preoccupation with the mouth? As Barratt observes, it is deeply ironic in a text written for an audience that is 'more than

72 Savage notes how inescapable culpability becomes when an anchoress permits herself to be seen by a man – even if his subsequent (and, we are to assume, inevitable) sin does not occur with her, she is still at fault should he sin with another woman. See Savage, '"The Translation of the Feminine': Untranslatable Dimensions of Anchoritic Works', in *The Medieval Translator* 4, ed. Roger Ellis and Ruth Evans (Binghamton: NY: Medieval and Renaissance Texts and Studies, 1994), pp. 181–99 (pp. 185–6).

73 Alexandra Barratt, 'The Five Wits and their Structural Significance in Part II of *Ancrene Wisse*', *Medium Ævum* 56.1 (1987), 12–24 (p. 22).

ordinarily silent, and abstemious'.[74] But it is only the mouth that (according to the *Wisse* author, at least) is capable of accomplishing every one of the deadly sins by its misuse.[75] Speaking on transgressions done by other people, the author reminds his charges that a 'deboneire' child, having been beaten, kisses the rod that has hurt it, should its father so command, and tells them that they should imitate this example and 'kiss' those who have caused them harm or mistreated them – but, so that they do not misunderstand, even here there is a caveat that the kissing should be done 'naw[t] wið muð, ah wið luue of heorte' (not with the mouth, but with the love of the heart, IV. 70–1). The notion of physical kissing is avoided even in analogy; the metaphorical kissing of the rod used in punishment must still be understood as the action of the heart, while the mouth is to be used and opened as little as possible. The message, again and again, is that unregulated or unsuitable speech and use of the mouth is the gateway to unspoken transgressions of increasing magnitude. It is significant that the sin of making confession inaccurately may be compounded by the perfidy of making confession 'al to wundre' (in a quite inappropriate way, II. 28). Confession made improperly seems to be a ruse to conceal sexual relations with a priest in the anchorhold.[76] Though the *Wisse* writer follows his own maxim not to name 'schendfule limes' explicitly, a later Middle English version written for a mixed audience (with possible Wycliffite leanings) notably substitutes for the unspeakable 'sin', the 'entrance' of which

[74] Barratt, 'Five Wits', p. 22.

[75] Sandy Bardsley charts the many 'sins of the tongue' that came to fill whole treatises from the thirteenth century onwards, in *Venonous Tongues: Speech and Gender in Late Medieval England* (Philadelphia, PA: University of Pennsylvania Press, 2006), see pp. 26–44. One of the most comprehensive treatments was Peraldus's *Summa de vitiis,* which contains a substantial section after the seven deadly sins that treats exclusively of the twenty-four sins of the tongue (*de vinginti quatuor peccatis linguae*). See Guilelmus Peraldus, *Summa de virtubtibus et vitiis* (Venice: Paganino de Paganini, 1497), 332b–350a. Sins connected with the mouth that are listed in the taxonomy of temptations in part IV comprise loquacity, blasphemy and contentious speech, species of Pride; denunciation, backbiting, derision, sowing of dissension and sulking – 'þe deofles silence' – species of Envy; invective and cursing, species of Wrath; complaining or negligence in saying or doing, species of Sloth; deceit, false witness (or perjury), species of Covetousness; all five species of Gluttony; finally, provocative words and kissing, species of Lechery (see IV. 75–9). However, earlier in part II the writer has warned against still more varieties of evil speech – that which is idle, foul and poisonous is later subdivided into flattery, lying, backbiting and heresy (see II. 33). See Barratt, 'Five Wits', on the complexity of these divisions and their analogues in thirteenth-century *summae* (pp. 18–20).

[76] See Bella Millett, ed. and trans., Ancrene Wisse*: A Guide for Anchoresses* (Exeter: Exeter University Press, 2009), p. 186 n. 55. Against this suspicion a good anchoress should therefore have a witness to her visits, even by her confessor, so that malicious gossips cannot spread lies and to set an example to those who would otherwise avail themselves of this 'unseli gile'.

the writer dares not speak or write.[77] Of all the ways into the (female) body, the one the writer appears most concerned with on the surface is the mouth; yet those sins that cause him most anxiety – certainly sexual, whether or not they include sodomy or masturbation as well as faked confessions – are concerned with the body parts and entrance(s) he doesn't speak of.

INSIDE OUT, OUTSIDE IN

The gendered materialism on which the *Wisse* insists, and against which the Old English *Mary of Egypt* pushes, holds that the body that is gendered female is also and necessarily impure, fallible, leaky.[78] The image of the virginal body under siege and the need to keep oneself sealed is a commonplace.[79] Bernau suggests that, in as much as confession is the curative response to all sins, language itself is therefore 'shown to be the condition of possibility for the virgin'.[80] Confession – letting words escape that have been suppressed – is therefore the means of the intact, enclosed subject's continued self-fashioning and performance. (Though Mary is, pointedly, not a virgin, confession therefore allows her the same performative possibility.) Confession is the culmination of a conspicuous tension between insides and outsides played out on several levels. As well as the linguistic, vocal level, such tension is evident in the intersecting domains of masculine and feminine that seem to encompass but not define, and in the vastly different environments from which the two protagonists are drawn: the enclosed and the nomadic. While both the desert and the monastery are clearly sacred sites, the former is such by virtue of its remoteness from the world, existing outside the social milieu; it is, in fact, outside the latter, which maintains its religious integrity precisely by functioning as an integrated, internalising order. When the masculine can exist inside the realms of the feminine (and vice versa), or the confining walls of a monastery are keeping someone *out* of a spiritual space (as well as

77 This is in the Pepys MS: see Mills, 'Gender, Sodomy, Friendship', p. 19. The Pepys MS is also associated with Wycliffite writings: see Eric Colledge, '*The Recluse*: A Lollard Interpolated Version of the *Ancren Riwle*', *RES* 15 (1939), 1–15, 129–45. Stevenson makes the point of the foot-kissing in the life of Mary of Egypt that 'The foot is the subject of much obsessive activity in the middle East in late antiquity […] In Hebrew, the word *regel*, "foot", is sometimes metonymic for the genitals': Stevenson, 'Holy Sinner', p. 37.

78 St Jerome in his commentary on Ephesians holds that a woman may only be considered equal to a man when she wishes to serve Christ completely and thereby ceases to be feminine – then she will be called a man (*mulier esse cessabit, et dicetur vir*). Jerome, *Commentarium in Epistolam ad Ephesios Libri III*, *PL* 26 (col. 658C).

79 Though see Sarah Salih, *Versions of Virginity in Late Medieval England* (Cambridge: D. S. Brewer, 2001), for an interrogation of the constructedness of this ideal.

80 Anke Bernau, 'Virginal Effects: Text and Identity in "Ancrene Wisse"', in *Gender and Holiness*, ed. Samantha J. E. Riches and Sarah Salih (Cardiff: University of Wales Press, 2002), pp. 36–48 (p. 42).

in), there is a lot at stake when considering the implications of internal and external politics.

As an individual, Mary demonstrates with great clarity the effects of inner and outer spaces on the formation of the subject. In her days of notoriety, she is rejected and cast out even as she dwells in the heart of one of the great cosmopolitan cities of the ancient world. The cast-out Mary craves food, drink and sex in ever-increasing quantities; not only is she a social outsider, but in her hedonistic pursuits she repeatedly constructs herself as the physical, literal 'outside', where her conspicuous consumption of food and wine are metonymic of the even more conspicuous way she ushers in male visitors. After her conversion, however, Mary moves from a place of excess, of wanting more and more, of drawing all she can into herself (in all the indelicate senses she later confirms), to a space where she is surrounded by openness, the outer limits – where she tries, in fact, to *inhabit* the abject. Despite its size, the desert encloses her to the extent that she has even less human interaction than does the tightly confined anchoress – who is visited by her confessor and perhaps other guests as well, looks in on the Church, might live with a maid or two and is famously permitted a feline friend.[81] The outcast, by casting herself even further out, ends up firmly in the centre. As a wandering outsider, she is the centre of her surroundings not only because there is no one else but because she is always in-between: between earth and sky; male and female; life and death; taking little inside her but, in her conversations with Zosimus, becoming the source of spiritual nourishment. She is clothed not only in borrowed garments but in the Word of God: unlike her previous male companions, Zosimus is not permitted to penetrate her even with a gaze. Her unspeakable, unnamed parts are taken out of the equation because it is now she, not a male counterpart, who is closed and immaculate.

Where Mary blurs the boundaries between inside and outside (and most of the other boundaries she encounters as well), the workings of innerness and outerness in *Ancrene Wisse* continually diversify and are held in a sophisticated suspension.[82] The very form of the text is pressed into this service, with the 'outer rule' framing the 'inner rule', so that the whole text is composed of concentric discussions: the core of temptation, confession and penance is encased in meditations on the senses that might admit entrance to sin; the meditation on thoughts and feelings is wrapped in a practical, meticulous

81 See the 'outer rule' for the author's arguments against the keeping of cows and concession on the keeping of a cat (VIII. 157).

82 On this suspension and the fluidity of the internal and external in *Ancrene Wisse*, see Wogan-Browne, '"Inner" and "Outer"', Sarah Beckwith, 'Passionate Regulation: Enclosure, Ascesis, and the Feminist Imaginary', *South Atlantic Quarterly* 93.4 (1994), 803–24. For a discussion of the relations between the *Wisse*'s readers and their spaces, and the 're-placing' of sex and pleasure, see Lara Farina, *Erotic Discourse in Early English Religious Writing* (Basingstoke: Palgrave Macmillan, 2006).

and nearly comprehensive outer guide to proper behaviour and style of living. The ins and outs of the zoomorphic deadly sins are even more striking, for when each class of sin will inevitably birth another sub-set of sin, each sin-animal becomes the outside of a further sin-animal buried in its womb. The womb in which the anchoress is invited to imagine herself, which doubles as a tomb, therefore echoes not only the womb of the Virgin, in which Christ was enclosed, or the 'wombe' of the dragon that swallowed up St Margaret, but also the womb of the sin-animal, where one transgression breeds and nurtures another. The anchoress who sins by looking outside the walls of her cell is accordingly nurturing the further transgressions that will gestate in the womb of her anchorhold; *Hali Meiðhad* goes one further by imagining both pious and impious thoughts as offspring, warning that 'vre licomes lust is þes feondes foster; vre wit is Godes dohter; ant ba beoð us inwið' (our physical desire is the Devil's offspring; our reason is God's daughter; and both are within us).[83] As the treatise on virginity also reminds its reader, of course, the virgin who permits herself to be tempted still further may well find herself growing and nourishing her own young in the literal sense to which the these allegorical procreating animals all gesture.

The manoeuvres of inner and outer, speakable and unspeakable, in these two texts also emphasise that, even in the telling of a life, the female subject is narratologically enclosed by the work of a male author. As is so often the case, the text that creates these women does so through the mediation of the masculine author, the monk entering the desert or the confessor looking into the anchorhold. The terms in which the interiority of the subject is enclosed are decided by, as it were, an outsider. The condition of being (on) the 'inside' or the 'outside' of a given social structure or community is one that is continually subject to change and which changes its subjects. This is never truer than in confession. Long before psychotherapy, confession was the talking cure: the *Wisse* likens unconfessed sin to the wound that kills the patient through being concealed from the doctor; the soul is therefore figured as a corporeal body that has been punctured. Whereas speaking outside conditions of confession opens up the body and allows the soul to become vulnerable, speaking under the conditions of confession will shut the figurative body even as it opens the entrances of the physical body, repairing the metaphorical wounds.[84] The

83 *Hali Meiðhad*, in *Medieval English Prose for Women*, ed. and trans. Bella Millett and Jocelyn Wogan-Browne, pp. 14–15. That sexual activity is physically *internal* also heightens its gravity: citing Paul, the author warns the virgin that since 'euch sunne þet me deð is wiðute þe bodi bute þis ane' (every sin that is committed is outside the body except this one alone), loss of virginity not only 'unwuðgeð [hire] bodi' (dishonours [her] body), it also 'suleð [hire] sawle' (defiles [her] soul, pp. 30–1).

84 Although such is the dilemma of non-confessional speech that even shutting up speech may also 'nurse' words that can leave the soul open to diabolical attack. As the *Wisse* insists, after Solomon, '*Qui custodit os suum custodit animam suam;* "Hwa-se witeð wel his muð, he witeð", he seið, "his sawle"' (II. 30) [translation from Millett: '*Whoever*

confessed soul is therefore analogous to the enclosed, imperforate body the anchoress is supposed to possess corporeally.

In a text that is so very much concerned with the physical and material in the enclosed life, the author's focus on the body and its importance to an effective understanding of the 'rule' he proposes makes corporeal analogies significant and this one especially so, since it is the patristic simile adopted by the canon for confession in Lateran IV. *Omnis utriusque sexus* institutionalised a practice for the faithful that had existed in a developing form for centuries, but it also laid out the role of the priest. The wording of the canon reflected the long-established tradition of confessor as soul's physician: the priest should be 'discerning and prudent, so that like a practised doctor [*more periti medici*] he can pour wine and oil on the wounds of the injured [*vulneribus sauciati*]'.[85] Lateran IV also specifies that a confessor who broke the seal of confession should be judged more harshly than the original transgressor. The priest was to be considered a grave sinner who revealed by word or sign (*verbo vel signo*) what was said in confession: for such a revelation, a priest would be deposed from his office and 'shut up to do penance for life in a monastery of strict [*arctum*] observance'.[86] Before the 'seal of confession' was enshrined in the Lateran canon, it had also been insisted upon by Burchard of Worms and by Gratian in his *Tractatus de penitentia*; it is interesting to note that here, the indiscreet priest is warned that his revelations will incur not only deposition but also that the remainder of his life is to be spent not in the *arctum monasterium* but in ignominious wandering (*ignominiosus peregrinando*).[87] Thus a confessor who uncovered an enclosed penitent's sins – made them speakable again – would theoretically incur a punishment that enclosed his body in a way that not only mirrored that of his spiritual ward (who may also be said

guards his mouth guards his soul; "Whoever guards his mouth well", he says, "guards his soul"'].

85 Lateran IV, constitution 21, in *Conciliorum Oecumenicorum Decreta*, ed. J. Alberigo et al. (Freiberg: Verlag Herder, 1962), p. 221. Translated in *English Historical Documents, 1189–1327*, ed. Harry Rothwell (London: Routledge, 1975), p. 654.

86 Lateran IV, 21, translated in Rothwell, *English Historical Documents*, p. 654.

87 Distinctio VI, canon ii: 'Nam si hoc fecerit, deponatur, et omnibus diebus uitae suae ignominiosus peregrinando pergat'. Atria A. Larson, ed. and trans., *Gratian's Tractatus de penitentia: A New Latin Edition with English Translation* (Washington, DC: Catholic University of America Press, 2016), p. 266. The 'seal of confession' is attributed to Gregory the Great by Gratian and other writers of canon law, but may date back to the fifth century. See Atria A. Larson, *Master of Penance: Gratian and the Development of Penitential Thought and Law in the Twelfth Century* (Washington, DC: Catholic University of America Press, 2014), p. 221. Alexander Murray observes how, prior to this, ecclesiastical authority had become increasingly involved in the pursuit of public justice in Carolingian France, being instructed to investigate and record certain crimes. The dilemma here was that 'the priest who "shopped" his parishioners is supposed to be the one who heard their confessions, in the pastoral manner'. See Alexander Murray, 'Confession Before 1215', in *Transactions of the Royal Historical Society*, 6.3 (1993), 51–81 (p. 59).

to be *arcta*, enclosed or of narrow custom) but also represented the impenetrable enclosure that his own person, his own unspeaking body, should have afforded the anchorite's sins in the first place.[88]

Thus, one last irony of confession rearranges the boundaries of gender and the speakable yet again. While in the telling of a life, the female subject is narratologically enclosed by the work of a male author, in confession the sins of a penitent's life are enclosed by the body of the priest. The ritual of confession ensures that the soul that is figured as a material body lacerated by wounds is absolved of its sins and metaphorically shut again, with the priest acting as both physician and guard of its welfare. Speaking out and externalising the internal feeling is the principal means by which experience, be it culturally speakable or unspeakable, may be made repeatable; thus an unspeakable sin, which *must* be articulated and spoken in confession, only becomes truly unspeakable post-confession. The unspeakable in a confessional exchange is only truly present in a male consciousness, not a female one. Indeed, even a minor or humdrum sin becomes unspeakable in and by the person of the priest. Whether this is read as another iteration of the male body as closed, the female as open, or of the higher degree of spiritual observance represented by the confessor as opposed to the fallible and flawed observance expected of the lay person, the paradox is the same: in confession, speaking up is the only way of ensuring something is unspeakable.

The fluidity of inside and outside articulates and enables the work of the unspeakable in these texts. Inner and outer converge in both narratives: unlike the anchoress, Mary is not and cannot be enclosed by anyone outside of herself, preferring instead to remain at large, yet neither saint nor recluse is truly part of the world they traverse and even manage to change. Where Mary is out in the open – a free-range, wandering saint – the anchoress is always closed up, closed off, shut up in both senses of the word. While Mary speaks of her unspeakable sins insistently and with determination, the anchoress of the *Wisse* is encouraged to think often on the dangers of letting speech escape, or of using the mouth impiously for any purpose. Yet, if unspeakability is about boundaries, where the physical and geographical in these texts become metaphoric of the boundaries and unboundedness of their expression, it is also – indeed, it is only – about their transgression. In confession, the unspeakable is rarely what it seems: this manoeuvre is not the drawing of a line, but rather the crossing of a border. To elicit a full confession means avoiding, with elaborate manoeuvres, the articulation of the full range of sins; yet to confess sin is to make it unspeakable, even if it would not have been so designated before. The (re)appearance of the unspeakable does not

[88] 'Þeos twa þing limpeð to ancre, neorowðe ant bietternesse; for wombe is nearow wununge, þer ure Lauerd wes recluse' (These two things are appropriate for a recluse: constriction and bitterness. For the womb, where our Lord was enclosed, is a constricted space to live in, VI. 142).

occur in a resurgent whoosh; it is a dance of seven veils, like the mortified scuffle between Zosimus and Mary, in which that which is already uncovered is hastily obscured and so made all the more noticeable. As Bachelard writes, insight does not always come from the internal: 'Sometimes, it is in being outside itself that being tests consistencies. Sometimes, too, it is closed in, as it were, on the outside.'[89] While the body may be undone by unspeakable acts, the soul may be repaired precisely by speaking them. For the out-of-bounds saint and the closed-in recluse, inside out is outside in: speaking up *is* shutting up, and the unspeakable must be spoken.

89 Bachelard, *Poetics of Space*, p. 215.

2

WHAT COMES UNNATURALLY: UNSPEAKABLE ACTS

The case of 'Johannes Rykener, se Elianoram nominans' was tried in 1395. The verdicts are still being written. It was an unusual case with all the right (or wrong) ingredients for a ripping yarn – sex, money, cross-dressing, nuns – but even for all that, those involved might scarcely have believed the celebrity it would achieve six centuries later. The defendant was caught with one John Britby in Sopers Lane and is accused of committing a crime that the recording clerk, in a suggestively reticent turn of phrase, refers to as 'illud vitium detestibile, nephandum et ignominiosum' (that detestable, unspeakable and ignominious vice).[1] At the time, he was dressed in women's clothes and calling himself Eleanor. Besides the encounter in question, Rykener states that he had sex as a woman with an Essex rector, three Oxford scholars, four Franciscans, one Carmelite, three chaplains and many priests; additionally, as a man, 'with many nuns and [...] many women both married and otherwise'.[2] As the case wears on, the need to record the unmentionable sin eventually effects the textual metastasis that yields 'illo vitium antedictum' (the aforementioned [unmentionable] vice). Even in 1932, in an edition of late-fourteenth-century Pleas and Memoranda that specifies names, locations and other particulars for almost every other contemporary case, the entry for 1 February 1395 reads only (but tantalisingly), 'Examination of two men charged with immorality, of whom one implicated several persons, male and female, in religious orders.'[3] Consequently, the case was very little known until the mid-1990s, when it was rediscovered and its tangled language and

1 Ruth Mazo Karras and David Lorenzo Boyd, 'The Interrogation of of a Male Transvestite Prostitute in Fourteenth Century London', *GLQ* 1.4 (1995), 459–65 (p. 462); Ruth Mazo Karras and David Lorenzo Boyd, 'Ut Cum Muliere: A Male Transvestite Prostitute in Fourteenth Century London', in *Premodern Sexualities*, ed. Louise Fradenburg, Carla Freccero and Kathy Lavezzo (New York and London: Routledge, 1996), pp. 99–116.

2 Karras and Boyd, 'Ut Cum Muliere', pp. 111–12.

3 Roll A34, membrane 2. See *Calendar of Select Pleas and Memoranda of the City of London, 1381–1412*, ed. A. H. Thomas (Cambridge: Cambridge University Press, 1932), p. 228. Although the editor states that he endeavoured to 'include all passages which seem to add in any way to our knowledge of the times', the omission of some 'formal entries and records of small debt actions' was inevitable (p. vii). While the Rykener case does not concern one of Thomas's main projects, struggles between city guilds, the intriguing synopsis suggests that, in the midst of pages and pages of assaults, debts and petty theft, it would make a welcome change, if nothing else.

arresting mix of frankness and ambiguity brought to critical attention by Ruth Mazo Karras and David Lorenzo Boyd.

The Rykener case has remained a mainstay of medieval, queer and gender studies ever since, and as such I will not dwell on it here;[4] it does, however, introduce some key issues. Firstly, it makes very pointed mention of the unspeakable act or vice and, moreover, the phenomenon of the aforementioned unmentionable act. This is one that Carolyn Dinshaw notes 'neatly exemplifies Foucault's point about sexuality in general as it developed out of premodernity: the sexual act here is defined as unspeakable, yet it is spoken of voluminously'.[5] Referring to something encumbered with the stigma of being 'unspeakable', even to further reinforce its base reputation and add weight to this same stigma, becomes rather a problem, as this case makes abundantly clear. However, the permutations by which the unspeakable may suddenly be progressed to the previously spoken, bypassing the customary intermediate act of *speaking*, are worth investigating.

Secondly, the case is marked by plurality of names and labels that also appear along with this unspeakable act. If the problem of the Rykener case for the Rolls writer is that the offence in question is unnameable, the difficulty for the reader, conversely, lies in the plethora of possible labels that might plausibly be applied to the actions of the defendant. Even a first name, a basic referent, is not to be pinned down – the subject of the case is called both John and Eleanor by the Rolls scribe and, by several critics, 'John/Eleanor', the two names mashed together in a single moniker of uncertain, unfixed or unreadable gender.[6] Karras, revisiting the Rykener record, uses the pronoun 'ze' to draw attention to the complexities of gender identity as well as sexual identity in the case.[7] The surfeit of signifiers attached to a sensitive signified reveals not only a desire to circumlocute or fudge, in the interests of reflecting a perceived popular opinion or a generalised desire, but a reality of speech and language with which Lacan is concerned through his works and which will inform the theoretical framework for this chapter. Although the relation

4 See, for example, Dinshaw, *Getting Medieval*, pp. 100–42; Carolyn Dinshaw, 'Queer Relations', *Essays in Medieval Studies: Out of Bounds* 16 (2002), 79–94; Conor McCarthy, *Love, Sex and Marriage in the Middle Ages: A Sourcebook* (London: Routledge, 2004); Ruth Evans, 'The Production of Space in Chaucer's London', in *Chaucer and the City*, ed. Ardis Butterfield (Cambridge: D. S. Brewer, 2006), pp. 41–56. Ruth Karras and Tom Linkinen have also revisited the case as the experience of a transgender individual rather than a transvestite, as the original scholarship had it. Karras and Linkinen, 'John/Eleanor Rykener Revisited', in *Founding Feminisms in Medieval Studies: Essays in Honor of Jane E. Burns*, ed. Laine E. Doggett and Daniel E. O'Sullivan (Cambridge: D. S. Brewer, 2016), pp. 111–21.

5 Dinshaw, *Getting Medieval*, p. 105.

6 Most notably Karras and Boyd in 'Ut Cum Muliere', whose convention is usually followed by subsequent critics.

7 See Karras and Linkinen, 'John/Eleanor Rykener Revisited', p. 112, n. 6 (and *passim*).

between words and meaning is the inheritance of the mature subject as he or she enters into language – and into a relation with the other – the problem with language lies precisely in its inability to perfectly represent, through its signifiers, that which it signifies. Even when the goal of speech is to express a concept in its entirety, the nature of language is to convey only in fragments.

Thirdly, the case exemplifies the interconnectedness in medieval thought of those sex acts considered unorthodox and the dissolution of gender norms. The language of the court clerk echoes that of the penitential writers – what is unspeakable? How do we indicate what that is? As Pierre Payer summarises, 'The medieval Christian sexual ethic was straightforward. Sexual intercourse was allowed only between a man and a woman legitimately married to each other, if done in the natural manner.'[8] That is to say, almost all sex acts might be considered unorthodox or unnatural. The collapse of gender binaries and the mutability of gendered roles that the cross-dressing sex worker exploits are part of the discourse that defines the act that precipitated the Rykener case as not only unspeakable, but unnatural.

This chapter is about unspeakable sin, non-heteronormative sexuality and the non-heteronormative experience and performance of gender, addressing a cluster of medieval texts that describe and explain same-sex desire, gender ambiguity and gender fluidity through a sexual grammar that was meant to reflect orthodox and 'natural' custom. These texts draw on the late medieval intellectual and literary inheritance that links the interventions and justifications of Nature and the results for speaking subjects, beginning with Alain de Lille's account of Nature's despair in the face of same-sex eroticism and non-binary gender, and extending to Geoffrey Chaucer and John Gower. The ironic proliferation of speech as the response to the imposition of the unspeakability trope is traced in Chaucer's 'Pardoner's Tale', while the latter half of the chapter is given over to considerations of the role of gender in the dynamics of unspeakability, drawing on Lacan but also the revisions and insubordination of Irigaray that address blind spots in Lacan's pronouncements on women. This section focuses on the (doubly unspeakable and naturally unnatural) women who love women and women who take on masculine roles in Gower's *Confessio Amantis* and the Old French *Roman de Silence*. While Chapter 1 explored how the gendering of bodies may inflect the (un)speakability of confession, this chapter will examine the (non-)articulation and (un)acceptability of sexual acts and the discourse of the natural that shapes understandings of gender – the confluence of norms on which the phenomenon of the unspeakable and unnatural vice is predicated. Since the logic of the natural privileges generation as the proof of orthodoxy, I am interested in what these unspeakable, unnatural acts produce, and what the

8 Pierre J. Payer, *Sex and the New Medieval Literature of Confession, 1150–1300* (Toronto: Pontifical Institute of Mediaeval Studies, 2009), p. 1.

implications of figuring sex acts as speech acts, and gendered individuals as gendered words, has for the preservation of Nature and for the suppression of 'vices' and voices.

THE SIN OF SODOM

There is a certain inevitability to the appearance of sodomy in the discussion of the unspeakable in the Middle Ages. In the medieval imagination, the problems of communicating it, confessing it, containing it, ensure that the 'sin against nature' achieves the distinction of becoming *the* unspeakable sin. However, the unspeakable is hardly a simple euphemism – the concepts of the unspeakable and the sodomitical are also elided, exchanged and, in the process, exploited to the point at which they may even function as virtual synonyms. It is thus liable to become confused (purposely or not) with a collection of other terms. It is an accusation that purports to be removed from orality and yet which seems to breed utterances. The 'unspeakable sin' both reflects – acting as the cipher for attitudes and meanings elsewhere attested – and deflects, resisting easy or fixed interpretations, and in this double performance it flags up the unutterable inherent in language itself.

Nor is sodomy the only sin against nature, of course; indeed, all sin should in theory be against nature.[9] The range of acts considered to be unnatural could be extensive. Usury, for example, could be unnatural, as in Gerard of Siena, who wrote that it 'causes a natural thing to transcend its nature [*faciebat rem naturalem supervalere sue nature*] and an artificial thing to transcend the skill that created it'.[10] Pierre D'Ailly, whose 'Radix Malorum Omnium est Cupiditas' echoes the Pardoner's own motto, affirmed that 'simony is against natural and divine law [*contra ius naturale et divinum*], has been shown.'[11] Tyrannicide was declared a form of heresy by the Council of Constance, 1415, since it was against sovereignty and therefore against nature. Poisoning was

9 John Boswell cites Aquinas in this connection (*Summa Theologiæ*, 1a. 2ae. 94.3 ad 2), commenting that since 'not only are all sexual sins "unnatural," but all sins of any sort are "unnatural"', it seems that '"natural" in this section is in fact simply the "moral"; and it seems circular, to say the least, to argue that homosexual acts are immoral because they are immoral'. Boswell, *Christianity, Social Tolerance and Homosexuality: Gay People in Western Europe from the Beginning of the Christian Era to the Fourteenth Century* (Chicago: University of Chicago Press, 1980), p. 324.

10 Lawrin Armstrong, *The Idea of a Moral Economy: Gerard of Siena on Usury, Restitution, Prescription* (Toronto: University of Toronto Press, 2016), pp. 82–3. See also John Thomas Noonan, *The Scholastic Analysis of Usury* (Cambridge, MA: Harvard University Press, 1957).

11 '[S]ymonia est contra ius naturale et divinum, ut patet ex dictis.' Pierre D'Ailly, 'Radix Malorum Omnium est Cupiditas', ed. Alan E. Bernstein in Bernstein, *Pierre d'Ailly and the Blanchard Affair: University and Chancellor of Paris at the Beginning of the Great Schism* (Leiden: Brill, 1978), pp. 197–236 (p. 209: 29–31; my translation).

also against nature, since men are not naturally venomous.[12] The issue of why some males enjoy having sex with other males is also posed in the Aristotelian *Problemata* (whose late medieval commentaries and responses Joan Cadden has recently investigated), where it is classified as unnatural in a passage that lumps together infanticide and cannibalism alongside such seemingly arbitrary vices as nail biting or eating dirt.[13] Not everything that is unnatural is sodomy, nor is everything that is unnatural unspeakable. Yet species of sexual sin exert a particular imaginative pull in later medieval thought, and same-sex acts even more so. From Jerome onwards, traditional etymology maintained that *Sodom* meant *mute,* reflecting the inhabitants' muteness before God and establishing the unspeakability of the sodomitical sin.[14] The connection between the city of Sodom and male–male or female–female sexual relations was made gradually. At the same time, the view that same-sex desire defied 'natural' gender (as Romans 1.26–7 was held to confirm), ensured that *sodomia* thus became both unnatural and unspeakable, and crystallised the links between the two concepts.

Payer highlights the generative aspect of the 'natural' as a measure for the degree of sexual sin: 'Acts that facilitate or at least do not impede procreation are in accord with nature, are natural. Acts that frustrate or that cannot result in procreation […] are against nature, are unnatural.'[15] As seen in Chapter 1, masturbation was a particularly worrisome vice, condemned as unnatural by Robert Grosseteste, Albertus Magnus and Jean Gerson, among others.[16] The logic behind this categorisation was also subject to variation: Peter of Poitiers deemed masturbation hermaphroditic (since the active and passive roles are performed by and combined in the same person), while Robert of Sorbon saw it as a species of incest (since to whom is one more closely related than oneself?). Should the active become the passive, this is likewise unnatural (thus the unnaturalness of unorthodox sex between a man and a woman is

[12] See Franck Collard, *The Crime of Poison in the Middle Ages*, trans. Deborah Nelson-Campbell (Westport, CT: Praeger, 2008).

[13] Joan Cadden, *Nothing Natural is Shameful: Sodomy and Science in Late Medieval Europe* (Philadelphia, PA: University of Pennsylvania Press, 2013). As Cadden remarks, the medieval responses to *problema* IV.26 from the *Ethics* demonstrate the capacious flexibility of the category of the unnatural: 'What question did medieval readers think was being posed by Aristotle in *Problemata* IV. 26? […] The commentaries and the margins of the manuscripts mention sodomites and shame; anuses, penises, thighs, and vaginas; habits and birth defects; bodily fluids and planetary conjunctions; boys, adolescents, and men; eunuchs and women' (p. 31).

[14] See Mark D. Jordan, *The Invention of Sodomy in Christian Theology* (Chicago: University of Chicago Press, 1997), pp. 106–13; Mark D. Jordan, *The Silence of Sodom: Homosexuality in Modern Catholicism* (Chicago: University of Chicago Press, 2000), p. 16 and *passim.*

[15] Payer, *Sex and the New Medieval Literature of Confession*, p. 132.

[16] See Payer, *Sex and the New Medieval Literature of Confession*, pp. 135–7.

stressed by writers such as Thomas of Chobham, William Peraldus and Alain de Lille). The unnatural may be commuted to heretical; the heretical is not to be enacted and therefore the cautious should not speak of it; the heretical and unnatural are therefore *unspeakable*.

The definitions begin to break down and dissolve together; discovering a characteristic of one of these concepts would, for practical purposes, legitimise the use of any and all the allegations of sodomy, acting against nature, unspeakable behaviour. Such was the pernicious and insidious nature of such a sin, the logic runs, that to mention it was tantamount to performing it. Yet in order to suppress mention of sodomy, it was first necessary to name names – or pseudonyms.

Foucault pithily condenses the stakes in his notorious summary:

> Discourse transmits and produces power; it reinforces it, but also undermines and exposes it, renders it fragile and makes it possible to thwart it. In like manner, silence and secrecy are a shelter for power, anchoring its prohibitions; but they also loosen its holds and provide for relatively obscure areas of tolerance. Consider for example the history of what was once 'the' great sin against nature. The extreme discretion of the texts dealing with sodomy – that utterly confused category – and the nearly universal reticence in talking about it made possible a twofold operation: on the one hand, there was an extreme severity [...] and on the other hand, a tolerance that must have been widespread.[17]

As John Boswell has shown, the prohibitions on sodomy did indeed counter a more tolerant attitude that was in evidence before the twelfth century and before the condemnation of sodomy – the unnatural vice – was encoded in the canons of Lateran III.[18] Thereafter, this tolerance was eroded in the wake of suspicion and persecution of anything deemed to be against the Church, and by implication against nature.

While this is not the place for an historical account,[19] even a brief survey gives an indication of the contradictions at work. In the taxonomies

17 Foucault, *The History of Sexuality I*, p. 101.

18 Canon 11: 'Let all who are found guilty of that unnatural vice for which the wrath of God came down upon the sons of disobedience and destroyed the five cities with fire, if they are clerics be expelled from the clergy or confined in monasteries to do penance; if they are laymen they are to incur excommunication and be completely separated from the society of the faithful', *Decrees of the Ecumenical Councils*, 2 vols, ed. Norman P. Tanner (Washington, DC: Georgetown University Press, 1990), I: 217.

19 For a more comprehensive history, see Michael Goodich, *The Unmentionable Vice: Homosexuality in the Later Medieval Period* (Oxford: Clio Press, 1978); Boswell, *Christianity, Social Tolerance and Homosexuality*; Jordan, *Invention of Sodomy*; Jordan, *The Silence of Sodom*; William Burgwinkle, *Sodomy, Masculinity, and Law in Medieval Literature: France and England, 1050–1230* (Cambridge: Cambridge University Press, 2004). Goodich surveys the penitential tradition and both he and Boswell in particular argue for a degree of tolerance towards same-sex partnerships in the early medieval period that was steadily eroded. The aim of Jordan's project, meanwhile, is to examine

of sin that make up medieval penitential and moral texts, the attempt to find a coherent definition soon becomes fraught with inconsistencies. Peter Damian's *Liber Gomorrhianus* (1049), for example, refers to four different acts (masturbation, mutual masturbation, interfemoral intercourse and anal intercourse) as sodomy,[20] while Thomas Aquinas's *Summa Theologiæ* (*c.* 1265–73) discusses sodomy as a form of 'vice against nature [*vitium contra naturam*]'. Aquinas classes unnatural vice as that which either conflicts with reason (*repugnat rationi rectæ*) or does not benefit the species (*repugnat ipsi ordini naturali venerei actus qui convenit humanæ speciei*). Accordingly, it may take the form of masturbation or self-abuse (*mollitiem*), bestiality, same-sex relations (he refers to both male and female same-sex relations as *sodomiticum vitium*) and finally intercourse in which 'the natural style [*naturalis modus*]' is not observed.[21]

The practice of enforcing prohibition, of containing sodomy so as to effectively abject it, came to be characterised (and problematised) by the epithet with which it was so frequently saddled: *peccatum nefandum,* the unspeakable sin. Both sodomy and heresy were called *contra naturam*, and called *nefandus*, to the point where 'sodomy' as a category might therefore be extended and attached to almost anything one wished to cast as viciously sinful.[22] It could also be evoked when referring to heretics or to the theologically suspect – the Old French *bougre,* referring to a Bulgarian sect of alleged heretical and sodomitical tendencies, was adopted into English as 'bugger' – as it was understood to be entirely 'against nature', *contra naturam.* That both heresy and sodomy are in like fashion called *nefandus* and unnatural therefore connects them in a way that runs somewhat deeper than the shared

the instabilities that exist within the works of single authors, or even within single texts (rather than attempting to survey the instances or trace an etymology for the term). Burgwinkle focuses on the homoerotic elements of high medieval popular literature and the interconnectedness of the sodomitical and the orthodox in constructed and idealised masculinities.

20 'Four types of this form of criminal wickedness can be distinguished in an effort to show you the totality of the whole matter in and orderly way: some sin with themselves alone; some by the hands of others; others between the thighs; and finally, others commit the complete act against nature.' See Peter Damian, *Book of Gomorrah: An Eleventh Century Treatise Against Clerical Homosexual Practices*, ed. and trans. Pierre J. Payer (Waterloo, Ont.: Wilfrid Laurier University Press, 1982), p. 29.

21 *Summa Theologiæ*, ed. and trans. Thomas Gilby et al., 60 vols (London: Eyre and Spottiswoode, 1968), XLIII: 2a2æ. 154, 11.

22 William Burgwinkle observes that the term 'ranges from being a simple description of homoerotic relations or attractions to a theological category synonymous with the sinful', while Allen Frantzen examines how this promiscuity of definition had the effect that 'sodomy became a weapon of invective and retribution that could be used against those who were sexually orthodox as well as against those who were not'. See Burgwinkle, *Sodomy, Masculinity, and Law*, p. 3; Frantzen, 'The Disclosure of Sodomy in *Cleanness*', *PMLA* 111.3 (1996), 451–64 (p. 454).

adjective, and as Dinshaw has shown, both accusations came to be used 'for the purposes of power, not for the reform of the true church'.[23]

In a collusive harmony of technical and rhetorical connotations, this single word 'sodomy' is so overused and overdefined that, as Michael Hanrahan remarks, extending as it does to 'potentially [...] all unnatural acts and practices, which, in turn, are readily substituted for it', sodomy as a term 'threatens to mean nothing'.[24] On the other hand, although linguistic switches with reference to sodomy can present this possibility for the modern reader, the problem for medieval writers was also that 'sodomy' meant too much. Indeed, it was at once uncompromisingly negative and (for the unfortunate target) wholly compromising. A transgression sometimes characterised as *delictum mixti fori* – a crime that came under both ecclesiastical and secular jurisdiction – the unspeakable, unnatural vice blurred and exceeded boundaries again when its actants were tried, with the result that it became a catch-all accusation, levelled not only at wretched sinners but at powerful orders (most notably the Templars), at high-ranking and even royal figures, when they came under political pressure. (Indeed, Jeremy Goldberg has recently read the Rykener case as a response to Richard II's suspension of the City of London's liberties in 1392, an angry political satire fabricated by clerks, in which Rykener/Richard is brought low and symbolically buggered).[25] When speaking of unspeakable transgressions, all were equals in as much as they were made 'abject'.

Designating a person's behaviour 'unspeakable' thus often owed less to a state of genuine gobsmack than to an intention of guaranteeing sufficient condemnation. In Latin, at least, *nefandus* (from *for*, to speak, comes *fandus*, 'that which should be spoken of') is often defined not as 'unmentionable' but simply as 'wicked', 'iniquitous': one can thus omit the element of 'mentioning' altogether, proceeding instead directly to dreadfulness. The association of sodomy and the unspeakable functions as a result of a comparable subtraction

23 Dinshaw, *Getting Medieval*, p. 68.

24 Michael Hanrahan, 'Speaking of Sodomy: Gower's Advice to Princes in the *Confessio Amantis*', *Exemplaria* 14 (2002), pp. 423–46 (p. 425).

25 Jeremy Goldberg, 'John Rykener, Richard II and the Governance of London', *Leeds Studies in English* 45 (2014), 49–70. Hanrahan also discusses the case of Richard II ('Speaking of Sodomy', p. 426). The deposition of Richard in 1399 was in part engineered through the insinuations made about members of his court and his counsellors, a time-honoured method of indirectly criticising the king. Robert Mills, who also discusses the crises of Richard II's reign, makes the point that sodomy's 'flexibility of reference and its associations with unmentionability provided medieval commentators with a means of critiquing power structures obliquely, by way of enigma and allusion, without putting themselves directly in the political firing line'; 'Male–Male Love and Sex in the Middle Ages, 1000–1500', in *A Gay History of Britain: Love and Sex Between Men Since the Middle Ages*, ed. Matt Cook, H. G. Cocks, Robert Mills and Randolph Turnbach (Oxford, Westport, CT: Greenwood World Publishing, 2007), pp. 1–44 (p. 18).

– though sodomy is said to be 'unspeakable', both in the sense of being unworthy of mention and in the sense of being depraved, the basis for this appellation, which might be supplied by *contra naturam*, is missing. In order to expand the formula (sodomy is *nefandus* because…), one would be obliged first to define sodomy and, by extension, to define what is natural.

Mark Jordan argues that this resistance to clear definition is not coincidental, insisting that:

> [C]onfusions and contradictions cannot be removed from the category. They are the stuff from which it was made. That is why 'Sodomy' has had such a long life in oppressive legislation and demagoguery. It is confused and contradicting in just the way that oppressors and demagogues find advantageous.[26]

Like other critics, Jordan follows Foucault in stressing the 'confusion' of the category, though this is not a truth universally acknowledged. Randy Conner, focusing on premodern French texts, proposes that terms like *sodomie* are 'subject to cornucopian interpretation' rather than 'utterly confused' and that in some instances it is, indeed, quite clear what is being referenced, since: 'As early as 1260 CE [...] *sodomite* referred primarily to a man accused of engaging in male–male anal eroticism.'[27] Meanwhile, Karma Lochrie provides a rebuttal to the assumptions and shorthand of 'presumptive sodomy', which she argues do the same injury to female same-sex relations that the privileging of heteronormative discourse does to same-sex relations.[28]

While Jordan counsels that more complete understanding of the instability of 'sodomy' and its counterparts begins 'by supposing that the terms have to be learned anew with each author', Conner's post-Foucauldian move cautions against the convenience of finding in a collection of multi-inflected referents only an 'utterly confused category'.[29] While being seduced by the anarchy

26 Jordan, *Invention of Sodomy*, p. 9.

27 Randy Conner, '"*Les Molles et les Chausses*": Mapping the Isle of Hermaphrodites in Premodern France', in *Queerly Phrased: Language, Gender, and Sexuality*, ed. Anna Livia and Kira Hall (New York, Oxford: Oxford University Press, 1997), pp. 127–46 (pp. 131, 129-30). Conner's methodology differs significantly from Jordan's: where Conner leads to construct an encyclopaedic vocabulary for same-sex eroticism and transgender, as opposed to 'limit[ing] ourselves to examining the presence, absence, or use in isolation of one or two terms, such as *sodomy*' (p. 141), Jordan's project lies precisely in such an examination; however, he exercises extreme caution in his treatment. Though a word can be matched with a definition, the fixity of 'meaning' is a façade: 'There is no linear progress in the genealogies of Christian moral terms. The terms condense results of contests between opposing tendencies or programs – or else show how the contests had no coherent results' (Jordan, *Invention of Sodomy*, pp. 3–4).

28 See Karma Lochrie, 'Presumptive Sodomy', *Textual Practice* 13 (1999), 295–310; Lochrie, *Covert Operations*, pp. 180–1.

29 Jordan, *Invention of Sodomy*, p. 5. Compare with Goodich, who declares that 'All forms of homoerotic relations were indiscriminately labelled as sodomy' (*Unmentionable Vice*, p. ix).

of Foucault's characterisation is not without its drawbacks, the advantage of persevering with his famous (perhaps by now infamous) description of sodomy is that by scrutinising the discursive fractures, the rules that interrogate behaviour are themselves interrogated and queered. Though irresistibly apt, the notoriety of his remark eclipses, and perhaps masks, the nuanced models for the workings of speech, silence and power in the passage in which it is contained. As Foucault also insists, 'We must not expect the discourses on sex to tell us, above all, what strategy they derive from, or what moral divisions they accompany, or what ideology – dominant or dominated – they represent.'[30] The notion that power is discursive opens up possibilities, as does an insistence that discourse and power are not inseparable. More than acknowledging or understanding something to be 'unspeakable', explicitly stating that something is unutterable channels and destabilises both the reinforcing, proactive weight of discourse, and the insidious, oppressive subjugation of silence. Sodomy may or may not be 'utterly confused', but in its harnessing of the forces that are both proper to and opposed to underlying matrices of power, the unspeakable confuses utterance in very productive fashion.

CONTRADICTING NATURE

While the sin against nature may also be the unspeakable sin, the two need not be the same act. There may exist transgressions against nature that may be spoken of – usury, for example – however, when a thing is called unspeakable there can be little doubt that it is also unnatural. Since the basis of Nature's authority in sexual ethics is the principle of generation, an act against nature is an act that confounds or perverts procreation, and referring to something as unnatural implies this should not be thought in any way productive or generative.[31] Yet Nature as an authority is rarely consistent, either in the ways in which she is presented or in the conditions she endorses. 'Natural' may refer to that which is observed in animals and of nature at large; it may equally (and in the same texts) refer to a set of circumstances in which what is 'natural' often boils down to what is unexceptional.[32] As Daston and Vidal point out, 'Nature's authority works by paradox and obscurity as well as by the clash of clear-cut positions' and the advantage of the allegorical is precisely that 'figurative language and images offer a rich and plastic repertoire for depicting nature's traits, which can be juxtaposed without necessarily being made consistent with one another'.[33] To accurately represent natural authority,

[30] Foucault, *The History of Sexuality I*, p. 102.

[31] See Payer, *Sex and the New Medieval Literature of Confession*, pp. 128–32, for the use of this idea in the high Middle Ages.

[32] On Christian ethics equating the good with the usual, see Boswell, *Christianity, Social Tolerance and Homosexuality*, pp. 312–13.

[33] Lorraine Daston and Fernando Vidal, 'Doing What Comes Naturally', in *The Moral*

it seems, is not to risk but to revel in contradiction. Certainly the personification of Nature in the Middle Ages has been repeatedly shown to be protean, incoherent and slippery – who better, then, to enable writers to speak of the unspeakable?

Barbara Newman observes, in her survey of Nature's territory in medieval culture, that ever since Bernard Silvestris made Nature a goddess, 'one of her favorite habitats [has been] ethical discourse about sex and gender, and in text after text she stakes out her position as goddess of the normative'.[34] This position is vividly established in the twelfth century by Alain de Lille's *De Planctu Naturae,* which relates a vision of the goddess Nature descending to earth to bemoan man's vices, especially those that are against nature and which she may take particularly personally. In a lengthy *effictio,* Alain describes Nature's appearance and her magnificent robe, which depicts all creation but is torn by philosophers; she tells him about her role as God's *uicaria* and how, despite her efforts, man perverts her laws. Nature has latterly chosen to dwell in heaven and therefore delegated the work of procreation to Venus, Hymen and Cupid; Venus, however, has entered into an adulterous liaison with Antigenius and the result is the proliferation of unnatural couplings. Nature's complaint ends with the appearance of the Virtues and the composition of a letter to Genius, her priest, who finally excommunicates those who commit offences against Nature. As Jan Ziolkowski has shown, *De Planctu* supplies Nature with the grammatical–moral equivalence of the period and enables her to imbue her complaints with rhetorical force that derives from the link between corruption of grammar and corruptness of sexual acts.[35] An act that is *contra naturam* is therefore not only against Nature's law but against Nature's grammar – correct usage extends to both words and bodies.

The reception and influence of Alain's text is demonstrated emphatically by the authors of the *Roman de la Rose,* the quintessential dream allegory.[36]

Authority of Nature, ed. Daston and Vidal (Chicago: University of Chicago Press, 2004), pp. 1–20 (p. 8). See also R. G. Collingwood, *The Idea of Nature* (New York: Oxford University Press, 1945); C. S. Lewis, 'Nature', in *Studies in Words* (Cambridge: Cambridge University Press, 1990); *The Concept of Nature,* ed. John Torrance (Oxford: Clarendon Press, 1992).

34 Barbara Newman, *God and the Goddesses: Vision, Poetry and Belief in the Middle Ages* (Philadelphia, PA: University of Pennsylvania Press, 2003), pp. 53–4.

35 Jan M. Ziolkowski, *Alan of Lille's Grammar of Sex: The Meaning of Grammar to a Twelfth-Century Intellectual* (Cambridge, MA: Medieval Academy of America, 1985).

36 On the subject of the *Rose*'s debt to Alain, its allegory, satire and readership, see in particular George Economou, *The Goddess Natura in Medieval Literature* (Cambridge, MA: Harvard University Press, 1972); Noah D. Guynn, *Allegory and Sexual Ethics in the High Middle Ages,* The New Middle Ages (Basingstoke: Palgrave, 2007); Sylvia Huot, *The 'Romance of the Rose' and Its Medieval Readers: Interpretation, Reception, Manuscript Transmission* (Cambridge: Cambridge University Press, 1993); Maureen Quilligan, *The Allegory of Female Authority: Christine de Pizan's 'Cité des dames'* (Ithaca, NY: Cornell University Press, 1991).

Amans, the lover, dreams of a garden where he is struck with the God of Love's arrows and becomes obsessed with the Rose he glimpses at the fountain of Narcissus; with the aid (and sometimes hindrance) of a string of helpers, led by Genius, he finally overcomes the guards and storms the castle where he wins his Rose. In this further transformation of the allegory of Nature's authority in sexual matters, as Schibanoff notes, Nature is not entrusted with the analysis of same-sex desire, and the grammatical argument is removed, 'affording Nature no chance to weaken the case against sexual perversity with grammatical metaphors that are so easily challenged'.[37] Her priest Genius rules Venus and co-opts her in his opposition not only to same-sex desire but to all who do not procreate, including those whose desires are heteronormative, but the work emphatically maintains the traditional pro-generative and homophobic position on the 'natural'. Genius concludes with the famous diatribe against 'those who do not write with their styluses', who do not forge with their hammers, or 'despise the straight furrow' and waste their seed plowing the desert instead, and especially followers of Orpheus (who 'did not know how to plow or write or forge in the true forge'), calling for their excommunication and castration: 'May their styluses be taken away from them when they have not wished to write within the precious tablets that were suitable for them!'[38]

This accords with the goddess of *De Planctu,* who condemns Helen for adultery, Parsiphae for bestiality, Myrrha for incest and Narcissus for self-love; the most vehement (and stylistically complex) denunciations, however, are reserved for homoerotic acts. Metre I describes those who deny Nature, men turned women (*femina uir factus*) who blacken the fair name of their sex (*sexus denigrate honorem*);[39] later, men who seek other men:

> Non modo Tindaridem Frigius uenatur adulter
> Sed Paris in Paridem monstra nefanda parit.
>
> (No longer does the Phrygian adulterer [Paris] chase the daughter of Tyndareus but Paris with Paris performs unmentionable and monstrous deeds.)[40]

37 Susan Schibanoff, 'Sodomy's Mark: Alain de Lille, Jean de Meun, and the Medieval Theory of Authorship', in *Queering the Middle Ages*, ed. Glenn Burger and Steven F. Kruger, Medieval Cultures 27 (Minneapolis: University of Minnesota Press, 2001), pp. 28–56 (p. 39).

38 Guillaume de Lorris and Jean de Meun, *The Romance of the Rose*, trans. Charles Dahlberg (Princeton, NJ: Princeton University Press, 1971 and subsequent), pp. 323–4; Guillaume de Lorris and Jean de Meun, *Le Roman de la Rose*, ed. Félix Lecoy, 3 vols, Societé des Anciens Textes Français (Paris: Firmin-Didot, Champion, 1914–24), vv. 19599–646.

39 Alain de Lille, *De Planctu Naturae*, ed. Nikolaus M. Häring, *Studi Medievali* 19 (1978), 797–879 (806: 17).

40 *De Planctu Naturae*, ed. Häring, 808: 51–2; Alain de Lille, *The Plaint of Nature*, ed. and

The problem has arisen because Nature has delegated the work of matching couples to Venus. Nature calls to the authority of grammar and subverts its usual operation in her transmutation of orthodox sexuality into orthodox language. Prose V details how Nature, 'with secret warnings and mighty, thunderous threats', instructs Venus that in accordance with reason she should 'concentrate exclusively in her connections on the natural union of masculine and feminine gender [*in suis coniunctionibus ratione exigentie naturalem constructionem solummodo masculini feminique generis celebraret*]', since these are the conditions that must obtain for reproduction.[41] Since, in this generative grammar, the masculine corresponds to the active form and to the adjective (which modifies the noun), and the feminine by implication corresponds with the noun and the passive form, masculine and feminine should join naturally and have no recourse to grammatical agreement that would pair masculine and masculine, and feminine and feminine. The active sense and the passive are not to be mixed, the adjective acts upon the noun and nothing else; intransitive constructions (with no direct objects) and reflexives (that refer back to the subject) should not be tolerated; deponents (passive/female in form, active/male in action) should not be adopted.[42] Should the masculine, 'by a certain violence of unreasonable reason [*irrationabilis rationis*]' desire 'a gender entirely similar to itself', this may not be defended 'as any kind of graceful figure but will bear the stain of an outlandish and unpardonable solecism [*inexcusabili soloecismi monstruositate*]'.[43] In *De Planctu*, however, Alain's complex discussion of the manifold grammatical constructions that do not obtain in the grammar of Nature also, of course, makes the point very well that all of these unspeakable constructions are indeed possible in speech, and precisely through the agreement of gender.

De Planctu holds forth on the pitfalls of unnatural behaviour, but it is not without its own internal inconsistencies, which marry persistent invective against 'unnatural' practice with persistent hints that Nature herself is inconsistent and lacks commitment to her work. Her garb features behaviours well-known from the bestiaries – the resurrection of the phoenix, the self-castration of the beaver, the bear whose offspring begin so ill-made they must be literally licked into shape – and throughout the characteristic violence,

trans. James J. Sheridan (Toronto: Pontifical Institute of Medieval Studies, 1980), p. 71.

41 *De Planctu Naturae*, ed. Häring, 846: 47–9; *The Plaint of Nature*, ed. and trans. Sheridan, p. 157.

42 *De Planctu Naturae*, ed. Häring, 846–7: 58–72; *The Plaint of Nature*, ed. and trans. Sheridan, pp. 157–9. See *The Plaint of Nature*, ed. and trans. Sheridan, n. 12–15, on this 'almost incredible mélange of words'.

43 *De Planctu Naturae*, Häring, 846: 54–7; *The Plaint of Nature*, ed. and trans. Sheridan, p. 157. The distance between figures of speech and barbarisms is also a preoccupation for Alain elsewhere. For his discussion of the rejection of figures of speech by grammar, see *Anticlaudianus, or The Good and Perfect Man*, ed. and trans. James J. Sheridan (Toronto: Pontifical Institute of Medieval Studies, 1973), 86: 417–35.

promiscuity and lack of reason that are commonly attributed to animals. Nature's coherence and consistency is repeatedly called into question. The night-owl is so demonstrably imperfect and sullied that it is as if Nature were napping during his manufacture. The parrot feigns human speech 'on the anvil of its throat' (*in sui gutturis incude*),[44] while among the fish there is 'a siren, part fish, but with a man's face'.[45] The elephant's size is attributed to Nature's original credit being multiplied through usury (*fenore duplicabat*).[46] Nature's robe also shows 'natural' instances of otherwise 'unnatural' acts: the bat, for example, is a 'hermaphrodite among birds [*auis hermafroditica*]' and appears to elide two forms and possibly two genders.[47]

Moreover, Nature's philosophy of language is also inconsistent; it vacillates between a Platonic eschewal of false poetry (in prose 4) and a resolve to beautify vice with golden phrases and honeyed words. Her insistence on the importance of measure, pattern and regularity is overthrown by the language that in her indignation against these transgressions exceeds limits and becomes strange and profane (*prophanas [...] nouitates*).[48] Alain's rhetoric amplifies Nature's objections to the sex acts that fall under the category of sodomy, and the gender instabilities that she likewise deplores, but, as several scholars have pointed out, the rhetorical bravura accomplishes this objective by resorting to precisely the type of sophistry that is used as a metaphor for the unnatural behaviour that is the cause of Nature's ire – the very form of *De Planctu* is a hybrid. While the unnatural is opposed to speakability and legibility, implying that Nature may act as the arbiter of access to speech and language, the natural often appears confusing and near unspeakable, too.

The fallout from unnatural acts seems to destabilise Nature herself in turn, but as she admits, these transgressions take place because Nature has delegated the work of matching humans to Venus, Hymen and Cupid, for reasons that, as Sheridan points out, are self-serving and insufficient.[49] This is a Nature who abandons the work with which she is tasked by God because she wishes to be nearer to heaven; who deputises unwisely; who speaks at length of the correct order and the rectitude of male–female pairings and

44 *De Planctu Naturae*, ed. Häring, 815: 181.

45 *De Planctu Naturae*, ed. Häring, 817: 212–13.

46 *De Planctu Naturae*, ed. Häring, 818: 240.

47 *De Planctu Naturae*, ed. Häring, 816: 192–3; *The Plaint of Nature*, ed. and trans. Sheridan, p. 94. The bat was regarded as being like a bird but not quite a bird; possibly a mixture of bird and mouse. Hugh of Fouilloy in *De Bestis et Aliis Rebus* deems the bat 'ignoble [*ignobile*]' (*PL* 177, col. 95C); this is translated by T. H. White as 'a paltry animal'; *The Book of Beasts: Being a Translation from a Latin Bestiary of the Twelfth Century* (Madison, WI: Parallel Press, 2002), pp. 140–1. Both texts note its distinction from other birds but do not call it hermaphrodite.

48 *De Planctu Naturae*, ed. Häring, 836: 95; *The Plaint of Nature*, ed. and trans. Sheridan, p. 137.

49 *The Plaint of Nature*, ed. and trans. Sheridan, p.147, n. 44.

the orthodoxy of gender roles and the singleness of gender in bodies, but whose robe displays *mixturae* that would have agitated Bernard of Clairvaux and, worse still, creatures who transgress these boundaries. Nature's acts and bodies would seem to be *contra naturam*, and all this without comment from the narrator. Indeed, just as Nature is shown to exhibit the inconsistencies of form, intent and action that she decries in creation, Alain 'exhibitionistically shows himself to be a practitioner of the *falsigraphia* he has Nature cite as the obverse of her orthography'.[50] While Larry Scanlon and William Burgwinkle's readings conclude that Alain revealed more of himself in *De Planctu* than in any other work, and perhaps more than he intended[51] (recalling Foucault's point that we cannot expect discourse on sex to tell us about whether it comes from a dominant or dominated position), David Rollo takes up their observations and takes these ideas further in his analysis of form, reading 'style itself [as] a covert message'.[52]

The *Rose* continues Alain's fascination with linguistic correctness and continues to muse on the relation of language to reality, with gleeful satire exemplified in the notorious passage in which Jean's Reason chooses the example of 'testicles' and 'relics' to point out the arbitrariness of words' relation to what they describe.[53] Though Reason makes light of blasphemy, Jon Whitman contends that the *Rose* 'participate[s] in a larger intellectual controversy that acquires new intensity in the late thirteenth century, the problem of formulating the relation between the created and divine worlds'.[54] Drawing on Aquinas, he sets out the stakes: creation and the Creator cannot be described in the same words with the same sense, yet if words could not describe both creation and Creator, how could we speak of God or acknowledge the connection to the Creator? Reason is no neoplatonist, declaring that one cannot speak too much of God; yet even here the *Rose* is also concerned with the confusion that comes about through prolixity, and Reason must concede

50 David Rollo, *Kiss My Relics: Hermaphroditic Fictions of the Middle Ages* (Chicago: University of Chicago Press, 2011), p. 116.

51 Larry Scanlon, 'Speaking the Unspeakable: Sexual Regulation and the Priesthood of Genius', *Romanic Review* 86.2 (1995), 213–42 (p. 226); Burgwinkle, *Sodomy, Masculinity, and Law*, pp. 193–9.

52 Rollo, *Kiss My Relics*, p. 216.

53 Responding to Amant's prim remark that a well-bred maiden should not know the word *testicles* (or *coilles*), Reason declares that 'If, when I put names to things that you dare to criticize thus and blame, I had called testicles relics [*coilles reliques apelusse*] and had declared relics to be testicles, then you, who here criticize me and goad me on account of them, would reply that "relics" was an ugly, base word.' *The Romance of the Rose*, trans. Dalhberg, p. 135; *Le Roman de la Rose*, ed. Lecoy, vv. 7079–85.

54 Jon Whitman, 'Dislocations: The Crisis of Allegory in the *Romance of the Rose*', in *Languages of the Unsayable*, ed. Budick and Iser, pp. 259–79 (pp. 269–70).

that, though silence 'remains a small virtue [.../ to speak the things to be kept silent [*dire les choses a tere*] is to commit a diabolical deed'.[55]

The scholastic evolution of Alain's theme is very much in evidence when Nature debates whether free will, predestination and divine prescience can co-exist; this discussion occurs during Genius's confession of Nature. Just as Alain's ornate and sophisticated stylings enthusiastically embrace grammatical flexibility, Jean's digression-filled work is fuelled by the pleasures of excess and prolixity. Even Nature, though she claims she does not want to tire herself talking, and that 'It is a good thing to flee prolixity [*bon fet prolixité foïr,* v. 18268]', does not know reason and measure in her speech. Where language is the metaphor for sexuality then Nature's own behaviour does not conform to the ideal.[56] She cannot keep her silence and so confesses not only her own failings but the sins of others, too:

> [S]ince he has done so much against me, I will tell the story of his [man's] fall before God, who gave him to me when he created man in his image. I am a woman and cannot keep silent [*Fame sui, si ne me puis tere,* v. 19188]; from now on I want to reveal everything, for a woman can hide nothing. Man was never better vilified than he will be now. It was an evil hour for him when he wandered so far from me. His vices will be recounted; I shall tell the whole truth.[57]

Jean's Genius (anticipating Derrida, but with an antifeminist slant) insists that no woman – even Nature – is capable of keeping secret anything that should not be said: the only reason a man could have for revealing to a woman anything he does not want subsequently broadcast is that he is drunk or mad (*ivres ou forsenez,* v. 16320). If he does, he has only himself to blame when his secret is spilled. 'But what does the wretch think he can do? He cannot keep his own tongue silent [*sa langue tere*]. Is he going to try now to restrain another's?'[58] Such is the censure of women in the *Rose*, of course, that it inspired the literary debate known as the *querelle de la Rose* or the *querelle des femmes*. Champions of virtuous women, led by Christine de Pizan, objected to the obscene language and satirical philosophy in the *Rose*, Jean's antifeminist rhetoric, which extended to the declaration that women are universally and necessarily whores,[59] and his cynical treatment of love.[60] Noah Guynn argues

55 *The Romance of the Rose*, trans. Dahlberg, p. 215; *Le Roman de la Rose*, ed. Lecoy, vv. 7001–13 (7005–6).

56 *The Romance of the Rose*, trans. Dahlberg, p. 304; *Le Roman de la Rose*, ed. Lecoy, vv. 18266–8.

57 *The Romance of the Rose*, trans. Dahlberg, p. 317; *Le Roman de la Rose*, ed. Lecoy, vv. 19184–94.

58 *The Romance of the Rose*, trans. Dahlberg, p. 279; *Le Roman de la Rose*, ed. Lecoy, vv. 16523–5.

59 *The Romance of the Rose*, trans. Dahlberg, pp. 165–6; *Le Roman de la Rose*, ed. Lecoy, vv. 9155–65.

60 See Christine de Pizan, Jean Gerson, Jean de Montreuil, Gontier and Pierre Col, *Le*

that it is precisely the *Rose*'s continual dislocations and authorial disavowals that serve to obscure and enable its antifeminist stance, by seeming to distance its writer from the ideology the romance describes and seemingly deconstructs.[61] While silence and secrecy may be the Foucauldian shelter for power, the deconstruction of ideological discourse and the multitude of voices may thus become equally effective in this regard. In this text, which as Guynn insists 'seeks a shelter for male power in the apparent disruption and demystification, but also the subtle affirmation and perpetuation, of a variety of patriarchal culture codes', there is a preoccupation with the dangers of speaking women.[62]

Where *De Planctu* is often seen as the archetype of high medieval homophobia, and the *Rose* of antifeminism (and both texts are coloured by both prejudices, of course), their biases also skew the representation of Nature. Nature is the authority in sexual ethics, but Nature is confused, open to interpretation and, inevitably (if ironically), bound up in custom as well. She is encompassed in Jean's misogyny just as she is party to the homoerotic preferences Alain decries. Thus Susan Schibanoff, in her brilliant reading of Alain and Jean, analyses the queerness of Nature and Genius and the fecundity of same-sex desire, and Guynn notes that, strictly speaking, *monstra nefanda parit* (in *De Planctu*'s opening verses) may be 'both the doing of monstrous misdeeds and the begetting of monstrous offspring, here through homosexual intercourse and male parturition'.[63] As Jordan remarks, 'Nature's rules seem to spawn their own violations in same-sex fertilities'.[64] She embodies traits that are supposedly shameful and even unspeakable. And yet, just as Nature is the term that makes the obfuscations of the confessional script clear, Nature is also the arbiter of that which is acceptable to speech. In texts about the unnatural, Nature enables the unspeakable to go on speaking.

PIECES OF PILGRIMS (AND WHY THEY MATTER)

The condemnation of the unspeakable is enabled by the conversion of a person into a sign, a word that is gendered. The remainder of this chapter now turns to this process and the speculation that it enables, tracing the unspeakable acts and clamour of voices around three queer protagonists of the late medieval

Débat sur 'Le Roman de la Rose', ed. Eric Hicks (Paris: Editions Honoré Champion, 1977).

61 'Is it possible that the poem's fascination with its own lack of unity, including its dislocation of the author from his signature, may actually serve to *privilege* antifeminist ideologies and shield them from attack, rather than exposing and unsettling the very foundations of medieval patriarchy?' Guynn, *Allegory and Sexual Ethics*, p. 153.

62 Guynn, *Allegory and Sexual Ethics*, p. 140.

63 Guynn, *Allegory and Sexual Ethics*, p. 109.

64 Jordan, *Invention of Sodomy*, p. 86.

canon. I begin with the figure who is now probably the most notorious (possible) exponent of the unspeakable sin in medieval literature – Chaucer's Pardoner. Among the motley crew of pilgrims on the road to Canterbury, it is arguably the Pardoner who best characterises the multivalence of that other collection of 'Fragments', *The Canterbury Tales*.[65]

The final member of the band that Chaucer describes in the Prologue, the Pardoner, is companion to the Summoner and carries a 'male' stuffed with the fake 'relics' he sells all over England. Though Harry Bailly requests a mirthful antidote to the distressing story of Virginia that the Physician has just told, the general company calls for something more edifying. The Pardoner obliges with a homiletic digression on the evils of greed (as he himself drinks ale and eats cake), followed by a tale of three rioters who, on hearing Death has taken one of their fellow drinkers, attempt to evade him but find instead a heap of gold that leads to their collective demise. Indeed, though unlike its gloomy predecessor in many ways, the 'Pardoner's Tale', like the 'Physician's Tale', calls attention over and over to the disparity between speech and truth, and makes rigorously the link between speaking and sinning. Truth and falsehood, natural and unnatural, are again superimposed. While Virginia is Nature's greatest achievement, a maiden of clear and simple speech with no 'countrefeted termes' (VI. 51), the judge Appius lies shamelessly, and the Pardoner's revellers are 'fals' and 'unkynde' (that is, unnatural, VI. 903).

Unfortunately for the edification of the company, not only does the Pardoner preface his tale by explaining his dodgy dealings with the lay folk who come to him for pardons and relics, he then caps his otherwise moral story by attempting to hawk his wares to the pilgrims. Bailly, in his disgust, silences the Pardoner by threatening to enshrine his 'coillons [...] in an hogges toord' (VI. 952–5), and it is left to the Knight – the first among the pilgrims – to make peace between them. The many critical readings of this pilgrim's tale also turn the tables on the *quaestor* and interrogate him for his 'secret', outing him as homosexual, exposing him as a eunuch and claiming him for queer theory.

The sheer volume of Chaucerian study produced in the centuries since Hoccleve declared him the father of English poetry can reveal a stunning array of interpretations on any issue, but even in this context the 'Pardoner's Tale' is remarkable for the range of critical assertions that all take their cue from a select few lines:

> A voys he hadde as smal as hath a goot.
> No berd hadde he, ne nevere sholde have;
> As smothe it was as it were late shave.

[65] References to *The Canterbury Tales* will be given from *The Riverside Chaucer*, 3rd edn, ed. Larry D. Benson (Oxford: Oxford University Press, 1988). Subsequent references will be given in the text by fragment and line number.

I trowe he were a geldyng or a mare.
But of his craft, fro Berwyk into Ware
Ne was ther swich another pardoner. (I. 688–93)

In large part on account of this first appearance, the Pardoner has been saddled with a plethora of assessments for his condition or identity, whether physical, psychological or psychical, as subsequent readers have tried to figure out who he 'really' is. The Summoner's hyper-masculinity has come in for scrutiny, but it is still the Pardoner who best 'fits' the image – if there can be said to be one – of a queer medieval character.[66] From George Lyman Kittredge onwards, the principal trend among scholars treating the 'Pardoner's Tale' and 'Prologue' has been towards the systematic construction first of his 'personality' and later his sexuality. Though Kittredge did not stray from the former (resolving the disparity of Chaucer's putting 'a beautiful story, wonderfully told [...] into the mouth of a vulgar, prating rascal' by examining 'all the available evidence as to the Pardoner's character'),[67] his character assessment spawned other analyses in a similar vein, whose focus gradually narrowed almost exclusively to discussions of the Pardoner's (homo)sexuality or, alternatively, whether or not he is a eunuch.[68] *The Canterbury Tales* are perennial favourites with medievalists studying sexual politics, but critics were 'outing' the Pardoner for decades before the advent of gender and queer theory.

The final section of Chaucer's *Canterbury Tales*, dominated as it is by the Parson's lengthy sermon for the improvement of the general company, famously rails against 'thilke abhomynable synne, of which that no man unnethe oghte speke ne write' (X. 909). For at least some of his travelling

66 The Summoner is described as 'hoot [...] and lecherous' (I. 626) and bears 'a stif burdoun' to the Pardoner as they sing together (I. 673); the Pardoner is taken to be effeminate and therefore potentially sodomitical. This pun on 'stif burdoun' ('strong bass', as the *Riverside* glosses it, but also a staff or stud, with inevitable phallic connotations) provides the basis for speculation as to the Pardoner and Summoner's relationship.

67 G. L. Kittredge, 'Chaucer's Pardoner', *The Atlantic Monthly* 72 (1893), 829–33 (p. 830).

68 In 1919, Walter Clyde Curry identified him, from his thinning hair and staring eyes, as a congenital eunuch, a verdict that was thereafter endorsed by critics well into the latter half of the century, and indeed still persists (albeit as a theory that is frequently problematised). Monica McAlpine probes possible implications of the word 'mare', suggesting the Pardoner 'may be seen as a frustrated heterosexual who associates himself with the lecherous Summoner in order to deny his own impotence [...] [or who is] ambivalent about disclosing his status, [but] nonetheless becomes suspect through the public display of this ambiguous friendship'. See Walter Clyde Curry, 'The Secret of Chaucer's Pardoner', *JEGP* 18 (1919), 593–606; Beryl Rowland, 'Animal Imagery and the Pardoner's Abnormality', *Neophilologus* 48.1 (1964), 56–60 (p. 58); Monica E. McAlpine, 'The Pardoner's Homosexuality and How it Matters', *PMLA* 95.1 (1980), 8–22 (p. 13); and Gregory W. Gross, 'Trade Secrets: Chaucer, the Pardoner, the Critics', *Modern Language Studies* 25.4 (1995), 1–36, for the development of the Pardoner's critical 'closet'.

companions, however, this is a bit late. The problem with the category of the 'unspeakable', as the Parson's allusion itself points out, is that even in order to impose the necessary censure, or (more charitably) to encourage appropriate confession, one is obliged to 'speak or write' about it. Naturally, in *The Canterbury Tales*, which function in and through an economy of enunciation – I'll tell you mine if you tell me yours – there is little chance of anyone or anything remaining silent. As Jean's Genius says, secrets breed speech.

The Pardoner becomes *The Canterbury Tales*' representative of the unspeakable, since he himself is concerned chiefly with the meaning of fragments and with oral control. In medieval terms, he may be seen as unnatural in several ways – his physical body is construed as unmanly, effeminate; he is spiritually hollow and a purveyor of fakes and blasphemy – but his narrative also exemplifies the unspeakable in that what goes unmentioned is routinely emphasised. He himself acknowledges the rhetorical force of saying what you will not say, telling people what you are not going to tell them. Confronted with a sceptic in his congregation, one of the 'folk that doon us displesances' (VI. 420), he appears to take particular pleasure in cutting this man down to size, but he derives equal satisfaction in doing it without naming names. Though the Pardoner will 'telle noght his propre name', he nevertheless ensures by the use of certain signs that 'Men shal wel knowe that it is the same' (VI. 417–19). Likewise, mention of the sin practised by men and women 'in diverse entente and in diverse manere' (X. 910) might suggest any or none of the pilgrims, but the audience might equally know by the signs who is meant.

Even a plain, bald statement becomes a veiled reference to an unspeakable alternative, when it comes from the Pardoner.[69] Of his double moral standards, he declares, 'I preche agayn that same vice / Which that I use, and that is avarice' (VI. 427–8). His personal motto, 'Radix malorum est Cupiditas' (VI. 334, 426), casts the original sin as greed, not pride. References to the Pardoner's own fiscal *cupiditas* are abundant; indeed, Walter Scheps argued that the notorious gelding/mare line was actually an indication of an avaricious character (following Gower's model in the *Confessio Amantis*, wherein Avarice is variously depicted as being both male and female and also riding on horseback).[70] It is nevertheless another critical commonplace that this vice is, as McAlpine terms it, a 'screen sin'[71] – the educated guesser might indeed

69 For a reading of the Pardoner's veils, both physical and metaphorical, see Robert S. Sturges, *Chaucer's Pardoner and Gender Theory: Bodies of Discourse*, The New Middle Ages Series (Basingstoke: Palgrave Macmillan, 2000), pp. 64–80.

70 Walter Scheps, 'Chaucer's Numismatic Pardoner and the Personification of Avarice', *Acta* 4 (1977), 107–23 (pp. 117, 120).

71 McAlpine, 'The Pardoner's Homosexuality', p. 14. See Carolyn Dinshaw, *Chaucer's Sexual Poetics* (Madison, WI: University of Wisconsin Press, 1989), p. 157; Lee Patterson, 'Chaucerian Confession: Penitential Literature and the Pardoner', *Medievalia et Humanistica* 7 (1976), 153–73 (p. 163).

argue that the Pardoner's true vice is the vice of (desiring) the 'same', since 'the shame that attends the naming of the sin even in the confessional seems a clear allusion to homosexuality'.[72]

Despite the Parson's admonitions, matters of which no man should speak or write make other guest appearances through the course of *The Canterbury Tales* regardless; in its silent yet persistent clamour, the unspeakable echoes through certain pilgrims' yarns, an elephant in the room. The flyting and quiting of the Miller and the Reeve early on in the tales indicate that, unspoken though it is, there is little doubt in the pilgrims' minds what is happening when Nicholas is penetrated by Absolom's hot coulter. As Daniel Pigg argues, the Miller is also subjected to 'male violence – male against male. It is a tale of symbolic rape.'[73] Where Nicholas and Absolom are engaged in a homosocial contest via the body of Alisoun, the Reeve's story implicates himself and the Miller in another male–male rivalry, triangulated again by the (unwitting) female body.[74] The 'Reeve's Tale' is thus a speech act equivalent to a performance: 'in "saying" his tale he is not merely talking, but also metaphorically "doing" something quite perverse to his adversary, the Miller'.[75]

The Host threatens to do something equally, if not more, perverse to the Pardoner. Having divulged frankly that the relics he carries around to sell are all forgeries, the Pardoner's subsequent attempts to flog these same goods to the audience of pilgrims do not sit well with Harry Bailly. In response to the Pardoner's behest that he 'kisse the relikes everychon' (VI. 944), Bailly snaps the famous retort:

> Thou woldest make me kisse thyn olde breech,
> And swere it were the relyk of a seint,
> Though it were with thy fundament depeint! (VI. 948–50)

The sexual undercurrent detectable in this scene has been thoroughly picked apart by a succession of critics (as will be discussed later in the chapter). In

72 McAlpine, 'The Pardoner's Homosexuality', p. 15.

73 Daniel F. Pigg, 'Performing the Perverse: The Abuse of Masculine Power in the *Reeve's Tale*', in *Masculinities in Chaucer: Approaches to Maleness in the Canterbury Tales and Troilus and Criseyde*, ed. Peter G. Beidler (Woodbridge: D. S. Brewer, 1998), pp. 53–61 (p. 60).

74 Pigg makes the point that 'Medieval records are all but silent on the issue of homosexual rape, not because it did not happen, but because it was ultimately an attack on the world of male authority [...] How much of a threat homosexual rape was will probably remain unclear, but it was certainly inscribed in the cultural mind [...] On the symbolic level of the tale, the Reeve has merely substituted the clerk's attack on the two women for his own verbal attack on the Miller' (Pigg, 'Performing the Perverse', p. 60). Given the inherently more 'speakable' nature of heterosexual rape, it is tempting to wonder how much hegemonic capital there was to be gained by telling stories about attacks on females that reinforced the subjugation of the feminine to the masculine.

75 Pigg, 'Performing the Perverse', p. 54.

an effort to persuade Bailly to buy, the Pardoner bids him 'Unbokele anon thy purs' (VI. 945), 'unbokele' carrying the connotations of both *undoing* and *displaying*, and 'purs' potentially referring to a purse of money, a receptacle for relics or, as the Wife of Bath uses the term in her 'Prologue', the 'nether purs' (III. 44b) or scrotum. Whether the Pardoner's motives are fiscal, sexual or owing to some other impulse, Bailly's reply to his solicitation puts him down firmly; in his own literal interpretation of Reason's relic-testicle aphorism, the Host would have the Pardoner's 'coillons' in his hand, so as to cut them off and make of *them* a relic. The Pardoner in his 'wrath' is left speechless, until the Knight's intervention restores the balance and the two kiss and make up.[76]

As Robert Sturges shows, the Pardoner is a figure who exposes ruptures and inconsistencies in medieval thought about sexual identity and gender identity. In his protean nature, cynical religiosity and fluid gender, the Pardoner riffs on Jean's Faux Semblant. False Seeming, who aids Amans but is eventually dismissed as an ally, declares all the guises in which he passes from town to town – all occupations, clerical and lay, all ages, both sexes. He is not only a trickster but spiritually vacant: no matter whether he disguise himself as monk, clerk, priest, nun or devotee, he cheerfully admits that when it comes to religion, 'I leave the kernel [...] and take the husk [*j'en lés le grain et pregn la paille*].'[77] The Pardoner's swagger is likewise built on undisguised disguises; he apes the Physician's medicinal tonics with a cure-all made from water that washed a shoulder-bone 'that was of an hooly Jewes sheep' (VI. 350–65); he likens himself to a serpent, admitting he defames others and uses preaching for the opportunity to 'spitte [...] venym under hewe / Of hoolynesse' (VI. 421–2). If his layers of physical, social, psychological and psychical camouflage have fed centuries of modern and postmodern reader controversies, the continuations of the Canterbury narrative contained in the anonymous *Tale of Beryn* and Lydgate's prologue to *The Sege of Thebes* suggest that medieval readers did not seem to know what to make of the Pardoner either. Whereas in the *Tale of Beryn* he gets into a fabliauesque scrape with the comely tapster of a Canterbury inn, attempting to seduce her but ending the night in a dog kennel, Chaucer's near-contemporary Lydgate continues to portray the Pardoner as a beardless wonder with a glassy stare.[78]

[76] On the Pardoner's apoplexy at the jokes on his relics, see also William Chester Jordan, 'The Pardoner's "Holy Jew"', in *Chaucer and the Jews*, ed. Sheila Delany (London: Routledge, 2002), pp. 25–42. While the other pilgrims can communicate in jokes and successfully battle with wits, Jordan argues, the Pardoner is speechless before the truth (that his relics fail in their function).

[77] *The Romance of the Rose*, trans. Dahlberg, pp. 196–7; *Le Roman de la Rose*, ed. Lecoy, vv. 11151–92 (vv. 11185–6).

[78] See *The Canterbury Tales: Fifteenth Century Continuations and Additions*, ed. John M. Bowers (Kalamazoo, MI: Medieval Institute Publications, 1992).

If the Pardoner's identity is a many-gendered thing, Sturges demonstrates the value of proliferating and plural interpretations, which may 'challenge all critical attempts to fix the Pardoner's body', and instead 'render it discoherent, to reactivate the contradictions erased by the ideology of unitary discursive truth and its attempts to control meaning'.[79] Implicitly allied with unnatural acts and religious fakery from his first appearance, the Pardoner evokes the emptiness of words, the fragmentation of bodies, the interchangeability of terms and genders, and the conversion of bodies into speech. He is a cipher, fragments of a persona made into different wholes in discourse (or holes in the discourse). Continually rearranging pieces of personas, the Pardoner makes heavy demands on any reader who attempts to pin him down.

Such slipperiness extends both to his speech and his fake relics. While Lee Patterson reconciles the attraction of psychoanalytic theory with its inherent drawbacks, particularly 'the way its seeming persuasiveness can foreclose access to relevant medieval materials and contexts',[80] the impact of theoretical trends from a historicist perspective is half-lamented, half-lampooned in Robyn Malo's essay 'The Pardoner's Relics (And Why They Matter the Most)'.[81] For the theoretically inclined, though, the Pardoner's relics are also crucial. Like a neat label for a lengthy thought process, a relic is a part for an inaccessible whole, connoting lack as well as connection. The similarities between fragments of language and the *materia* of the 'Pardoner's Tale' are crystallised in Carolyn Dinshaw's compelling reading of his relics as 'partial objects' – those items 'used by the subject in the attempt to fill the lack brought into being by the loss of an original ideal, an original wholeness and plenitude'.[82] For this technique of strategic, flawed but ceaseless substitution in the face of glaringly obvious deficiency, Dinshaw coins the name 'eunuch hermeneutics'. The Pardoner's relics become constitutive of his self-image in a manner that recalls the *méconnaissance* of the Lacanian mirror-stage: despite

79 Sturges, *Chaucer's Pardoner and Gender Theory*, p. 36. Sturges is borrowing Jonathan Dollimore's term from *Sexual Dissidence: Augustine to Wilde, Freud to Foucault* (Oxford: Oxford University Press, 1991).

80 Lee Patterson, 'Chaucer's Pardoner on the Couch: Psyche and Clio in Medieval Literary Studies', *Speculum* 76.3 (2001), 638–80 (p. 656).

81 Robyn Malo, 'The Pardoner's Relics (And Why They Matter the Most)', *The Chaucer Review* 43.1 (2008), 82–102. Malo responds to McAlpine, 'The Pardoner's Homosexuality and How It Matters', and Richard F. Green, 'The Pardoner's Pants (And Why They Matter)', *Studies in the Age of Chaucer* 15 (1993), 131–45, by pointing out that in the forty-five lines introducing the Pardoner in the *General Prologue*, the longest segment (I. 686–700) is devoted to his relics.

82 Dinshaw, *Chaucer's Sexual Poetics*, p. 165. Dinshaw is adopting Melanie Klein's usage here: in Kleinian object relations theory, in which the infant's early experiences provide the pattern for the individual's expectations of people and situations in later life, these internalised impressions – objects – begin with fragmentary images of the infant's physical relation to the world and others (such as the image of the breast); these, Klein terms as part objects.

knowing the imperfections of his phony patents and relics, the Pardoner 'uses them – aggressively, desperately – in the belief that they can make him whole, somehow part of the body of pilgrims'.[83] This same belief or desire informs the critical wish to settle on a solution to the Pardoner problem – is he a geldyng or a mare? From this partial description, there is no possibility of getting at 'the secret' or 'the truth' without speculating or extrapolating – even faking it. The illusion of the Pardoner's relics, metonymic parts pointing but not equating to an imagined whole, is the illusion of the Pardoner's own appearance in *The Canterbury Tales*, snippets of information that indicate some indefinable, unspeakable *something* the reader can only imagine beyond the limits of the text. This hermeneutic of the partial, Dinshaw posits, reveals 'a truth about language' as well as the Pardoner: namely that it was 'understood to be at best a fragment'.[84]

Critical discourse on the Pardoner, in its plurality of conclusions about him, is likewise composed of fragments that resemble and represent, but cannot express, a truth – a catalogue of scraps all attempting to describe the same persona. In his appearance and behaviours, the Pardoner breeds speech even (or especially) about the unspeakable, and though he may represent a specific unspeakable sin for pilgrims and medievalists, the Pardoner himself is also frequently concerned with the sins of speaking and of the mouth. According to this tale, the unnatural (or 'unkynde') acts with which the pilgrims *should* be concerned are not the usual unmentionable suspects, but the sins of gluttony – the tale includes detailed surveillance of everything that goes in and out of the revellers' mouths, and even goes so far as to cast gluttony as the sin that should not be spoken of[85] – and particularly blasphemy, which is an unnatural betrayal of God. The Pardoner bemoans profane language in one of his most sustained rants (VI. 629–60): oaths are grisly and foul, swearing 'a thyng abhominable' that tears apart Christ's body (VI. 631). While relics might be invoked in legitimate oaths, to swear by God's heart, nails or arms (VI. 651, 654), to speak of the Creator as if he were a creature, was blasphemous.[86] That the merchant of fake relics is preoccupied with swearing and

83 Dinshaw, *Chaucer's Sexual Poetics*, p. 177.

84 Dinshaw, *Chaucer's Sexual Poetics*, p. 173. Patterson remarks that, 'Although Dinshaw sounds like Lacan, and explicitly invokes Melanie Klein, this reading depends ultimately on Freud's account of fetishism. For Freud, the fetish is a sexually arousing object that substitutes for the mother's missing penis […] The Lacanian turn to Dinshaw's argument is to include in this economy of castration language itself' (Patterson, 'Chaucer's Pardoner on the Couch', p. 658).

85 It is, he says, a 'foul thyng […] / To seye this word' (though the deed itself is fouler: VI. 524–5).

86 On medieval oaths and blasphemy, see Jonathan Michael Gray, *Oaths and the English Reformation* (Cambridge: Cambridge University Press, 2012), pp. 22–30; Edwin D. Craun, '"Inordinata Locutio": Blasphemy in Pastoral Literature, 1200–1500', *Traditio* 39 (1983), 135–62.

blasphemy is another facet of his hypocrisy, but the Pardoner also unwittingly embodies the logic of orthodox swearing. While his body is similarly torn apart by witnesses, critical focus on this mysterious body and its subsequent reduction to discourse shows with great accuracy how very much a creature he is. Readers unmake and remake the Pardoner by participating in the play of semiotic fragmentation he represents, invoking the Pardoner's fragmented body in the analysis of the unspeakable. The ironic prolixity of discourse around the unspeakable both illuminates and obscures the persona of the Pardoner, with the effect that, the more is said of him, the more difficult it is to speak of him. This meta-criticism is admittedly a point that might be made of other pilgrims and indeed other texts; however, it is one that Chaucer's Pardoner demonstrates with particular abundance and with special resonance to an exploration of unspeakable sin, gender and sexuality.

Less a process of selection than of innumerable, simultaneous occurrences and meanings, the many differences of opinion concerning the Pardoner in particular echo the lack of consensus on medieval sodomy in general – that which, as the Parson says, men and women do with diverse intent and in a variety of ways.[87] The fascination with this character and why he represents something unspeakable has, to some extent, served only to make the Pardoner more mysterious, less understandable; he has been so thoroughly 'defined' as to defy description. He remains dissembling and disassembled but creates through his unspeakability a surfeit of speech. The fragments that make up the Pardoner's image – the body parts, the relics and the relics of discourse from which he is composed and decomposed – might therefore be understood not as somehow fitting together, but as representing a collection of pieces whose separateness performs more work than any amalgamation. Surrounded by relics and accoutrements in the tale, surrounded by identifications and speculations that not only reduce him to words but to only five words in particular, the Pardoner reveals – both in relation to the unspeakable sin and to medieval constructions of gender more widely – the vital and generative importance of the partial.

LIKE AN UNNATURAL WOMAN

Sturges concludes his survey of the multiplicity of gender identities open to the Pardoner with a logical extreme – once it is established 'just how "utterly confused" not only sodomy, but all categories of sex, gender, and erotic practice are, especially when brought together in a single figure', it is even possible to see him as 'a lesbian'.[88] As revisionist scholarship on medieval lesbianism indicates, however, this concept in medieval literature and medieval

[87] *Canterbury Tales*, X. 910.

[88] Sturges, *Chaucer's Pardoner and Gender Theory*, pp. 58–9.

studies has suffered less from confusion than from obscurity.[89] Lochrie makes the point that sodomy as a category was by no means exclusively male. Just as the presumptive heteronormativity of medieval discourse does so at the expense of other gendered positions and sexualities, 'presumptive sodomy has the effect of privileging a version of medieval sodomy that excludes women and gender and replicates the very misogyny of the medieval category'.[90]

Robert Mills points out that, just as Alain's narrator asks Nature why she occupies herself so obsessively with the activities of men, or rather, mortals, as opposed to the gods of classical antiquity who indulged in these acts as much if not more, we may ask why he and Nature focus on the activities of men with men and seem to overlook those of women with women. Pointing to the kisses between Nature and the Virtues, Mills suggests that this 'apparent contradiction between the text's allegorical celebration of intense female fellowship and its condemnation of male–male relations elsewhere may thus be symptomatic of the difference gender makes to the interpretation of same-sex bonds'.[91] Jacqueline Murray encapsulates the status of the medieval lesbian and female same-sex relationships when she writes that they are 'twice marginalised and twice invisible'.[92] Though since the 1990s there has been given much more attention to this area of medieval studies, part of the challenge to such studies continues to be the lack of material in the medieval record and the lack of inscription in discourse. Brundage concludes that writers of canon law 'rarely mentioned lesbianism. The few references that do occur indicate that sexual relationships between women were thought more shocking than male homosexual relationships. Despite this, however, canonists apparently did not perceive lesbian practices as a major problem or as a serious threat to the social order'.[93]

Lochrie, on the other hand, emphasises that an evaluation drawn from lack (in this case of evidence in legal records) might be misleading when

89 For an overview of scholarship addressing and redressing this obscurity, see Jacqueline Murray, 'Twice Marginal and Twice Invisible: Lesbians in the Middle Ages', in *A Handbook of Medieval Sexuality*, ed. Vern L. Bullough and James A. Brundage (New York: Garland, 1996), pp. 191–222; Francesca Canadé Sautman and Pamela Sheingorn, *Same-Sex Love and Desire Among Women in the Middle Ages* (New York: Palgrave, 2001); Karma Lochrie, *Heterosyncrasies: Female Sexuality When Normal Wasn't* (Minneapolis: University of Minnesota Press, 2005); *The Lesbian Premodern*, ed. Noreen Giffney, Michelle M. Sauer and Diane Watt (Basingstoke: Palgrave Macmillan, 2011).

90 Lochrie, 'Presumptive Sodomy', p. 296.

91 Robert Mills, *Seeing Sodomy in the Middle Ages* (Chicago: University of Chicago Press, 2015), p. 255. Mills does acknowledge that this may simply indicate that Alain would have expected a male audience.

92 See Murray, 'Twice Marginal and Twice Invisible', pp. 191–222.

93 Brundage, *Law, Sex, and Christian Society in Medieval Europe*, p. 400. Brundage notes that sixteenth-century prosecutions for sex between women outnumber those of the Middle Ages but still do not amount to many (pp. 570–1).

women were included in the category of sodomy, though paid less attention, and cites Albertus Magnus, Thomas Aquinas and evidence from penitentials and *summae* from the seventh century to the thirteenth, as 'all include among the unnatural sexual sins a woman's fornication with another woman'.[94] Though instances of female sodomy crop up much less often than cases of sodomy involving men, Helmut Puff has brought attention to the case of Katherina Hetzeldorfer (tried in Speyer, 1477), which documents the masculine behaviour and cross-dressing of a woman accused of conducting a long-standing sexual relationship with another woman; Judith Bennett and Shannon McSheffrey also note the case of 'Thomasina' (London, 1493), who kept a female *concubina* dressed in male clothing.[95] Joshua Burson, meanwhile, has investigated the case of Hans Hall (from Constance, 1388), in which a female child (Catharina) who self-identified as male (Hans) was married to a woman.[96] The terminology in each case is revealing, as are the conclusions of the investigators. Puff notes that nowhere in the case is Hetzeldorfer's misdeed referred to as *sodomy*, while Bennett and McShaffrey point out the rarity of same-sex desire as a motivation for female cross-dressing.[97] Burson's case is made more complex by the fact that the individual involved, having considered himself a man, later finds herself developing breasts and appears on examination to be intersex, having 'both what a man should have and what a woman should [*baidn umb ain mann, unnd ain frow haben sölln*]'.[98] Hetzeldorfer was drowned and Thomasina's case was dismissed, for reasons not made clear; however, the council of Rotweil ruled that Hans and his wife had a legitimate marriage, despite both having been born women. Murray points out that when female homosexuality became subsumed under the category 'sodomy' or 'unnatural acts', as in Thomas Aquinas, it was thereby 'rendered [...] even more invisible, while at the same time it acquired the more serious overtones of sodomy' – the fate of the medieval lesbian, it

94 Karma Lochrie, 'Between Women', in *The Cambridge Companion to Medieval Women's Writing*, ed. Carolyn Dinshaw and David Wallace (Cambridge: Cambridge University Press, 2003), pp. 70–88 (p. 78).

95 See Helmut Puff, 'Female Sodomy: The Trial of Katherina Hetzeldorfer (1477)', *JMEMS* 30.1 (2000), 41–61; Judith M. Bennett and Shannon McSheffrey, 'Early, Erotic and Alien: Women Dressed as Men in Medieval London', *History Workshop Journal* 77 (2014), 1–25 (pp. 8–9).

96 I am grateful to Joshua Burson for sharing his article 'Gender Identity in Late-Medieval Germany: The Strange Case of Hans Hall'.

97 Cross-dressing might be associated with unnatural behaviour, with carnival traditions, with bids for increased social status, with fugitives from the law or danger, or with attempts to preserve virginity. For a discussion of cross-dressing and social status in the Middle Ages, see Vern L. Bullough and Bonnie Bullough, *Cross Dressing, Sex, and Gender* (Philadelphia, PA: University of Pennsylvania Press, 1993), pp. 45–73.

98 Translation Burson's.

seems, was to have the worst of both worlds.[99] Not only stigmatised under the charge of sodomy, female homosexuality was also suppressed in discourse in as much as it was not permitted to exist on its own terms, but rather defined by its relation to male sexuality and 'not taken seriously except insofar as it threatened male privilege or the natural hierarchy of the genders'.[100]

Lochrie therefore argues persuasively for the 'complicity of sodomy and "heterosexuality"' in this discourse.[101] Episodes of female same-sex desire are accordingly characterised and driven by cross-dressing and often miraculous transformation,[102] that is, by a heterosexual matrix. A woman who looked or behaved like a man, especially a woman who desired another woman, acted in a man's office, transgressing or ignoring male authority. Foucault notes the condemnation of women having sex with other women, rather than men with other men, since in the former case the masculine role is usurped by a feminine body.[103] A union in which one man adopted a 'feminine' role was bad enough – how much more unnatural must one be that contained no men at all and in which the 'male' agency could only be appropriated by a woman or abandoned altogether?

The latter part of this chapter focuses on narratives that give prominence to cross-dressed female protagonists and female same-sex relationships: Gower's tale of Iphis, as told by Genius in the *Confessio Amantis*, and the *Roman de Silence*. Both tell stories of female children brought up male and the complications this causes for them in maturity in social orders predicated on the authority of Nature, where biology is supposed to be destiny. They question which desires can be said to be natural, how 'natural' gender is decided, and by whom, and find an unspeakable component even in the 'unspeakable sin'.

'NATURE CONSTREIGNETH HEM': THE TALE OF IPHIS AND IANTE

John Gower's *Confessio Amantis*, composed in the 1380s and revised significantly in the ensuing decade (following the poet's perceived shift in allegiance from Richard II to Henry of Lancaster), draws again on the sovereignty of Nature and the ministry of Genius, but unlike Alain and Jean, Gower makes his Genius the priest of Venus, not Nature, and his Lover is schooled in confession, not seduction. The 'Tale of Iphis' comes midway through the

99 Murray, 'Twice Marginal and Twice Invisible', p. 200

100 Murray, 'Twice Marginal and Twice Invisible', p. 198.

101 Lochrie, *Covert Operations*, p. 226.

102 See for example William Robins, 'Three Tales of Female Same-Sex Marriage: Ovid's "Iphis and Ianthe", the Old French *Yde et Olive*, and Antonio Pucci's *Reina d'Oriente*', *Exemplaria* 21.1 (2009), 43–62.

103 Michel Foucault, *The History of Sexuality III: The Care of the Self*, trans. Robert Hurley (London: Penguin, 1986), p. 24.

Confessio as an exemplar that demonstrates the need to defeat Sloth in love, and the rewards of overcoming pusillanimity. The story of the king's daughter, cross-dressed and brought up as a boy to avoid detection by a femicidal father, is briefly but densely told. After King Ligdus decrees that no female child of his should be permitted to live and be his heir, Isis takes pity on Ligdus's wife and advises that her baby girl should be disguised and brought up as a boy. This deception is practised to such success that not only does Ligdus believe he has a son but arranges the marriage of 'Iphis' to another girl, Iante. The two fall in love and develop a sexual relationship that is untaught and natural – the two girls practise precisely that to which 'Nature [...] / Constreigneth hem' (IV. 484–6). This un/natural situation is once more resolved through the pity and intervention of a god, this time Cupid, who transforms the girl – at this juncture pointedly referred to as 'Iphe' – into a man in order to 'sette kinde above' and to enable Iphis to win 'the kinde love [...] / Of lusti yonge Iante his wif' (IV. 490, 502–3). Gower's retelling of the Ovidian tale thus juxtaposes radically not only the heterosexual and same-sex desires it deals in but also the expression of nature, which both moves the pair to the use of 'Thing which to hem was al unknowe' (IV. 477) and then later 'corrects' the situation so that the love between Iphis and Iante might be 'to kinde non offence' (IV. 505), or not against nature.[104] While critics are divided as to Gower's motives for telling this tale and in the way that he does, the emergence of nature as a contradictory, unpredictable, inconstant force is more uniformly observed.

The unspeakable vice is addressed here in a very different manner. While Chaucer is suggestive, the Pardoner and the unspeakable sin allied by implication, Gower's Iph/is and Ianthe are paired quite deliberately in a narrative that does not raise the question of the speakability (or not) of their coupling. C. S. Lewis concluded that the problem with *Confessio Amantis*, finally, is that Gower nearly ends perfectly but does not know when to stop; this is not the case in the 'Tale of Iphis'.[105] The tale serves as an example of how female same-sex desire in medieval writing can be denied or undeclared, both in the text and by its readers. It is presented as both natural and unnatural, as both problematic and unproblematic; it is not punished, but nor is it permitted to go uncorrected.

While the same-sex female couple of Iphis and Iante are not said to engage specifically in unspeakable acts, this union *is* deemed to be untenable by the narrative and by nature (or 'kinde'). For Gower and for Cupid, it is a relation that should not be preserved and cannot be written unproblematically – Gower's Latin gloss here, as elsewhere in the *Confessio*, tells a different story

104 See Hugh White, *Nature, Sex, and Goodness in a Medieval Literary Tradition* (Oxford: Oxford University Press, 2001), pp. 192–3; Lochrie, *Covert Operations*, pp. 214–16; Dinshaw, *Getting Medieval*, pp. 10–11.

105 C. S. Lewis, *The Allegory of Love: A Study in Medieval Tradition* (Oxford: Oxford University Press, 1936), pp. 221–2.

from the English in which Iphis is troubled by an inability to fulfil her desire. The two versions signify simultaneously on the page, both written out in words and written out of the vernacular tale. The tale also serves to illustrate an example of that which for Lacan, who infamously claimed that 'there's no such thing as Woman', is uninscribable in the symbolic; for Irigaray too the jouissance of a(nother) woman is inadmissible to a phallic and phallocentric symbolic, but with very different effects and possibilities.

Lacan holds that the unconscious is structured like a language, and that language is made up not of signs but, revising Saussure, signifiers.[106] The corollary to the formula of Lacan's Rome Discourse, that the subject seeks the response of the other in speech, is that man's ultimate desire is always desire for the big Other – God, Nature, Law, Language itself, the unattainable signifier that licenses all other signifiers that stand in for it but cannot encompass it. Reinterpreting Freud's Oedipus complex as the entry of the subject into language, he posits a form of castration anxiety that is therefore experienced by both male and female subjects, and is predicated on their differing (lack of) access to what he calls the symbolic order, the order of the linguistic. Thus 'the privileged signifier of that mark in which the role of the logos is joined with the advent of desire' is none other than the phallus.[107] Lacan's relation of the signifier to signified is cast as the relation between the symbolic and the order he terms the 'real', in which the former provides incomplete access, or the illusion of access, to the latter (as the image in the mirror enables the subject to 'see' but not 'be' the mirror-image). In this system the word is 'a presence made of absence' and if 'man speaks [...] it is because the symbol has made him man'.[108]

This advent of desire and induction into the order of *logos*, because it is predicated on access to the symbolic phallus (that is, the signifier with no signified), happens differently for the two sexes, and in Lacan's schema is intimately bound up in the issue of sexuation; to feminist readers, the challenge is therefore to explain how this entry into knowledge and language, and the jouissance or enjoyment of the Other, is experienced by the female subject as anything other than lack. This challenge is also taken up in part by Lacan in *Seminar XX* – famously the seminar 'on women'.[109] By this time, Lacan's three orders (the real, the imaginary and the symbolic) are firmly established in his work, as is the phallus as the signifier of the desire of the

[106] Lacan, 'Subversion of the Subject', in *Écrits*, pp. 323–60 (pp. 330–1).

[107] Lacan, 'Signification of the Phallus', in *Écrits*, pp. 311–22 (p. 318). Elaborating further, 'The fact that the phallus is a signifier means that it is in the place of the Other that the subject has access to it', pp. 319–20.

[108] Lacan, 'Function and Field', in *Écrits*, pp. 71, 72.

[109] Jacques Lacan, *On Feminine Sexuality: The Limits of Love and Knowledge* (*The Seminar of Jacques Lacan Book XX: Encore 1972–1973*), ed. Jacques-Alain Miller, trans. Bruce Fink (New York: W. W. Norton & Co., 1998).

Other. If 'man's' desire is the desire of the Other, what is woman's? Taking the phallus as both the signifier of the Other and of the entry into the symbolic order means that, by this logic, to identify as a woman is to be situated not wholly in the phallic function.[110]

Seminar XX is also on writing, inscription and the lack of inscription, writing that gets unwritten. The inadequacy of speech, the fragmentation of language, are felt again in the written word, which does not and cannot encompass the 'real'. Accordingly, the big Other of desire, which because not marked by lack is therefore illusory, can only be adequately expressed for Lacan when it is barred or struck through – *l'Autre* becomes ~~A~~.[111] Because *la femme* cannot exist as a tangible entity either, woman (or, rather, Woman) can likewise 'only be written with a bar through it. There's no such thing as Woman, Woman with a capital *W* indicating the universal. There's no such thing as Woman because, in her essence [...] she is not-whole.'[112] By extension, then, '~~Woman~~ cannot be said' and, because a third party, the Other, is always standing between the sexes, the sexual relationship 'doesn't stop not being written'.[113]

For Irigaray, Lacan's formula for this lack of inscription is also the inscription of lack. The 'discourse on truth', she writes, is 'a *phallic* one'.[114] Though Irigaray follows Lacan's interpretation of the understanding of the body as being imaginary and culturally influenced, in her essay 'Cosí Fan Tutte', her response to *Seminar XX*, she rejects the supposed ahistoricity of the Lacanian symbolic and the claim that the phallus, relation with which guarantees the subject's entry into the symbolic and thus into language, is unconnected to the male body. In as much as a woman is supposed to represent the desire of the Other – desire of the phallus – and all this without wholly existing in the phallic function, Irigaray concludes that:

> Psychoanalytic theory thus utters the truth about the status of female sexuality, and about the sexual relation. But it stops there. Refusing to interpret the historical determinants of its discourse [...] and in particular what is implied by the up to now exclusively masculine sexualization of the application of its laws, it remains caught up in phallocentrism, which it claims to make into a universal and eternal value.[115]

110 Lacan, *Seminar XX*, p. 72.

111 Lacan's algebra first appears in 1955; see *The Ego in Freud's Theory and in the Technique of Psychoanalysis* (*The Seminar of Jacques Lacan Book II: 1954–1955*), ed. Jacques-Alain Miller, trans. Sylvana Tomaselli (New York: W. W. Norton & Co., 1991).

112 Lacan, *Seminar XX*, pp. 72–3. It is important to note that in the French Lacan bars ~~*la*~~ as the demonstrative, not the word *femme*.

113 Lacan, *Seminar XX*, pp. 81, 144.

114 Luce Irigaray, *This Sex Which Is Not One*, trans. Catherine Porter (Ithaca, NY: Cornell University Press, 1985), p. 86 (original emphasis). Quotations from the French from Irigaray, *Ce sexe qui n'en est pas un* (Paris: Éditions de Minuit, 1977).

115 Irigaray, *This Sex Which Is Not One*, pp. 102–3.

While the separation of sexuality and sexuation from biological materialism is echoed in Irigaray, the Lacanian phallus is rejected as encouraging a one-sex model in which man 'seeks her [Woman] out, since he has inscribed her in his discourse, but only as lack, as fault or flaw'.[116]

Since Iphis is disguised as to appear to be the possessor of a physical phallus so that she may be the object of Iante's desire (also, significantly, so that she may be the object of her father's desire), the transformation seems to valorise the phallocentric discourse and access a missing phallus that will make the relationship intelligible. However, the omission of Iphis's lament in the adaptation from Ovid to Gower is telling here: this is a female subject who does not see the need for any intervention.[117] 'Iphis' is a test case for Gower's (a)morality; in this framework, the *Confessio* is particularly interested in 'transgressive' gendered identities, and not simply as negative exemplars.[118] Taking a cue from Genius, however, some readers still make a point of stepping around this issue. Thus Peter Nicholson writes of 'Iphis' that it reveals 'an optimistic view, both of the power of love and of its benevolence',[119] while Matthew McCabe suggests that, while Watt views the transformations of Iphis as transvestism and transgendering, 'if we compare "Iphis" to its analogues in the fourteenth-century moralised Ovids, it is unlikely the tale would have seemed quite so heterodox to Gower's contemporaries'.[120] These readings of Ovid interpret Iph/is as an evil person while female who must be made male to symbolise her becoming virtuous, allowing for the possibility of an 'unironic Christian reading' of Gower.[121] On the other hand, this reading still cannot

116 Irigaray, *This Sex Which is Not One,* p. 89.

117 The Latin here reads 'Set cum Yphis debitum sue coniugi unde soluere non habuit, deos in sui adiutorium interpellabat' (But when Yphis did not possess the wherewithal to render her debt to her bride, she called upon the gods for help; taken from John Gower, *Confessio Amantis*, ed. Russell A. Peck, with Latin translations by Andrew Galloway, 3 vols, 2nd edn (Kalamazoo, MI: Medieval Institute Publications, 2013, vol. 2). Watt notes that Iphis's lament that her desire is unnatural does not make it from Ovid to Gower. Diane Watt, *Amoral Gower: Language, Sex, and Politics* (Minneapolis: University of Minnesota Press, 2003), p. 74.

118 Watt, *Amoral Gower*, p. 64. Watt here diverges from Lochrie's reading of the *Confessio Amantis,* which concludes that Gower's text is 'not finally subversive'; Lochrie, *Covert Operations*, p. 224.

119 Peter Nicholson, *Love and Ethics in Gower's* Confessio Amantis (Ann Arbor, MI: University of Michigan Press, 2005), p. 216.

120 T. Matthew N. McCabe, *Gower's Vulgar Tongue: Ovid, Lay Religion, and English Poetry in the* Confessio Amantis (Cambridge: D. S. Brewer, 2011), p. 181. Watt does in fact note that 'according to certain theories of medicine, the one-sex model, the transformation from female to male was not in itself contrary to nature. Indeed, because women were perceived to be inferior to men, such a transformation could only be seen as an improvement, a change from an imperfect state to a perfect one'; Watt, *Amoral Gower*, p. 75.

121 McCabe, *Gower's Vulgar Tongue,* p. 182.

completely get around the fact that Gower's version does not 'circumvent the question of homosexuality' as decisively as the moralised Ovids, nor can it be said that he 'neutralizes' the homoerotic content in the way that they do.[122] The issue of Iphis and Iante's age – ten years, in Gower – might likewise be noted, since it could be interpreted as precluding them from adult responsibility.[123] While the age of legal accountability (for girls) was generally twelve years, Iphis is said to be married when (s)he is 'of a ten yer age' (IV. 475) and the two young spouses are 'of on age' (IV. 480). The age at which a marriage was considered binding was also twelve for girls (fourteen for boys). On the other hand, Shulamith Shahar notes that age seven was generally the *annis discretionis,* the age at which children were held to be capable of distinguishing good from evil, but also that some canonists increased this to ten years.[124] Gower does evade to some extent the issue of whether or not to condemn the lovers, but it is equally significant that his Iphis does not lament her lack in the fulfilment of the marriage debt.

Indeed, Cupid's pity is inspired by his own attachment to 'kinde' rather than a self-reproaching plea from either of the lovers. Lacan concludes that a woman 'can but be excluded by the nature of things, which is the nature of words',[125] and Iphis is indeed excluded by 'Nature' – from the relationship on which she is embarking, to be reimagined and reshaped as something that will be 'to kinde non offence' (IV. 505). Irigaray's verdict on the impossibility of a system of phallic signification allowing for another logic that evades or challenges its own, echoes the regendering of Iphis as the only means of legitimating the female–female sexual relationship (into which two women cannot be written without reinscription). Iphis's transformation thwarts the possibility of same-sex desire in the name of Nature, but also introduces (or, perhaps it would be more accurate to say, highlights) a sense of confusion and instability; as White puts it, 'something morally anarchic at the bottom of the totality one calls Nature'.[126] Nature's authority is called into question even as it is seemingly restored, and not least because the deity who effects the

122 McCabe, *Gower's Vulgar Tongue,* p. 181.

123 See Shulamith Shahar, *Childhood in the Middle Ages* (London: Routledge, 1990), pp. 24–6. Bracton put the age of criminal responsibility at 12 and 14 for girls and boys respectively. On the subject of age, see also Watt, *Amoral Gower*, p. 75. Watt notes the reduction in age for the betrothed pair, from thirteen in Ovid, but also that children would be expected to distinguish good from evil at age seven.

124 Shahar, *Childhood in the Middle Ages,* p. 24.

125 Lacan, *Seminar XX*, p. 73.

126 White, *Nature, Sex, and Goodness*, p. 193. On the ambiguities of Gower's Nature, see R. F. Yeager, 'Learning to Read in Tongues: Writing Poetry for a Trilingual Culture', in *Chaucer and Gower: Difference, Mutuality, Exchange*, ed. R. F. Yeager (Victoria, BC: University of Victoria, 1991), pp. 115–29; Kurt Olsson, 'Natural Law and John Gower's *Confessio Amantis*', in *Gower's* Confessio Amantis: *A Critical Anthology*, ed. Peter Nicholson (Cambridge: D. S. Brewer, 1991), pp. 181–213. Yeager examines the

transformation is not Nature, but Cupid. As Genius narrates, no longer priest of Nature but priest of Venus, Nature's work is done by he who, according to Alain, 'change[s] the shape of all mankind' *per antifrasim*, the rhetorical figure in which words are used to imply their opposite sense.[127] The boy who makes trouble for the Nature of *De Planctu* acts in the name of orthodoxy here in the *Confessio*, but he does so by a formal inversion of Nature's work.

'SILENCE, YOU TALK TOO MUCH': THE STRUGGLE OF NATURE

Cupid here changes the game, unwriting and rewriting bodies and sexual relationships, in a way that recalls the contest between Nature and Nurture in another tale of doubled gender – the *Roman de Silence*. Another story of a young girl disguised from birth as a boy, *Silence* extends Alain's treatment of grammar as analogous with sexual and gender orthodoxy. Heldris of Cornuälle's romance aligns so provocatively with 'modern' studies of gender that, as Simon Gaunt observes, it obliges us to rethink our notions both of gender and of modernity.[128] Its author has been the subject of readerly speculation concerning his or her gender – is this a text written by a man or a woman?[129] The text was itself silent for centuries after it was committed to parchment, languishing in a collection of papers marked 'of little value' until it was rediscovered in the twentieth century and edited by Lewis Thorpe. Even into the 1980s, little was written on the text, but as medieval studies took up the critical turn to gender and queer theory, so too did *Silence* become increasingly prominent. Just as in the Iphis myth, the protagonist is gendered first male and then female, in grammatical nomenclature and in physical appearance. In similar fashion, echoing and revising Alain, whose Nature in *Anticlaudianus* finds she is unable to make the perfect man without the aid of God, *Silence* sees Nature likewise setting out to create the perfect woman, only to find her efforts are open to interpretation from others and even correction by God.

To circumvent a decree that no female shall be permitted to inherit, the protagonist of *Silence*, identified by Nature as female, is raised by her parents

distinction between 'nature' and 'kinde' whereas Olsson argues that *Confessio* is an examination of *jus naturae* from its lowest forms to the highest.

127 *De Planctu Naturae*, ed. Häring, 842: 21; *The Plaint of Nature*, ed. and trans. Sheridan, p. 150.

128 Simon Gaunt, *Gender and Genre in Medieval French Literature* (Cambridge: Cambridge University Press, 1995), p. 20.

129 See Kathleen C. Brahney, 'When Silence Was Golden: Female Personae in the *Roman de Silence*', in *The Spirit of the Court: Selected Proceedings of the Fourth Congress of the International Courtly Literature Society*, ed. Glyn S. Burgess and Robert A. Taylor (Cambridge: D. S. Brewer, 1985), pp. 52–61; Lorraine Kochanske Stock, 'The Importance of Being Gender "Stable": Masculinity and Feminine Empowerment in *Le Roman de Silence*', *Arthuriana* 7.2 (1997), 7–34 (pp. 28–9).

a male known as Silentius, or, more often, simply Silence. Though her parents, Eufemie and Cador, view the situation as an open-ended arrangement, observing that their son's name may be grammatically altered if the child should have cause to revert to the feminine gender, Silence's upbringing becomes the occasion for a debate between the personifications of Nature and Nurture, both determined that their work shall be the decisive factor in the gendering of the child. Silence's adventures see him become a minstrel, then a knight, but his secret is threatened when Eufeme, wife of King Ebain, falls in love with the youth. Angered by Silence's resistance to her attempted seduction, Eufeme fakes her own rape and (when her husband prefers to pass over the accusation in silence and avoid making scandal) engineers Silence's banishment, doctoring a letter calling for the King of France to execute Silence. When Ebain's ally writes back to verify his intention, Ebain is mortified by the mistake and Silence is recalled to fight against the Count of Chester's uprising. Eufeme once more attempts to seduce Silence, is again rebuffed, and this time tries to procure Silence's permanent exclusion from court by having him sent on an impossible quest to find Merlin. The magician said he would only be captured by a woman's trick; for a man to bring him back should be impossible, but Silence, naturally, succeeds. Returning to court, Merlin reveals that Silence is a woman. Eufeme, whom Merlin exposes as having kept a lover at court dressed as a nun, is banished; women's right to inherit is restored; Silence is married to Ebain.

In the *Rose,* Jean's Genius declares that women by nature (even Nature) cannot keep secrets. Silence both appears to confirm this and at the same time defy Nature. By name, Silence appears to be neither male nor female, yet physically – with a female biological form but conforming in all other respects to the appearance and behaviours of a man – might be considered either male *or* female or perhaps both male *and* female. The narrative both suggests that gender identity may be subject to change or external influence and insists that silence is an integral part of this possibility. Is this a disenfranchising repression, or does *Silence* exploit a truth about language and its relation to the material and the lived body?

The pragmatism of this plot to conceal the child's native sex is shown in the passage explaining the two names Cador proposes, which compresses the romance's interlinking of naturalness, gender and grammar:

> Il iert només Scilenscius;
> Et s'il avient par aventure
> Al descovrir de sa nature
> Nos muerons cest -us en -a,
> S'avra a non Scilencia.
> Se nos li tolons dont cest -us
> Nos li donrons natural us,
> Car cis -us est contre nature,
> Mais l'altres seroit par nature.

> He will be named Silentius,
> and if it happens by chance
> that his true nature is discovered,
> we will change the *-us* to *-a*,
> and she will be named Silentia.
> If we removed this *-us* from her
> we will give her more natural custom [*-us*],
> for this *-us* is against nature,
> but the other would be according to nature.[130]

The particle *-us* denotes not only the masculine gender of the name and its bearer, but the notion of 'custom' as well. As Peter Allen summarises, 'Silence's gender depends, then, not on nature but on custom or usage (*us*).'[131] *Silence* again links the deviation from nature with grammatical deviation, but unlike Alain does so in a vernacular context, with the result that the protagonist possesses three versions of the same name (in addition to a selection of pragmatic aliases) – the Latin Silentius and Silentia, and the French Silence. This last is the most frequently used and, indeed, is most 'silent' with regards to gender.[132] Indeed, Jane Bliss notes that 'the name Silence is effectively non-existent…';[133] Allen characterises it as more 'a placeholder for a name' than a real proper noun.[134]

Both male and female pronouns are used in the narrative for its protagonist, with her parents assigning male pronouns in order to maintain their deception; later, Silence himself appears to self-identify as male, while also acknowledging the native physical limitations of a woman's body. When Silence is inevitably uncovered as a woman, signalling the end of the romance, the change of name is, on the surface, as simple as Cador and Eufemie predicted: 'Silence atornent come feme. / […] Ostés est -us, mis i est -a /Si est només Scilentiä' (They dressed Silence as a woman […] the *-us* was removed and *-a* put in its place, and she was named Silentia, vv. 6664–8). The word

130 *Le Roman de Silence: A Thirteenth-Century Arthurian Verse-Romance by Heldris de Cornuälle*, ed. Lewis Thorpe (Cambridge: W. Heffer & Sons, 1972), and Heldris de Cornuälle, *Le Roman de Silence*, trans. Regina Psaki, Garland Library of Medieval Literature 63 (New York and London: Garland, 1991), vv. 2074–82. Subsequent quotations will be cited in parentheses.

131 Peter L. Allen, 'The Ambiguity of Silence: Gender, Writing and *Le Roman de Silence*' in *Sign, Sentence, Discourse: Langauge in Medieval Thought and Literature*, ed. Julian N. Wasserman and Lois Roney (Syracuse, NY: Syracuse University Press, 1989), pp. 98–112 (p. 106).

132 See Allen, 'The Ambiguity of Silence', p. 100; Erin F. Labbie, 'The Specular Image of the Gender-Neutral Name: Naming Silence in *Le Roman de Silence*', *Arthuriana* 7.2 (1997), 63–77 (p. 65).

133 Jane Bliss, *Naming and Namelessness in Medieval Romance* (Cambridge: D. S. Brewer, 2008), p. 134 (on *Silence*, see pp. 134–54).

134 Allen, 'The Ambiguity of Silence', p. 106.

Silence is 'dressed' as a woman with the exchange of suffix, just as the female child became a boy with a change of clothing; when her body is finally dressed in women's clothes, Silence is thereafter designated 'she' for the remainder of the narrative. It is as if grammatical gender is enough to change the form of the body.

On the other hand, earlier in the romance, in the double reading stressed by several critics, Silentius himself has already concluded that to be stripped of this name is to be uncovered – literally, *nus*, nude – and a nobody:

> 'Donques sui jo Scilentius,
> Cho m'est avis, u jo sui nus.'
> Dont se porpense en lui meïsme
> Que Nature li fait sofime:
> Por cho que l'-us est encontre us
> N'a pas a non Scilentius.
>
> 'So I *am* Silentius,
> It seems to me, or I am no one.'
> He thought to himself
> that Nature was speaking in sophistries;
> because the *-us* was against natural law,
> his name was not Silentius. (vv. 2537–42)

Do clothes make the man? As Jane Burns puts it, 'The female body is here shown to be a nobody, a nonperson, and further an unknowing body. Perhaps better put: as a woman, Silence is reduced to body alone, to being just a body.'[135] Allen elaborates on the text's ambiguities and its challenges to readers to let themselves be read. To resolve *Silence*'s doublings and uncertainties would be objectifying the text, 'breaking its silence': the only option is to make the text 'the *subject* of our study: the text itself – both as a poem and as a manuscript – tells us how to read.'[136] These verses epitomise this textual challenge, compacting paradox (nobody, and yet all about a body) and social comment (either a named man, or exposed as a nameless woman) into a single charged syllable, whose formal excess is as arresting as Alain's, but in which form and message are shown in cohesion and collaboration, rather than in productive but deeply ironic contradiction.

Silentius is also concerned here that Nature 'li fait sofime' – that she speaks in sophistries (still her weakness, as it was for Alain's Nature) when she insists that the child she made was female, and not male (v. 2540). However, a few lines later, and despite his 'cuer diviers' – his divided heart (v. 2681) – he

135 Jane L. Burns, *Bodytalk: When Women Speak in Old French Literature* (Philadelphia, PA: University of Pennsylvania Press, 1993), pp. 243–5 (p. 243); see also Kate Mason Cooper, '*Elle* and *L*: Sexualised Textuality in *Le Roman de Silence*', *Romance Notes* 25 (1985), 341–60.

136 Allen, 'The Ambiguity of Silence', p. 99 (original emphasis).

decides that, all things considered (particularly the role he might have to adopt in bed), 'miols valt li us d'ome / Que l'us de feme' (a man's life is better / than a woman's, vv. 2637–8). The bedroom is the one arena in which Silence doubts his ability to perform in the role in which he identifies, and when the queen's eye falls on him the romance does not pass up the opportunity to use the suggestion of a same-sex encounter for provocative as well as narrative ends. The possibility that *Silence* also features covert but conscious same-sex desire (as opposed to simply a mistaken or unwitting same-sex attraction) has been raised by Kathleen Blumreich, who argues that Eufeme may be read as a woman who desires women, albeit one whose would-be female lover is dressed as a man and whose male lover is disguised as a woman. Eufeme's dominant erotic role, her desire for masculine power and her 'unnatural', quasi-heretical behaviour, are all concordant with the medieval understanding of a 'covert lesbian attraction'.[137] This unorthodox, unnatural desire becomes a further and even final proof of her depravity, and something she must keep quiet at all costs.

Even if Eufeme is to be read as straight, the text keeps her more silent than Silence. The romance frequently plays with and plays out the possibilities of the unspoken, silent and unspeakable, a fascination that the episode of the false message Eufeme sends to the French king, ordering Silence's execution, shows most clearly:

> Cho me dist ceste letreüre
> Que il a fait al roi tel honte
> Que il ne violt pas metre en conte.
>
> This letter tells me
> that he did such wrong to the king
> that Ebain does not want to narrate it. (vv. 4442–4)

Here again – as in her acidic, ironic put-down, 'Silence, you talk too much' – Eufeme tells more truth than she knows, more truth than she is given credit for. In writing to the French king of Silence's unspeakable crime, so terrible that 'Ebain' does not wish to name it, she is describing the scenario in a manner firstly congruent with the terminology of the day, if she knew it was an encounter between two women that she envisaged; secondly, in the terms that Ebain encourages when he refuses to confront a suspected rapist in his court (he urges silence on the matter instead); and thirdly, in ontologically correct terms since it is indeed impossible to speak of 'Silence's crime' when he committed none.

The silencing of women and undoing of women's deeds even extends to Nature herself. *Silence* is what Howard Bloch has called, in a Foucauldian turn,

137 Kathleen M. Blumreich, 'Lesbian Desire in the Old French *Roman de Silence*', *Arthuriana* 7.2 (1997), 47–62 (p. 58)

a 'biopolitical drama'.[138] This drama is as much Nature's as Silence's. During an argument over who will determine Silence's gender, Nurture crows to Nature that she has indeed triumphed in her actions and transformed Silence to the point that Nature may as well retire. 'I have completely denatured [*desnaturee*] her', Nurture declares (v. 2595), taunting Nature that her continued presence only serves to prove the point, and concluding:

> Jo te desferai tolt ton conte.
> Nature, envoiés o sa honte.
>
> I will undo all your speech.
> Nature, begone, and take the child's shame away with you. (vv. 2603–4)

Nurture frames her work as speaking away Nature, undoing her *conte* – her reckoning or tale – and rewriting Silence's person. The line even has the ring of corporeal rewriting in that it contains the protean particle *con*, which as Bloch points out is almost always open to interpretation.[139] If Nurture also means to pun on *con* and boast of 'undoing' Nature's cunt, it is only one in a series of methods that Heldris uses to revise Alain's transformation of bodies into discourse.

The role of Nurture is also scrutinised: in *Silence* as in the story of Iphis, gender is decided for the child by a parent and reinforced by the child's later behavioural patterns and, most strikingly in the case of Silence, their decisions. The matter of Iphis's gender is directed by her mother, Isis, and later Cupid. In Silence's case, the arbiters of her gender are, in order: Nature (who forges the beautiful female child), her father (who persuades Eufemie to bring up their child as a male), Silence himself (who decides that a man's lot is preferable to a woman's), Merlin (who exposes Silence as having been born female) and, finally, the king (who wishes to marry Silence). When Cador introduces his plan to Eufemie, he recounts and inverts the creation of Eve from Adam, justifying the change he proposes for their child by reminding his wife that there is 'grant commune' (great community) between men and women (v. 1711).[140] Yet Nature is opposed to this exegetical interpretation of gender difference, lamenting angrily that the actions of Cador and Euphemie alter her work, and setting out with grim determination to 'correct' these alterations.[141]

[138] R. Howard Bloch, *Etymologies and Genealogies: A Literary Anthropology of the French Middle Ages* (Chicago: University of Chicago Press, 1983), p. 195.

[139] R. Howard Bloch, *Scandal of the Fabliaux* (Chicago, University of Chicago Press, 1986), pp. 106–9.

[140] See Julie Orlemanski, 'A Silence in the Family Tree: The Genealogical Subject in Heldris of Cornwall's *Silence*', in *Individualism: The Cultural Logic of Modernity*, ed. Zubin Meer (Lanham, MD: Lexington Books, 2011), pp. 33–46

[141] *Silence*, vv. 6669–73.

This contest between the will of God and the will of Nature reaches a crisis point when Silence prays to God while endeavouring to withstand the attack of the Count of Chester:

> Silences dist: 'Bials Dex, chaieles,
> Ki m'a jeté de maint anui,
> Done moi vertu viers cestui!
> Cho qu'afoiblie en moi Nature
> Cho puist efforcier T'aventure.'
>
> Silence said, 'Fair God, for pity's sake,
> who have delivered me from great trouble,
> give me strength against this man!
> That which Nature makes weak in me,
> may Your providence strengthen. (vv. 5604–8)

Silence defeats the Count, indicating that God grants his prayer and appears to supply the deficiency of Nature of which Silence despairs. The miraculousness of Silence's victory seems on the one hand to be predicated on the naturalness and normality of a female body being less robust than a male body, but on the other hand, Silence is also asking God to 'correct' Nature.

Keeping one's gender a secret, illegible and therefore unspeakable for onlookers, refusing to be read, seems itself to be deemed unnatural. Yet, though it appears that 'natural' gender will out in the end, Nature's influence also seems utterly subordinate to parental control, the efforts of Nurture, and even the will of God. If God corrects Nature, does this amount to an endorsement of Nurture, of Silence's determination that biology should not be destiny? For certain, doing the right thing – here, subduing the insurrection of the king's rebellious subject – comes 'unnaturally' for Silence. However, here and throughout the narrative, the text does not imply that Silence's unnatural behaviour should be condemned.

WRITTEN OUT AND WRITTEN OUT: ONE TO(O) MANY

On the recognising or neutralising of women's pleasure (or jouissance), Irigaray's sceptical reading of Lacan focuses especially on his claim that 'women […] don't know what they're saying'.[142] Lacan's 'woman' is not a universal category and a woman's jouissance is not that which is designated by the phallic function. For precisely this reason, however, Lacan also claims that 'she has a supplementary jouissance compared to what the phallic function designates by way of jouissance […] there is something more (*en plus*)'.[143] The trouble with this 'jouissance beyond the phallus' for she who may experience

142 See Lacan, *Seminar XX*, p. 73.
143 Lacan, *Seminar XX*, pp. 73–4.

it, is that it is a relation of which 'woman knows nothing'; indeed, if women complain they are excluded from the nature of words, 'they don't know what they are saying'.[144] Irigaray argues that this reveals, rather, the belief that 'Women are not worth listening to, especially when they speak of their own pleasure' and muses that:

> The question whether, in his logic, they can articulate anything at all, whether they can be heard, is not even raised. For raising it would mean granting that there may be some other logic, and one that upsets his own. That is, a logic that challenges mastery.[145]

Since the symbolic of Lacanian discourse leaves for women 'only lacks, deficiencies [...] their negative(s) [*leur(s) négatif(s)*]', and by 'speaking the same language together, we're going to reproduce the same history',[146] Irigaray in her more poetic moments calls instead for multivalency, for fluidity, a model of language that incorporates the mechanics of fluids, rather than signifiers and lack.

By Irigaray's reimagining of Lacan it is untrue to say that Gower's Iphis and Iante approach a jouissance that does not know itself – rather that they do not know what this jouissance of one another means in the (masculine) discourse they inhabit (and yet do not). Woman cannot be said? 'And yet that woman-thing [*la femme*] speaks'![147]

Gower's Genius bookends his tale by moralising on how the god of love valorises 'hem that ben of a love stable' (IV. 444) and rewards those whose pursuit of love is 'continuende' (IV. 508), while insisting that instability and transformation is essential in the exemplar he chooses. Material and corporeal stability is apparently not the aim here, but what is? The stability and continuity of emotion, of virtue? In a text and a discourse that insists that women do not have the same access to virtue as men? We might paraphrase Irigaray and wonder, whose stability are we talking about here?[148] Silence, likewise, has to change form by the end of the narrative, in order to suit a prospective partner and make possible the conditions for marriage; it is significant that although in theory Silence should not have to physically change, Nature is obliged to work hard. However, it also is the irony of both tales that, whosever it is, 'natural' continuance comes only at the price that 'Every "body" is transformed by it.'[149]

[144] Lacan, *Seminar XX*, pp. 73–5.

[145] Irigaray, *This Sex Which Is Not One*, p. 90.

[146] Irigaray, *This Sex Which Is Not One*, pp. 207, 205.

[147] Irigaray, *This Sex Which Is Not One*, p. 111.

[148] Irigaray's response to Lacan's suggestion that, to understand the jouissance about which women know nothing, one should go and view Bernini's statue of St Theresa in Rome: 'What pleasure are we talking about? Whose pleasure?' *This Sex Which Is Not One*, p. 91.

[149] Irigaray, *This Sex Which Is Not One*, p. 88.

Taking apart the Lacanian mirror-stage, Irigaray critiques the strangely sexed and sexless net result of one and other, a distinction 'henceforth undecidable between which would truly be the one, which the other, which would be the double of whom'.[150] The sex of which she writes is not 'one', but nor is it a split mirror image, a mirage that reproduces one in the other. While it may be a stretch too far to claim Gower for a camp that constructs 'some other logic', in his natural coupling of 'sche and sche', Iphis and Ianthe are portrayed sympathetically and are united by narrative (whereas the Pardoner is systematically fragmented by Chaucer, other pilgrims and then the critics). It is a 'solein' tale (IV. 448), not only singular but strange and lonely.[151]

Women are also written as one from two in the *Roman de Silence*. Eufeme is in some ways as significant an indicator of the parameters of gender and its performativity as Silence, and so she is again in the events that lead to Silence's exposure. Merlin has said, to Eufeme's knowledge, that he will only be captured by a woman's trick. Yet the trick that Silence executes is not his own: it is conceived in every particular by the old man, not the young knight – Silence does not even have to fetch the meat and drink by which the wizard will be tempted and incapacitated, only prepare it in the way the old man specifies. Perhaps cooking might be called a woman's art,[152] but it seems imprecise to conclude that Silence tricked Merlin when the means and method were provided by someone else. Yet there *is* a woman's trick behind Merlin's capture, but it is the work of Eufeme, who is once more silenced. Merlin hides the agency and authority of one woman even as he unveils the agency of another – the unveiling of Silence as the woman who caught him in fact veils the role of Eufeme in the whole enterprise. Like Iphe and Iante's relationship, female agency in *Silence* comes to be written out, even as it is written out. Silentius thus becomes Silentia, but not through Silence's own trick – it is through Eufeme's. Indeed, Eufeme succeeds in driving *Silentius* out of the kingdom but the narrative also needed to be rid of Silentius, in order to restore Nature's authority. Thus the two-natured person is made into one of orthodox and singular gender, and Merlin's exposure also means there cannot be two women in Ebain's life – the one who has lost (masculine) agency remains.

As Lacan insists, 'This "There's such a thing as One" is not simple – that's the word for it [...] it is announced by the fact that Eros is defined as the

150 Irigaray, *This Sex Which Is Not One*, p. 118.

151 Macaulay has 'strange' at I. lvii, followed by 'alone, lonely' at I. 503, which Russell Peck follows; see John Gower, *Confessio Amantis*, ed. Russell A. Peck, trans. Andrew Galloway, 3 vols, 2nd edn (Kalamazoo, MI: Medieval Institute Publications, 2013). *MED* offers 'different', which may certainly apply as well.

152 On Silence's movement from one set of gendered behaviours to another, see Stock, 'The Importance of Being Gender "Stable"', p. 25.

fusion that makes one from two.'[153] Irigaray, too, finds this 'One' problematic; when she speaks of the mother and daughter relationship, she wonders:

> Really, two? Doesn't that make you laugh? An odd sort of two. And yet not one. Especially not one. Let's leave *one* to them [...] And the strange way they divide up their couples, with the other as the image of the one.[154]

Whereas *Silence* silences its queer woman, for Gower's text to effect this strange way of dividing its couple, the beguiling simplicity of the middle part of the tale undergoes a marked change.

From the simultaneously doubled and unitary 'sche and sche, / Whiche of on age bothe be' (IV. 479–80), the scene becomes strikingly confused and confusing when Cupid – God is 'the third party in this business of human love' – intervenes.[155] Cupid's reasons are that:

> love hateth nothing more
> Than thing which stant ayein the lore
> Of that nature in kinde hath sett. (IV. 493–5)

As in Alain, where erotic love is evoked in a dizzying series of oxymoronic phrases, a tumult in which 'Pax odio fraudique fides, spes iuncta timori / Est amor et mixtus cum ratione furor' (Love is peace joined to hatred, loyalty to treachery, hope to fear and madness blended with reason),[156] the results of Desire/Cupid's intervention defy description and can only be expressed in what de Certeau called the realm of the metasememe and the deictic, where two-part paradox and opposition are used in place of the adequate third term.[157] Just as the Pardoner exceeds a single body to become many possibilities through two signifiers, in a mass of equivocal discourse, so from this singular tale, with its beautifully matched pair of protagonists, is made a confusion in which 'love hateth', Nature vies with Kind,[158] and Cupid can see (IV. 493, 499).[159] Thus confusion is introduced, not by the spectre of sodomy or

153 Lacan, *Seminar XX*, p. 67.

154 Irigaray, *This Sex Which Is Not One*, p. 207 (original emphasis).

155 Lacan, *Seminar XX*, p. 70.

156 *De Planctu Naturae*, ed. Häring 842: 1–2 (translation from *The Plaint of Nature*, ed. and trans. Sheridan, p. 149).

157 Michel de Certeau, *The Mystic Fable. Volume One: The Sixteenth and Seventeenth Centuries, trans.* Michael B. Smith (Chicago: University of Chicago Press, 1992), p. 143.

158 On this point, see Yeager, who proposes that the two must be understood as representing different parts of the same function; however, since this is one in which Nature, despite being Gower's referent for '*Natura*, God's vicar', that is 'a different force, pre-existent to "kinde" and, for that reason (as well as others) superior' (Yeager, 'Learning to Read in Tongues', pp. 121, 124), will nevertheless 'step aside for "kinde"' in the cause of procreation (p. 125), it is hardly less confusing.

159 Although Amans laments that 'love is blind and may noght se' (I. 47), Peck suggests at I. 138–41 that Cupid's 'yhen wrothe' indicate that Gower does not present Cupid as blind;

the questioning of gender, but with the imposition of the heterosexual matrix. Love stands opposed to the 'lore' of that which Nature has set 'in kinde'. This is generally translated as the 'teaching' of nature, but of course it also means loss. Here, teaching is the same as loss, and only one is 'permitted' to continue being a woman. 'Sche and sche' cannot simply remain, 'continuende': they must through Cupid (or Eros) conform to the fusion that makes one from two. Not simply the two that may procreate, but one woman from two. If the tale is to be resolved in the same schema in which it began, it only needs one woman. As multiple as their identities become, 'Iphis' and *Silence* both do and do not show how there may be more – *en plus* – for women.

KISSING AND TELLING

To end with an ending, I return to the kiss between the Pardoner and the Host. The Knight's insistence that the two make peace crystallises the chaotic spectacle of the unspeakable in a striking image, described by Glenn Burger as 'a "speaking picture" in which a variety of voices – and no voice – is heard'.[160] A kiss that stills time, brings peace to the pilgrims, makes war among critics and restores the balance of masculine paradigms even as it threatens to subvert them, there is a cacophony of noise surrounding this image, and yet, in itself, it is one of silence, effected by closed lips and shut mouths. Kisses represent turning points in all three texts, and are unspeakable precisely because one cannot speak a kiss. The restoration of order in Gower's 'Iphis' also takes place mid-kiss – when the lovers are not looking, Cupid removes, reinscribes, redraws their 'speaking picture', makes it say something else. Normative sexual grammar seems to obtain in these kisses, where conventional male authority acts on a problematic feminine or feminised body (Cupid on Iphe, Ebain on Silence, the Knight on the Pardoner). Yet even as Cupid does the work of Nature, he (or Gower) has a significantly unorthodox moment – while it is true that Gower's 'Iphe' (as opposed to Iphis) doesn't even appear until she is about to disappear, it is a kiss that shows Iphe precisely as a woman for the first and only time in the text. Kissing is a particularly vexed activity in *Silence*. Does Silence's refusal to kiss the queen in the way Eufeme would like indicate that Silence is obeying Nature? Or is this social conformity, as to do otherwise would be to commit treason against the king? A female–female kiss

see *Confessio Amantis*, vol. 1, ed. Peck. When Cupid casts the fiery dart into Amans' heart, however, he has previously turned his face 'aweiward fro [him]' (I. 141–5) and does not appear to watch the flight of the arrow. Theresa Tinkle notes the variety of characteristics displayed by both Venus and Cupid in the poetic tradition and suggests that, in the case of Gower's Cupid, his blindness is at some points transferred to Venus and at others a species of 'psychological sightlessness'; see Theresa Tinkle, *Medieval Venuses and Cupids: Sexuality, Hermeneutics, and English Poetry* (Stanford: Stanford University Press, 1996), pp. 178–97 (p. 193).

160 Glenn Burger, 'Kissing the Pardoner', *PMLA* 107.5 (1992), 1143–56 (p. 1147).

disguised as a male–female kiss (between Silence and Eupheme) results in a death sentence; an outwardly male–male but actually male–female kiss results in exoneration (the sign of peace between Silence and the king of France that precludes Silence's execution).[161] When the bodies are the same, the consequences are more sinister than when the bodies are different.

Though these are texts that could – and do – occupy far more space, I want to conclude with the notion of the unspeakable as a manoeuvre responsible on the one hand for shutting down in narrative, but also, on the other hand, for opening up and productivity. This chapter has explored the unspeakability of acts both in the sense of the acts that are not spoken of and the actions accomplished by the unspeakable. We have seen in Alain how bodies are not only affected but *effected* by Nature. The unspeakable queers Nature, the cases of female sodomy perhaps even more so than male, and the effects of the trope here go beyond the implications of the morally or sexually transgressive. As in the Parson's imprecise definition of the unspeakable sin, the onus is on the reader or listener to compose their own coherent interpretation from the 'diverse' pieces of information with which they are provided. The Pardoner, descendent of False Seeming, reveals truths about language, and how language transforms bodies – how the physical is sought in place of the metaphysical. The substitution of words for bodies, meanwhile, is shown most clearly in *Silence*, where Alain's model allows bodies to be recast with grammatical substitutions and to perform their gender.[162] Where women come into the equation, the unspeakable act becomes even more unspeakable, and the conversion of bodies into discourse is even more pronounced in its ramifications, since the alteration or 'correction' of gender in the narratives and the gendering of the nouns is so prominent and is presented as naturalising and necessary to the completion of the story. Having been multiple and non-heteronormative, female–female relations involve a change of form (whether physical or cosmetic) in order to finish the story. Lacan's difficult 'One' is shown by Irigaray to be especially difficult for women. Though Irigaray speaks of twoness, Iphe and Iante are made one flesh in marriage only by being made one woman, from two; Silence is made one female person from being a person of two possible genders, in order that Ebain's potential partners may be reduced from two to one as well.[163]

The role of language and unspeakability comes to hinge on the precepts of Nature. In sexual matters, the unnatural is consistently understood as that which prohibits procreation, but the unnatural is also aligned with grammatical

[161] 'Li baiziers senefie pais. / Nel puis deffaire ne lasscier' (The kiss signifies peace. / I certainly cannot abandon him or put him to death; vv. 4488–9).

[162] On Butlerian readings of *Silence*, see Peggy McCracken, '"The Boy Who Was a Girl": Reading Gender in the *Roman de Silence*', *Romanic Review* 85.4 (1994), 517–36.

[163] The political implications of a double identity or a hybrid body will be investigated in Chapter 3.

constructions that obtain in language but not in procreative 'nature'. Though these naturalising effects serve the purposes of a procreative impulse, in the allegorical narratives of which they are part they bring generation to an end, sterilising and smothering the story. (Nor are these 'natural' endings necessarily the work of Nature.) Yet in the logic of substitution of speech for sexual acts, same-sex relations are clearly not those that do not generate speech. As Schibanoff remarks of the ending of the *Romance of the Rose*, 'Genius's wish to castrate perverse writers like Orpheus – "may their styluses be taken away from them" [...] – not only recalls but empowers Ovid's bard by reminding us that homosexual Orpheus made a lasting mark indeed.'[164] The stories of queer women are not memorable for their conclusions but for their challenges and confrontations.[165] The twoness and plurality of 'Iphis' is foreclosed by the imposition of a 'natural' state, but Gower's multi-lingual text still says what it does not say. The final legibility of Silence's 'restored' feminine body is hardly an aid to reading the text as a whole. The point here is not that same-sex desire would be any more 'natural' in generative terms to a conventional medieval schema than usury (which bears fruit from matter that should be non-productive). Rather, it is to show the generative possibility of the same, of the unspeakable, of the unnatural, which disrupts the logic of non-generative: therefore should not be done: therefore should not be mentioned.

Ultimately, one does not declare something unutterable as a means procuring only silence. It is precisely through the unspeakability topos that the 'unnatural vice' results in generation: the proliferation of discourse. Moreover, this generative possibility stems from the insistence that only one kind of relation and understanding of gender identity and sexual difference can be generatively orthodox. The unspeakable is a figure that shows the queerness of nature. In attempting to undermine the 'unnatural', advocates of 'nature' who transform bodies into speech – the extended metaphor that is supposed to valorise only one set of relations – instead participate in a rhetoric that enables the fecundity it is meant to prove cannot exist, and which is the basis for justifying the strategic use of this unspeakability topos in the first place. When power is articulated by suppression, then to discuss what has been labelled unmentionable may indeed thwart this power, yoking vocal exposure of its flaws to the exposure of the secret places over which it has no dominion. There is a lot to be gained from the unspeakable – but only if you speak about it.

[164] Schibanoff, 'Sodomy's Mark', p. 47.

[165] As Allen puts it, 'To remove ambiguity from this text means to tear it, to falsify it, to lose its essence' ('The Ambiguity of Silence', p. 110). On this point, see also *Silence*, trans. Psaki (pp. xxxi–ii).

3

CRYING WOLF: GENDER AND EXILE IN *BISCLAVRET* AND *WULF AND EADWACER*

In the eleventh century, the sentence of exile was codified in English law with the famous decree, *caput gerat lupinum*: let his be a wolf's head. This particular designation for the outlaw is commonly attributed to statutes from both before and after the Conquest and was retained for centuries, feeding into a sprawling pan-European literary tradition of exile and animality along the way.[1] In this chapter I look at two texts connected to this tradition: Marie de France's *Bisclavret* and the Old English elegiac poem *Wulf and Eadwacer*. They are also texts that depend for their narrative force on the effects of the abject, the suspension of linguistic norms or organised language, and the return of the outside/r.

The unspeakable has so far been explored as the space *between*: the distance between language and what it represents – between signifier and signified – and the figurative ground left undetermined by the conditions of socio-historical norms or categories. As such it becomes a repository for a diverse collection of unvocalised, conflicting descriptions, and (for the advocate of the hegemonic order) the defining characteristic of the wayward, transgressive body or pattern of behaviour. However, in looking at the various epistemological positions in which the concept of the unspeakable appears to be rooted, it also becomes clear that what cannot be captured in words does not cease to exist, but is present in these very epistemes. While the unity of theological or socio-economic or gendered or any other class of cultural norms is maintained through a systematic process of abjection, the abjected does not disappear, nor can it be allowed to do so; the paradox of the unified, regulated centre is the marginal, uncontainable, fragmented outside to which it is diametrically opposed but upon which it is fundamentally reliant.

The unspeakable, then, points not only to a space *between* but to a place *beyond*; yet in both these cases it is, crucially, nevertheless inextricably bound up in the workings of those supposedly cohesive forces between or beyond which it is found. Present both within and outside the prevailing order, the

1 See Sabine Baring-Gould, *The Book of Werewolves* (London: Smith and Elder, 1865), pp. 53–69; Kirby Flower Smith, 'An Historical Study of the Werewolf in Literature', *PMLA* 9.1 (1894), 1–42; Philippe Ménard, 'Les histoires de loup-garou au moyen âge', *Symposium in Honorem Prof. Martin de Riquer* (Barcelona: Cuaderns Crema, 1985), pp. 209–38.

continued manifestation of the unspeakable serves as a constant reminder of the formative exclusion upon which the spoken – the nameable, the representable portion of reality – is founded. Nor is this function merely a historiographical one; as the loading of possible meanings onto the term demonstrates, there is great power and latent potential in the concept of the unspeakable. In tracing a 'way to language', Martin Heidegger points out that, 'The unspoken is not merely what is deprived of sound: rather, it is the unsaid, what is not yet shown, what has not yet appeared on the scene.'[2] The key notion here is the implication of that word 'yet'; there is not simply silence, a blank, but always expectation – the unspoken seems to announce even as it keeps quiet, seems to herald more to come.

If the unspoken creates an air of non-specific, ethereal anticipation – *something* is yet to be revealed – then this suspense is both heightened and dissolved by the logical progression into the *unspeakable*. Heidegger continues, 'Whatever has to remain unspoken will be held in reserve in the unsaid. It will linger in what is concealed as something unshowable. It is mystery.'[3] That which '*has to remain* unspoken' – more than the simply unstated – is no longer *en route* to the utterance, leaving the listener waiting in breathless attendance to find out what it is, but a lingering, mysterious presence. Though the speaker assumes control over the mechanics of what is voiced and unvoiced, spoken and unspoken, the unspeakable is present regardless of the stage management. In contrast to the passivity of the constrained, indeterminate unspoken, there is an active, almost physical manifestation that can be inferred from Heidegger's description; like one who has been banished, the unspeakable can and must be set apart, but it is never forgotten.

The previous chapters have explored the unspeakable in its relation to spaces and to the idea of nature, texts in which location and boundaries – between insider and outsider, masculine and feminine, civilised and animal – are both drawn and erased. Taking further the material and topographical aspect of the unspeakable, and the evaluation of crises of the natural as crises of the speakable, I turn here to the non-speech of animals and outcasts. Whereas Chapter 1 concerned women as described and defined by men and male-authored narratives, and conceptualised *inside* bounded spaces, this chapter deals largely with the opposite scenario – in which men's access to language is described and defined by female voices, and driving someone (or something) *out* from a bounded central space results in the realisation that they, or it, is found to remain firmly *within*. This is the situation of the exile, the bandit, or the wolf's head. The exile's sphere is the outside or, rather, the exile is to be found outside a particular sphere. However, as with the wandering saint and the mediating anchoress, it is overstating the case to

2 Martin Heidegger, 'The Way to Language', in *Basic Writings: Revised and Expanded Edition*, ed. David Farrell Krell (London: Routledge, 1994), pp. 394–426 (p. 409).

3 Heidegger, 'Way to Language', p. 409.

simply leave it at that. In as much as the exile is obliged to remain at the edge, always outside, there is nevertheless a zone peculiar to the one who is outside; in being outside, they are necessarily inside. However, the crucial condition that governs the zone of the exile is not individual perception or performance, but the intervention of the law. Banishment thus is evoked and controlled through the quintessential performative utterance: this is a state founded on an originary statement. Whereas the purgatorial sentence for other transgressions may be alleviated through confession and penance – a burden that can be shared and even bequeathed after death – the sentence of the exile may be lifted only by the sovereign, and the purgatorial waiting, neither in one place nor in another, is on earth.

Both *Bisclavret* and *Wulf and Eadwacer* play on the tension between the acceptable and the intolerable in society, what should be retained within the boundaries and what should be ejected from them – and how language is implicated in this process. Both tell the story of a 'wolf' and a woman. Giorgio Agamben analyses the first, in *Homo Sacer* (2001); the second has furnished debates about gender in Old English poetry when read through the writings of Julia Kristeva.[4] The link between the texts is thematic – they have both been studied as literary and cultural perspectives on exile, with an interest in gender – but they also bear a contiguous relationship to Agamben's argument in *Homo Sacer*, and thereby to each other. Agamben draws on *Bisclavret* as a case study for the relation between the sovereign ban and the wolf's head, and at other points appeals to the Germanic association of wolf and exile (specifically in law) that arises in the scholarship on *Wulf and Eadwacer*. As such, my argument is not for a clear-cut connection between the two texts – though they do both appear to reflect cultural and, to some extent, legal formulations of exile that did not differ greatly from the pre- to post-Conquest period – but rather that it may be illuminating to explore the thematic link suggested by Agamben's literary and legal case studies. While considering Anglo-Saxon and Anglo-Norman texts alongside one another entails a certain historical complexity, in the spirit of recent scholarship that brings literature from either side of the Conquest into contact and articulates this caesura more clearly, I

4 Both Patricia Belanoff and Helen Bennett have contributed to the literature on *Wulf and Eadwacer* and sexual difference using Kristeva as a theoretical framework. See Patricia Belanoff, 'Women's Songs, Women's Language: *Wulf and Eadwacer* and *The Wife's Lament*', in *New Readings on Women in Old English Literature*, ed. Helen Damico and Alexandra Hennessey Olsen (Bloomington, IN: Indiana University Press, 1990), pp. 193–203; Helen Bennett, 'Exile and the Semiosis of Gender in Old English Elegies', in *Class and Gender in Early English Literature: Intersections*, ed. Britton J. Harwood and Gillian R. Overing (Bloomington: Indiana University Press, 1994), pp. 43–58. Paul Acker analyses the role of the 'monstrous' feminine in *Beowulf* by drawing on the Kristevan abject, in 'Horror and the Maternal in *Beowulf*, *PMLA* 121.3 (2006), 702–16.

suggest that a study of the nature of gender and exile in *Bisclavret* may have something to gain from an Old English analogue – *Wulf and Eadwacer*.[5]

Agamben's work contrasts *homo sacer* – the sacred man, a juridico-political cipher often associated with the outlaw or exile – with the sovereign, arguing that both exist in and are constitutive of a threshold that is neither inside nor outside the law, and thus opening up places of indistinction or exception to critical application.[6] Kristeva also theorises a threshold, the boundary between subject and object that is habitually threatened by the abject, which is both of the subject and yet which must be cast away for the subject to emerge – that which 'does not respect borders [...] The in-between, the ambiguous, the composite', all being intimately linked with the first abjection: that of the maternal body.[7] To explore the usefulness of these two approaches to the concept of gendered medieval exile, I will be looking not so much at the (sacred) men of these texts but at their female counterparts, considering the place of 'place' for the exiles – and who the wolves really are. The participation of medieval studies in the animal turn has been significant, bringing as it does a corresponding return to the high medieval interest in the human–animal divide. While the question of the animal had been debated in philosophical and ethical discussions for some time, particularly with regard to the rights of the animal, Derrida's late work 'The Animal That Therefore I Am' opened up further questions that humanities scholars are still addressing.[8] Joyce Salisbury, whose work on animal studies has been foundational for later medieval surveys, ends her investigation of the roles of the animal in the Middle Ages with the question 'What is a human?', a question Karl Steel takes up in his own critically agile take on the animal turn – *How to Make a Human* – in which he argues that violence against what is perceived as the animal constitutes the space in which we create and understand the human.[9] Cary Wolfe, drawing on Heidegger, Foucault and Agamben in his analysis of the cultural processes that enable and obscure the conversion of animal lives into bare lives, shifts the focus of the discussion onto the intersection of

5 Christopher Cannon, for example, argues that 'the very distinction between Old and Middle English is the most compelling and general procedure employed for ignoring the extent to which substantially different kinds of English coincide in the long moment between them' (Cannon, 'Between the Old and the Middle of English', *New Medieval Literatures* 7 (2005), p. 212).

6 Giorgio Agamben, *Homo Sacer: Sovereign Power and Bare Life*, trans. Daniel Heller-Roazen (Stanford: Stanford University Press, 2001).

7 Julia Kristeva, *Powers of Horror: An Essay on Abjection*, trans. Leon S. Roudiez (New York: Columbia University Press, 1982), p. 4.

8 Jacques Derrida, *L'animal que donc je suis* (Paris: Éditions Galilée, 2006); *The Animal That Therefore I Am*, trans. David Wills (New York: Fordham University Press, 2008).

9 Joyce Salisbury, *The Beast Within: Animals in the Middle Ages*, 2nd edn (London and New York: Routledge, 1994, 2011), p. 146. Karl Steel, *How to Make a Human: Animals and Violence in the Middle Ages* (Columbus, OH: Ohio State University Press, 2011).

the study of the animal and the biopolitical.[10] While this chapter will focus on gender and space as opposed to animality, the meditation on the animal confronts and deconstructs traditional binaries that construct and divide human from animal, thinking from unthinking, language possessing from language lacking, in ways that inevitably shade these topics.

Like a wild animal, the exile's place is on the margins: beyond the limits of the city, cast out of the community, relegated to uninhabited, even feral areas. If a person's slippery description can make them almost impossible to place, a person's place can position them beyond the remit of language. For the wolfish characters in these texts it is their literal – physical – location that has the most significant effect on their 'place' as defined in language; one of the protagonists under discussion is at large, while another is (literally) isolated. *Bisclavret*, the tale of a nobleman who turns into a wolf and is shut out of court life, obliged to slink off to the forest, concerns a man silenced by female action who finds his experiences become inarticulable in speech. The characters of *Wulf and Eadwacer* are set apart on islands; Wulf is narrated in a 'feminine' form so equivocal that it is not possible to say what he is or where, and the speaker grieves that there is a difference between them – *ungelic is us*. In what this difference consists is only one of the ambiguous features of this notoriously evasive poem.

The animal turn has a bearing on a final consideration in this chapter, which again stems from Agamben's analysis of *Bisclavret*. Agamben notably does not treat the end of the story and pays little attention to the wife; critics have also pointed to the lack of attention to women or gender in his work more generally. As Penelope Deutscher puts it, 'women's bodies are impressively absent from Agamben's writing, as are reproductive bodies'.[11] I therefore want to push Agamben's model further by focusing on the female exile, taking a cue from Kristeva's theory of the abject – that which 'confronts us, on the one hand, with those fragile states where man strays on the territories of *animal*' and, on the other hand, 'with our earliest attempts to release the hold of *maternal* entity even before existing outside of her' – as an alternative filter.[12] By comparing a Kristevan approach to *Wulf and Eadwacer* – which considers

10 Cary Wolfe, *Before the Law: Humans and Other Animals in a Biopolitical Frame* (Chicago: Chicago University Press, 2013).

11 Penelope Deutscher, 'The Inversion of Exceptionality: Foucault, Agamben, and "Reproductive Rights"', *South Atlantic Quarterly* 107.1 (2008), 55–70 (p. 59). Deutscher, who asks if it is 'possible to open a debate with Giorgio Agamben concerning the role of women's bodies in the politicization of life?' (p. 55), foregrounds one area in which Agamben's reworking of biopolitical life has come in for criticism: his limited engagement with race also is picked up by Ewa Ziarek, who insists that 'bare life cannot be regarded in complete isolation from all cultural and political characteristics'; see Ziarek, 'Bare Life on Strike: Notes on the Biopolitics of Race and Gender', *South Atlantic Quarterly* 107.1 (2008), 89–105 (p. 103).

12 Kristeva, *Powers of Horror*, pp. 12–13 (original emphasis).

precisely this maternal, reproductive body – with Agamben's approach to *Bisclavret*, my intention is also to consider how the relations between bare life and sovereignty, between language and silence, and between the wolf and the exile, are all affected by a gendered agenda.

SACRED MEN

Walter Benjamin famously attributed the character of the law to an uneasy alliance between it and the fundamental workings of violence in civilisation and society, when he wrote that, 'All violence as a means is either lawmaking or law-preserving.'[13] The law that preserves a particular status quo by infringing upon or constraining certain behaviour necessarily entails the strategic use of violence to make its point, as surely as the penalty for attempting to nullify that point will also be met with violence in retribution. Violence that does not fall into either of these categories is therefore threatening to the law: as Benjamin continues, 'If [an act of violence] lays claim to neither of these predicates, it forfeits all validity. It follows, however, that all violence as a means, even in the most favorable case, is implicated in the problematic nature of law itself.'[14] Thus the law is both made and preserved, but also threatened by violence; like the lingering presence of the unspeakable, violence that is unsanctioned by either function in the law is both rejected by and yet underpins the law. However, if the overriding influence governing the action of law is violence, its articulation is less straightforward. Benjamin looks at the active agents of legal violence (military forces, the police), but inasmuch as his critique deals with the means and ends of violence, it concerns the law as it is imposed and maintained – and to some extent expressed – but not communicated. The impetus behind the actions of law is violence, but the medium through which it is disseminated is language; more precisely, the force of performative language, which makes an action lawful or unlawful by declaring it so.

This interplay of violence, language and law is powerfully displayed in the workings of banishment. The law that ejects an individual from society is maintained by the threat of violence, but brought into effect by an utterance. This utterance may take the form of a legal formula or a judicial sentence, but it was originally conceived as the declaration of the sovereign. The ban shows up the stark contrast between the exiled individual – the target of the law – and the sovereign, the speaker whose word is law, but it also reveals the crucial connection between them. This connection is probed by Agamben in his exploration of the workings of sovereign political power as it relates to what he characterises as 'bare life'. His investigation is motivated in part by Foucault's

13 Walter Benjamin, 'Critique of Violence', trans. Edmund Jephcott, in *Walter Benjamin: Selected Writings, Vol. 1, 1913–1926*, ed. Marcus Bullock and Michael W. Jennings (Cambridge, MA: Belknap Press, Harvard University Press, 1996), pp. 236–52 (p. 243).

14 Benjamin, 'Critique of Violence', p. 243.

conclusion to the first volume of *The History of Sexuality*, proposing that anxiety over and scrutiny into sexual matters exemplify a historico-political shift in the mechanisms of power leading into the modern era, when 'classical' sovereign authority over death was 'supplanted by the administration of bodies and the calculated management of life' – a phenomenon Foucault terms 'biopower' or 'biopolitics'.[15] Agamben's thesis energetically endorses the existence of biopolitics, but he also challenges Foucault's assumption in arguing for a far more comprehensive historical application of biopolitical power. Drawing on the distinction in the classical Greek lexicon between *zoē* (the simple fact of living) and *bios* (a politically qualified form of living), Agamben considers both sides of Foucault's watershed – the sovereign's power over the life and death of his subjects, and a biopolitics of widespread control over life as a totality – not as historically consecutive structures of power but as politically concurrent, mutually productive concepts. Sovereign power thus has its ultimate expression (and its fundamental prerequisite) in the dispensable quality of pure *zoē*, bare life, which is defined by acts of sovereignty. Agamben goes so far as to suggest that '*the production of a biopolitical body is the original activity of sovereign power*'.[16] He supports this premise and its implications for the study of Western politics with an analysis of the nature and significance of banishment, conducted via the biography of a figure of paradox called *homo sacer*.

Homo sacer is a name found in archaic Roman legal codes; it translates literally as 'the sacred man'. A juridico-political cipher often associated with the outlaw or exile, Agamben investigates the strange status of this figure in order to locate the forces that underpin it. The very definition of *homo sacer*, taken from archaic Roman legal codes, is characterised by an extraordinary double bind: Agamben cites Pompeius Festus's *De verborum significatione*, in which the sentence for such a man stipulates, 'neque fas est eum immolari, sed qui occidit, parricidi non damnatur' (it is not permitted to sacrifice this man, yet he who kills him will not be condemned for homicide). [17] For this reason, a 'bad or impure man' might traditionally be called 'sacred'. At its Latin roots the idea of sacredness, or *sacratio*, is related to the verb *sacrare*, to consecrate in the sense of giving over to the gods – setting entirely apart. This setting apart gives the early penal sentence *Sacer esto* – literally, 'let him be consecrated' – its force. Agamben traces the similarities and possible ties to the personage of the *devotus*, a warrior consecrated to the gods of the underworld in order to save a city, who is expected to die and whose unanticipated survival occasions a ritual burying of an effigy or *colossus* in place of the corpse. In the case of the surviving *devotus*, what has been consecrated to the gods has not

15 Foucault, *The History of Sexuality I*, p. 140.

16 Agamben, *Homo Sacer*, p. 6 (original emphasis).

17 Pompeius Festus, *De verborum significatione* (quoted in Agamben, p. 71; trans. Heller-Roazen).

been delivered in death to the divine, but nor can it, precisely because it *was* consecrated, be reintegrated into the secular world. The transaction between the human and divine can be resolved and completed with the ritual forfeit of the *colossus*, symbolising that part of the *devotus* that ties him to life; however, though closure is achieved on the episode as a deal with the gods, the physical life – *zoē* – of the surviving man is not ended. Though his continuing to live serves as a reminder of the 'life' given over to the gods, divine law no longer recognises him once his function has been fulfilled, and neither does human law.[18] In the same way, though his ostracism was the result of a ban, and not self-sacrifice, the sacred man was thus 'outlawed [...] This involved exclusion from the community, from divine and human protection.'[19] The intrinsic 'ambivalence of the sacred' supplies Agamben with one of the central tenets of his thesis: the double exception or the double exclusion. The figure of *homo sacer* is made remarkable by the fact that he finds himself in a zone excluding him from both from divine and profane law. This is a state pertaining to only one other personage: the sovereign.[20]

The double exclusion from the human and the divine places the sovereign as much outside the usual spheres of interaction as is *homo sacer*. The sovereign is, as Foucault points out, the one with the right to decide life and death;[21] the link between power and the law is made clear by Benjamin when

18 It should be pointed out that earlier interpretations of *homo sacer* have not always aligned the figure with the outlaw but, rather, with one condemned to death, albeit in oblique terms (as is the *devotus*). Harold Bennett, for example, specifically argues that 'the *sacer homo* was never a picturesque outlaw, running the gauntlet of a thousand chances of death, his goal a sanctuary beyond the borders of his country, but that he was merely a citizen condemned to death for a heinous criminal offence, and regularly executed'; see Bennett, 'Sacer Esto', *Transactions and Proceedings of the American Philological Assocation* 61 (1930), 5–18 (pp. 17–18). Agamben gestures to those critics who 'see *sacratio* as a weakened and secularized residue of an archaic age in which [...] the death sentence appeared as a sacrifice to the gods' (*Homo Sacer*, pp. 72–3), but does not elaborate; his conception of outlawry, though, is somewhat less than 'picturesque'.

19 Adolf Berger, *Encyclopedic Dictionary of Roman Law: Transactions of the American Philosophical Society*, vol. 43, part 2 (Clark, NJ: The Lawbook Exchange, 2002), p. 687.

20 Agamben also interrogates this connection elsewhere, again with reference to Benjamin's writings on law; see Agamben, *Potentialities: Collected Essays in Philosophy*, ed. and trans. Daniel Heller-Roazen (Stamford: Stamford University Press, 1999), pp. 160–77.

21 Foucault first discusses biopower in the first volume of *History of Sexuality* (pp. 135–45), where he defines the classical sovereign right as the power to take or spare life, literally 'the right to *make* die or *let* live [le droit de *faire* mourir ou de *laisser* vivre]'. See *Histoire de la sexualité 1: La volonté de savoir* (Paris: Éditions Gallimard, 1976), p. 178 (original emphasis). Biopower, by contrast, is the power to 'make live or let die'. In *Society Must Be Defended*, he suggests that this development came about when the right of sovereignty 'came to be complemented by a new right which does not erase the old right but which does penetrate it, permeate it. This is the right, or more precisely the opposite right. It is the power to "make" live or "let" die. The right of sovereignty was the right to take life or let live. And then this new right is established: the right to make live and to let die.'

he declares: 'Lawmaking is powermaking, assumption of power, and to that extent an immediate manifestation of violence.'[22] He who has the power to decide the limits of the law is, in one sense, above the law; however, the fact that his word *is* law also locates him inside it. The crucial point about sovereignty to Agamben's thesis is the implication of supreme executive power for both the sovereign and his subjects, the fact that 'the sovereign is, at the same time, outside and inside the juridical order'.[23] The 'sovereign sphere' thus incorporates this state of double exclusion in the same way as does sacredness or *sacratio*. The sovereign, in fact, is also called *sacer* in legal texts: the 'other' definition of *sacer* is simply 'imperial', and in later constitutions 'is applied to everything connected with the emperor (*sacrae sententiae*, *sacra oratio*, *sacrum auditorium*, etc.)'.[24] Kristeva similarly identifies '[s]everal structurations of abjection [...] each one determining a specific form of the sacred'.[25] The two meanings of *sacred* are thoroughly entwined; Georges Bataille (on whom both Agamben and Kristeva draw) summarises the paradox thus:

> Whatever is the subject of a prohibition is basically sacred. The taboo gives a negative definition of the sacred object and inspires us with awe on the religious plane. Carried to extremes that feeling becomes one of devotion and adoration [...] Men are swayed by two simultaneous emotions: they are driven away by terror and drawn by awed fascination.[26]

It is the sense of being set apart, made taboo, from which the two meanings of the sacred stem: the sacred may be set apart so that it is forbiddingly divine or, conversely, subject to divine prohibition. Divinity and taboo, therefore, 'are opposed to each other in one sense only, for the sacred aspect of the taboo is what draws men towards it and transfigures the original interdiction'.[27] Moreover, Agamben insists that, in their exclusion and politico-juridical isolation, the parallel circumstances of the sacred man and the king are not

Foucault, *Society Must Be Defended*, trans. David Macey, ed. Mauro Bertani (London: Penguin, 2003), p. 241.

22 Benjamin, 'Critique of Violence', p. 248.

23 Agamben, *Homo Sacer*, p. 15. This correlation between the sovereign and *homo sacer* is also emphasised with regard to the two bodies, and their capacity to be killed: 'If the symmetry we have tried to illustrate between the body of the sovereign and that of *homo sacer* is correct, then we ought to be able to find analogies and correspondences in the juridico-political status of these to apparently distant bodies. [...] It does not matter, from our perspective, that the killing of *homo sacer* can be considered as less than homicide, and the killing of the sovereign as more than homicide: what is essential is that in neither case does the killing of a man constitute an offense of homicide' (p. 102).

24 'Sacer' in Berger, *Dictionary of Roman Law*, p. 687.

25 Kristeva, *Powers of Horror*, p. 17.

26 Georges Bataille, *Death and Sensuality: A Study of Eroticism and the Taboo*, trans. Mary Dalwood (New York: Walker and Co., 1962), p. 68.

27 Bataille, *Death and Sensuality*, p. 68.

merely coincidental but mutually supportive and enabling: 'At the two extreme limits of the order, the sovereign and *homo sacer* present two symmetrical figures that have the same structure and are correlative: the sovereign is the one with respect to whom all men are potentially *homines sacri*, and *homo sacer* is the one with respect to whom all men act as sovereigns.'[28] The sovereign sphere, a space of double exclusions and non-habitation – of being in neither one state nor, paradoxically and yet simultaneously, in the opposite state – is thus perpetuated by these two 'extreme limits'.

The nature of the violence committed in executing the law is therefore subject to confusion that extends to the execution of law in language. He who has been banned is not, Agamben stresses:

> [s]imply set outside the law and made indifferent to it but rather *abandoned* by it, that is, exposed and threatened on the threshold in which life and law, outside and inside, become indistinguishable. *It is literally not possible to say whether the one who has been banned is outside or inside the juridical order.*[29]

The 'threshold' between inner and outer, between life and death, is also the boundary between language and its object. With regard to *homo sacer*, therefore, it is genuinely impossible to state in words to which state he belongs in law. The unspeakable that governs speech corresponds to the lawlessness that dictates legality. The former in both instances is the 'outside' that holds in place all that falls within the sphere of the latter, but as such it is always already at the core as the founding repudiation. As the sovereignty of language requires the existence of what is *not* utterable in order to validate what is, so too the sovereign builds his power on the wretched state of the outlaw. Agamben in fact locates the structure of law exactly in this constitution of language: 'It [law] expresses the bond of inclusive exclusion to which a thing is subject because of the fact of being in language [...] To speak [*dire*] is, in this sense, always to "speak the law".'[30] The combination of language and law, then, and more specifically their twin overlapping make-ups, has produced this state of exception, concentrating the implicit expression of the ineffable and the juridical necessity of the (with)out-law in one figure.

The state of exception that Agamben elaborates is potentially a useful means of exploring literary depictions of exile and its spatial limits. In the extension (if not correction) of Foucault's concept of the biopolitical sphere from a gradual but discrete shift, taking place at the beginning of the modern era, to an apparatus that was always already in place, at least from the earliest Roman legal codes, Agamben's paradigm encompasses the medieval period in a way Foucault did not necessarily envisage. Robert Mills argues that Agamben's

28 Agamben, *Homo Sacer*, p. 84.
29 Agamben, *Homo Sacer*, p. 28–9 (my emphasis).
30 Agamben, *Homo Sacer*, p. 21.

version should resonate with medievalists because 'what he is suggesting is that bare life played a political role – albeit in a more secretive manner – long before the modern period'.[31] Accordingly, Agamben's investigation of the *homo sacer* figure offers a fertile ground for literary scholars exploring sovereign power and the threshold between animality and humanity, including its implications for readings and constructions of gender.[32] As Miranda Griffin notes, Agamben 'has become important to medievalists'.[33]

Agamben's resonances also stem from the particular case studies he addresses. He refers specifically to the Anglo-Saxon wolf's head – the exile who can be executed with impunity, his head struck off like a wolf's – and develops a second (similarly lycanthropic) medieval test case for *homo sacer* from the twelfth-century Old French tale of *Bisclavret*. Drawing a close parallel between *homo sacer* and the werewolf of Anglo-Saxon and Germanic law, Agamben argues that the origin of the latter is to be found in the fear of the former:

> That such a man is defined as a wolf-man and not simply as a wolf [...] is decisive here. The life of the bandit, like that of the sacred man, is not a piece of animal nature without any relation to the law and the city. It is, rather, a threshold of indistinction and of passage [...] [it] is the life of the *loup garou*, the werewolf, who is precisely *neither man nor beast*, and who dwells paradoxically within both while belonging to neither.[34]

31 Robert Mills, 'Sovereign Power and Bare Life in Poetry by François Villon', *Exemplaria* 17.2 (2005), 445–80 (p. 453).

32 Emma Campbell has re-examined the *Lais* through the lens of Agamben's study of humanity and animality, *The Open*, stressing 'the importance of the wife's transformation as the product of a human savagery of power that approximates – while never quite becoming – animal savagery'; likewise, Miranda Griffin turns to *Bisclavret* and other lais to suggest that 'these animals can be read as more civilized than their human counterparts, often functioning as a repository of the anxieties, transgressions and violence which are part of the medieval courtly text and figuring the anxious boundary between the human and the animal'. McClellan, meanwhile, uses Agamben to reveal how Chaucer treats 'the ethical ambiguity at the heart of the sovereign's relation to those he subjects' in a reading of Walter as sovereign and Griselda as the bare life. See Emma Campbell, 'Political Animals: Human/Animal Life in *Bisclavret* and *Yonec*', *Exemplaria* 25.2 (2013), 95–109 (p. 98); Miranda Griffin, 'The Beastly and the Courtly in Medieval Tales of Transformation: *Bisclavret, Melion* and *Mélusine*', in *The Beautiful and the Monstrous: Essays in French Literature, Thought and Culture*, ed. Amaleena Damlé and Aurélie L'Hostis, Modern French Identities 87 (Bern: Peter Lang, 2010), pp. 139–50 (p. 140); William McClellan, '"Ful Pale Face": Agamben's Biopolitical Theory and the Sovereign Subject in Chaucer's *Clerk's Tale*', *Exemplaria* 17.1 (2005), 103–34 (p. 105); Victoria Blud, 'Wolves' Heads and Wolves' Tales: Women and Exile in *Bisclavret* and *Wulf and Eadwacer*', *Exemplaria* 26.4 (2014), 328–46.

33 Griffin, 'The Beastly and the Courtly', p. 142.

34 Agamben, *Homo Sacer*, p. 105 (original emphasis).

This formulation ties in neatly with *Bisclavret*, the story of a knight who turns periodically into a wolf. Tricked into lupine exile by his fearful wife, he roams the forest, both not-man and not-wolf, and a year later he is almost put summarily to death – *homo sacer* style – when the king and his retinue discover him while hunting and nearly mistake him (if it can be said to be a mistake) for a real wolf. Yet, as scholars have been quick to note, this is only half the story – there is another, female, exile in this twisting tale.

THE WOLF AND HIS WIFE

Bisclavret is also the tale of Bisclavret's wife. In her opening lines Marie defines this word *bisclavret* against the Norman term *garwaf*, distinguishing her courteous Breton wolf from the 'savage' Norman variety, which '[h]ummes devure, grant mal fait, / Es granz forez converse e vait' (vv. 11–12; devours men, causes great damage and dwells in vast forests, p. 68).[35] By the end of the story, however, it is gender, not region, that distinguishes between the two 'wolves' in her *lai*.

At the beginning of the *lai*, the nobleman's wife is concerned by her husband's weekly disappearances (vv. 25–7). During these absences, he undergoes his change and spends three days each week as a wolf. The division is not only temporal, a matter of days, but also of place and space; as a man, he is the head of his household, but as a wolf, he removes himself entirely from the social sphere. When his wife coaxes from him the reason for his disappearances, he tells her:

> 'Dame, jeo devienc bisclavret:
> En cele grant forest me met,
> Al plus espés de la gaudine,
> S'i vif de preie e de ravine' (vv. 63–6)

> 'Lady, I become a werewolf: I enter the vast forest and live in the deepest part of the wood where I feed off the prey I can capture' (p. 69)

When she probes further, he tells her where he leaves his clothing during his transformation, despite his protestations that if he were to lose them while still a wolf, he should remain in this state indefinitely. The wife, frightened by what she has learned, enlists the assistance of another knight and makes her wolfish husband 'disappear' by stealing his clothes from the chapel where he hides them. Bisclavret is left to wander the forest, neither recognisably human, nor wholly wolf.

[35] I refer to *Bisclavret* in Marie de France, *Lais*, ed. Alfred Ewert, pp. 49–57. References are given by line number. Translations are taken from *The Lais of Marie de France*, trans. Glyn S. Burgess and Keith Busby, pp. 68–72, and subsequent references are given by page number.

Agamben's synopsis of the story ends, to all practical purposes, with the king's discovery of Bisclavret in the forest while hunting one day, a year after the wife's deception and the nobleman's seemingly permanent transformation. The king spares the werewolf's life when he observes Bisclavret's intelligence and nobility and takes the knightly beast to live at his court. While Agamben's thesis is undoubtedly compelling, its application to *Bisclavret* also raises questions, especially when the estranged feminine element of the tale dramatically returns.

The story continues as the knight who married Bisclavret's wife after contriving his disappearance visits the court. The werewolf attacks first the knight, then, on a subsequent meeting, his estranged wife, tearing her nose from her face. The king infers a connection among the three and finally the wife, under torture, confesses her crimes and reveals where the nobleman's clothes are hidden. Bisclavret, upon receiving his attire, returns to his human state. Despite the wife's apparently villainous role in the narrative, critics have pointed out that her actions are principally motivated by her fear of the violent wolf she takes her husband to be – she assigns the *bisclavret* and the *garwaf* the same conceptual space, just as they are set alongside each other by Marie in her opening lines. (It is worth noting that Bisclavret describes his lupine retreat in the same terms Marie uses for that of the ferocious *garwaf* – the 'grant forest'). The wife's mistake, according to Carolyn Walker Bynum, stems from the distinction Marie notes between the Norman and Breton werewolf traditions – the wife's 'crime' is actually 'to confuse her bisclavret with the *garvalf* tradition' or, to put it another way, 'stereotyping'.[36] Leslie Dunton-Downer likewise points out that she 'acts out of understandable fear', a justified fear given the violence inflicted on her over the course of the narrative.[37] Not only does Bisclavret mete out painful facial mutilation to her in his rage, but in order to get to the truth, the king authorises her confession to be extracted under torture. Elaine Scarry in her seminal work on the subject insists that the analysis of the body in pain reveals the interconnectedness of torture not only with power but with language and narrative, emphasising the intimate relation between the infliction of pain, the interrogation and the confession. In this way, the extraction of confession – whose truth or fiction in the case of Bisclavret's wife does bring about the end of the narrative, but which in Scarry's analysis is part of the fiction of torture itself – reflects again that 'what is quite literally at stake in the body in pain is the making and unmaking of the world'.[38] Agamben, meanwhile, though he stresses a 'special proximity of werewolf and sovereign', skips the details of the 'inevitable encounter with the

36 Carolyn Walker Bynum, *Metamorphosis and Identity* (New York: Zone, 2001), p. 172.

37 Leslie Dunton-Downer, 'Wolf Man', in *Becoming Male in the Middle Ages*, ed. Jeffrey Jerome Cohen and Bonnie Wheeler (New York: Garland, 2000), pp. 203–18. (p. 210).

38 Elaine Scarry, *The Body in Pain: The Making and Unmaking of the World* (Oxford: Oxford University Press, 1985), p. 23.

ex-wife and the punishment of the woman' and concludes that the important result is that 'Bisclavret's final transformation back into a human takes place on the very bed of the sovereign.'[39]

The omission of these details from the remainder of the narrative is significant. As Mills points out, as much as Bisclavret metes out punishment, he displays 'more in common with the figure of the sovereign than with a state of living inside/outside the law, a deployment of power made possible by exposing the outsider status of the former wife'.[40] Like sovereign powers, who occupy themselves in the creation of bare life that might be disposed of according to their sovereign wishes, Bisclavret imposes his (violent) will on his unfaithful wife, and the results of his action deny her any recourse to or defence from the law. The significance of Bisclavret's violence – whether or not it is 'valid' as lawmaking or preserving violence, as in Benjamin's paradigm – is that Bisclavret, of whom it is *not possible to say* whether he is man or beast, within or without the law, has suddenly erupted into the sphere of representation, of Heideggerian showing and 'appearing on the scene'... in short, of speech. In consigning him to his lupine state, his wife removed language from him, and him from language, making him unspeaking and also unspeakable in the zone of double exception. However, like Bisclavret himself, the unspeakable not only lingers but makes its presence felt, inscribing itself upon her very face.

Bisclavret is of course one of a number of high medieval werewolf narratives, which all deal to a greater or lesser degree with who is able and permitted to speak, and who is not. Susan Crane reads *Bisclavret* in the context of the Aristotelian and Platonic tradition that animals are living beings without *logos*, without *ratio*, exploring how Marie emphasises indeterminacy in her speaking-wolf protagonist, while Peggy McCracken emphasises the twelfth-century interest in language and animality and the implications of animal 'language' of gesture.[41] The themes and narrative motifs form a familiar pattern: the courtly werewolf, who is transformed through female duplicity and redeemed through the actions of the king towards whom he has shown courteous and loyal behaviour, is found in similar fashion to Marie's lay in the fourteenth-century *Biclarel* (whose narrative is structurally almost identical to Marie's);[42] again, in the much longer *Guillaume de Palerne*, translated into

39 Agamben, *Homo Sacer*, p. 108.

40 Mills, 'Sovereign Power and Bare Life in Poetry by François Villon', p. 455.

41 Susan Crane, *Animal Encounters: Contacts and Concepts in Medieval Britain* (Philadelphia, PA: University of Pennsylvania Press, 2012), pp. 42–68. Peggy McCracken, 'Skin and Sovereignty in *Guillaume de Palerne*', *Cahiers de recherches médiévales et humanistes* 24 (2012), 361–75 (pp. 372–3).

42 Amanda Hopkins summarises the differences and similarities between *Bisclavret*, *Melion* and *Biclarel* in her edition and translation *Melion and Biclarel: Two Old French Werewolf Lays*, Liverpool Critical Editions of French Texts, 10 (Liverpool: University of Liverpool, 2005), p. 16.

Middle English as *William of Palerne*; and again with an Arthurian framing device in the twelfth-century Old French lay *Melion* and the Latin *Arthur and Gorlagon*. The romance *Guillaume* features an additional narrative, in which the eponymous protagonist, supposedly a foundling but in fact heir to the king of Apulia, falls in love with the emperor's daughter, Melior, and is protected by the werewolf of the tale – here Alphonse, a Spanish prince turned into a wolf by his jealous stepmother. The lovers disguise themselves in bearskins and are the beneficiaries of the courtly werewolf's aid and loyalty when they flee Rome to escape Melior's engagement to the Greek emperor. *Melion* and *Arthur and Gorlagon*, with their additional Arthurian narrative elements (Melion is Arthur's knight, while Gorlagon tells Arthur a long story of a werewolf and a faithless wife, at the end of which it transpires he was indeed that werewolf), place the emphasis on the treachery of women and the actions – mostly punishments – of kings. Melion, who is transformed into a wolf by a magic ring his wife retains in order to pursue an affair with his squire, attacks the squire on the latter's reappearance at court but is dissuaded from inflicting corporal or capital punishment on his wife at Arthur's intervention; the denouement of *Melion* is, in the event, not violent but the wife is abandoned in Ireland. *Arthur and Gorlagon*, however – an 'anti-romance', as Sîan Echard has called it – contains probably the most unpleasant and vicious depiction of kingship, misogyny and violence.[43] Here, the unfaithful wife of the king who fosters the werewolf, her trysts exposed by her husband's unusual pet, is torn limb from limb and her lover flayed alive; in the final section, the werewolf's estranged wife, who tricked him into lupine exile in the first place (in order to take another husband), is tortured until she reveals how his transformation may be reversed, and her punishment is to kiss the embalmed head of her executed lover every time Gorlagon kisses his new wife.

As even brief synopses suggest, the werewolf legends unfold with varying degrees of misogyny and violence. While the stepmother of *Guillaume* is eventually the agent of transformation for the better as well as for the worse, Melion's wife is eventually abandoned, though not killed or burnt as the Irish king (her own father) suggests;[44] Gorlagon's wife is tortured and forced to perform a gruesome and macabre ritual penance; Bisclavret's wife is tortured and mutilated. From this point onwards, the wife in *Bisclavret* is unspeaking, despite still being human, in contrast with her earlier inquisitiveness. She is also banished from the kingdom, like her husband before her, and (in common with all the women who are violently punished) reduced to an unspeaking

43 Sîan Echard, *Arthurian Narrative in the Latin Tradition* (Cambridge: Cambridge University Press, 1998), p. 213.

44 *Melion*, vv. 568–70. See *Les Lais anonymes du XIIe et XIIIe siècles: édition critique de quelques lais bretons*, ed. Prudence Mary O'Hara Tobin (Geneva: Droz, 1976), pp. 289–318; *Eleven Old French Narrative Lays*, ed. Glyn S. Burgess and Leslie C. Brook (Cambridge: D. S. Brewer, 2007), pp. 413–66 (pp. 437–66).

state, closer to the animal she almost seems to become. (Significantly, Melion's preferred revenge for his wife is to transform her into a wolf in turn.) Scarry shows that the 'unmaking' of the world of the body in pain is linguistic: 'Physical pain does not simply resist language but actively destroys it, bringing about an immediate reversion to a state anterior to language, to the sounds and cries a human being makes before language is learned.'[45] Moreover, as well as bringing the human subject closer to a prelinguistic or an unspeaking – animal – state, the tortured subject is also excluded from community, from humanity, precisely through this removal from language. Pain achieves its ends through inaccessibility of suffering to anyone other than the sufferer, and it 'ensures this unsharability through its resistance to language'.[46] As Campbell argues, the brutal treatment Bisclavret's wife receives 'identifies the lady with Agamben's *homo sacer* figure', and she, along with her lover, is banished from the kingdom.[47] She, too, becomes a wolfish exile through the performance of her wolfish husband. Is Bisclavret still far from legal protection, or does Marie's depiction of a courtly werewolf leave open the position of the true outcast? Does the 'beste salvage' of the Norman tradition show his dripping jaws… or is this a different sort of wolf, a Breton wolf who, being 'une sorte de chien-loup qui baise le pied du roi' (a sort of dog-wolf who kisses the king's foot), has his violence sanctioned at the highest level?[48] Who is the real wolf?

If Bisclavret appears, with the king's acquiescence, to be finding his way out of the binds of bare life – perhaps appropriately, given that the end of the *lai* is nigh; his redemption is imminent, his abject status is becoming untenable – what implications does this have for sovereignty? If the originary activity of sovereignty is the creation of the bare life against which it is defined, then to maintain the status quo, the outlaw who came in from the cold must be replaced. This is a narrative full of very marked contrasts – sylvan and urban, bestial and courtly, loyalty and treachery, nobility and ignominy – and very little occurs in *Bisclavret* that does not find, somewhere along the line, an inverted 'other' supplying the flip side of a particular coin. Bisclavret, doubled in his own self, also parallels the king, the sovereign who, as the polar opposite to *homo sacer*, paradoxically shares in the sphere of double exception. The lover who seduces Bisclavret's wife can likewise be seen to mirror the husband he displaces. Even Marie herself – called by the retroactive *nom de plume* constructed by editors of her *Fables* and localised to the indeterminate site she both hints at and hides when she claims she is 'de France' – shares the zone of double exclusions (named, unnamed; placed, placeless) with her protagonist.[49]

45 Scarry, *The Body in Pain*, p. 4.

46 Scarry, *The Body in Pain*, p. 4

47 Campbell, 'Political Animals', p. 105.

48 Phillippe Ménard, *Les Lais de Marie de France: contes d'amour et d'aventures du Moyen Age* (Paris: Presses Universitaires de France, 1979), p. 177, my translation.

49 While scholarship generally operates around assumptions that Marie was a French

For all the efforts that have been made to locate Marie, geographically, dynastically, historically, she remains merely a three-word composite that may or may not correspond to a name. Bloch declares that, despite her seemingly contradictory possession of a name, Marie 'comes as close as one can imagine to being anonymous'.[50] It is worth noting, too, that scholars frequently infer a 'special proximity' between Marie and the sovereign, the 'nobles reis' to whom the *Lais* are dedicated (Prologue, l. 43).

Bisclavret finds himself stranded between two opposing spaces, existing partly in one and partly in another, yet at the same time, doubly excluded. In the case of one banned from the community, as we saw earlier, it is *impossible to say* whether he then lies within or outside the reach of the law; this same inability to give expression to the condition of the subject – even to the point of declaring if he *is* a subject – also prevails in the case of the werewolf. Bisclavret is both not man and not wolf: it is as impossible to say whether he belongs to the human or animal sphere as it is to determine if he is inside or outside

woman, the ration of hard facts about her 'is so meager as to render imprudent anything but the most militant skepticism about almost every aspect of her life': see R. Howard Bloch, *The Anonymous Marie de France (*Chicago: University of Chicago Press, 2003), p. 1. As June Hall McCash summarises, 'most scholars seem to agree on a few points [...] a) that Marie lived in the second half of the twelfth century – possibly into the early thirteenth; b) that she was a noblewoman who came into contact with the court of England during her lifetime; c) that she was born in the Île-de-France or territories attached to the crown of France'; see McCash, 'Sidney Painter (1902–1960): The Issue of Patronage for Marie de France', in *The Reception and Transmission of the Works of Marie de France, 1774–1974*, ed. Chantal A. Maréchal (Lewiston, NY: Mellen Press, 2003), pp. 171–208 (p. 196). On the subject of Marie's domicile and career history, see R. N. Illingworth, 'La chronologie des *Lais* de Marie de France', *Romania* 87 (1966), 433–75; Illingworth proposes (on the basis of nomenclature throughout the work) that the *lais* be divided into two groups reflecting a move from France to England. Burgess endorses this analysis and maintains: 'Everything suggests that, between writing her first group of lays and beginning the second, Marie had come to Britain, either as a result of marriage or because she wished to further her career'; see *The Lais of Marie de France: Text and Context* (Manchester: Manchester University Press, 1987), p. 18. Burgess hypothesises such a move to have taken place *c.* 1160. For an overview of the suggested identities of Marie and her patrons, see McCash, 'Sidney Painter (1902–1960): The Issue of Patronage for Marie de France'.

50 Bloch, *Anonymous Marie*, p. 7. However, he makes two points regarding this anonymity: firstly that it does not prevent readers forming a picture of her, filling in the blanks, and secondly that Marie was not, stylistically, an 'anonymous' writer. Indeed, she asserted her authorial identity vigorously: she is identified as the common author of the *Fables* and *Lais*, not via the coincidence of their both being signed Marie but on the linguistic and characteristic integrity of her writing. See also Diane Watt, *Medieval Women's Writing: Works by and for Women in England, 1100–1500* (Cambridge: Polity Press, 2007). Looking at the issue of authorship and authority in the writings of medieval women, Watt argues that Marie's works are 'preoccupied with questions about the role of the poet, compiler and translator [...] about the reasons for writing and the purposes writing serves, and about problems of reception and reputation' (p. 62).

the law. Even the name 'Bisclavret' – like 'Marie de France' – is a compound made up of two concepts, whose synthesis hints at meanings ranging from the philosophical (*bleiz-lavaret*: speaking or rational wolf; *bleiz-claffet*, wolf-sick) to the seemingly random (*bisc-lavret*: short trousers).[51] For Bloch, this is an exemplary instance of Marie's linguistic mastery, which runs through the *lais* and makes them 'in some deep sense about language as a flawed, uncontrollable, and sometimes fatal medium [...] this tale [*Bisclavret*] is about the irresistibility of the question'.[52] Questioning who, where and what Bisclavret is (or what 'bis clavret' means) returns the same answer over and over – neither one thing, nor another, and consequently both: it is, as before, 'not possible to say'. The situation of the werewolf is not in either state and, therefore and at the same time, not stateable, unstated. With regard to unspeakability, the most significant comparison is always between the werewolf and the woman. Although the fate of Bisclavret's wife is only discussed briefly at the close of the narrative, it is clear that the mantle of deformity and exile passes to her. As Griffin observes, in the wolf-man's act of mutilation, '[t]he bare life of the werewolf is displaced [...] from the wolf's body to the woman's'.[53] Like Ovid's Lycaon, the werewolf of classical myth, her crimes in the narrative are betrayal and deception, and she, too, finishes the tale with a 'wolf's head'.

In legal writings of the period, as in *Bisclavret*, the concepts of outlawry, exile and wolf-hood became increasingly conflated. While Agamben handles the Germanic laws with relative brevity – *Bisclavret* and the whole excursion into medieval culture is largely confined to one eight-page chapter – this is coincidentally in keeping with Marie's penchant for alluding to archaic laws and customs, including those of the Anglo-Saxon and Germanic inheritance.[54] These incorporations are sensitive to – and to some extent a reflection

51 Bloch includes a brief survey of suggested translations (*Anonymous Marie*, p. 82), as does Glynn S. Burgess, *The Lais of Marie de France, Text and Context* (Manchester: Manchester University Press, 1987), p. 9.

52 The first *lai* includes the declaration, 'Oëz, seignurs, ke dit Marie, / Ki en sun tens pas ne s'oblie' (Hear, lords, the words of Marie who in her time does not neglect her obligations. *Guigemar*, vv. 3–4). The 'de France' fragment is from the epilogue to the *Fables*:

> Al finement de cest escrit,
> Qu'en Romanz ai traitié e dit,
> Me numerai pur remembrance:
> Marie ai num, si sui de France.
>
> (At the conclusion of this text, which I have written and narrated in French, I shall name myself for posterity: Maries is my name, and I am from France. Epilogue, vv. 1–4).

Marie de France, *Les Fables: Edition critique accompagné d'une introduction, d'une traduction, de notes et d'un glossaire*, ed. Charles Brucker (Louvain: Peeters, 1991); *The Fables of Marie de France*, trans. Mary Lou Martin (Birmingham, AL: Summa Publications, 1979).

53 Griffin, 'The Beastly and the Courtly', p. 145.

54 On Marie's use of antiquated cultural tropes and laws, see Emanuel J. Mickel, Jr,

of – the relatively conservative content of Norman and Angevin law. Just as Marie (in her *Fables*) claims inheritance from King Alfred, the laws of Henry II – sometimes assumed to be Marie's 'nobles reis' – descend from those of Henry I, who maintained those of William the Conqueror, who claimed to conserve those of Edward the Confessor. Marie's wolf-man exile is therefore both an archaism and an allusion to contemporary jurisprudence, who appears in various guises through early English law. While the *wargus* of Salic law is referenced in the *Leges Henrici Primi*,[55] in the compendium written in the reign of Henry II (Glanvill's *Tractatus*, *c.* 1188), outlawry is addressed mainly from the sovereign's perspective.[56] However, the wolf's-head motif remains in common currency: Bracton's revised law code from the early thirteenth century – which borrows much from Glanvill and from the Anglo-Saxons – retains for the outlaw or 'friendless man' the term 'wolf's head' from earlier codes; aiding such a man will in turn incur a sentence of outlawry.[57] Bracton's code also stipulates that 'one who is under twelve years of age, cannot be outlawed or put outside the law because until he reaches that age he is not under any law [...] any more than a woman, who cannot be outlawed because she is not under the law': strictly speaking, an outlaw – the *utlag* – may only be a man.[58]

However, even if (as Pollock and Maitland put it) a woman 'can never be outlawed, for a woman is never in law', a provision addresses the case of delinquent females.[59] Women and children who take flight for a felony are said to be 'waived [*wayvari*]'; moreover, Bracton specifies that they 'bear the wolf's head [*gerunt caput lupinum*] and in consequence perish without judicial inquiry'.[60] Although the woman and the child are technically not termed outlaws, in as much as they are neither inside nor outside the law, they occupy

'Antiquities in Marie's *Lais*', in *In Quest of Marie de France: A Twelfth-Century Poet*, ed. Chantal A. Maréchal (Lampeter, Wales: Edwin Mellon Press, 1992), pp. 123–347.

55 See Felix Liebermann, ed. and trans., *Die Gesetze der Angelsachsen*, 3 vols (Halle: Niemeyer, 1903–16), I. 600.

56 Glanvill stipulates that an outlaw's inheritance escheats to his lord, and an outlaw who receives royal pardon will not be restored to his former position, as 'the lord king does not wish, when pardoning wrongdoing and outlawry [*utlagariam*], to infringe thereby the rights of others'; *Tractatus de legibus et consuetudinibus regni Anglie qui Glanvilla vocatur; The Treatise on the Laws and Customs of the Realm of England Commonly called Glanvill*, ed. G. D. G. Hall and M. T. Clanchy (Oxford: Clarendon, 1993), 7.17.

57 *Bracton, De legibus et consuetudinibus Angliæ: Bracton on the Laws and Customs of England*, ed. George E. Woodbine, trans. Samuel E. Thorne, 3 vols (Cambridge, MA: Harvard University Press, 1968), II. 361–2.

58 *Bracton*, II. 353.

59 Frederick Pollock and Frederic William Maitland, *History of English Law before the Time of Edward I*, 2 vols (Cambridge: Cambridge University Press, 1898), I. 482.

60 *Bracton*, II. 354.

a state of exception, one that suggests that they may reasonably share the outlaw's expectation of attack because to attack them is no longer unlawful.

The assumption of the wolf's head is thus linked to exile even when it is not specifically an outlaw in question; certainly Bisclavret's wife is marked by Bisclavret's rhinectomy, even before she leaves the courtly enclosure. Valentin Groebner argues that this moment in the tale is 'a distinct speech act of male patriarchal violence',[61] and the legibility of facial mutilation also agrees with Agamben's characterisation of the face itself, in *Means without End*, as another kind of threshold – 'the threshold of de-propriation and of de-identification of all manners and of all qualities […] in which only the latter become purely communicable'.[62] The loss of a medieval nose was undoubtedly a communicator of (negative) qualities, a disfigurement steeped in legal, spiritual and punitive significance. As the legend of St Æbbe – who supposedly advised her nuns to escape Viking rape by cutting off their noses to spite their faces – indicates, the loss of the nose might be deployed as the ultimate turn-off to avoid unwanted male claims on a woman's body.[63] It is also worth pointing out that having no nose was a copper-bottom sign of advanced leprosy,[64] with all the disenfranchisement that entailed: Carole Rawcliffe notes that 'the decision to exclude a leprous person from the community, and thus from the right to plead in a court of law, might be taken in cases of serious and visible deformity […] [which] presupposed extreme facial disfigurement' (Dunton-Downer also calls her a '*lepra-lupa*', a female leper-wolf).[65] However, arguably the most potent medieval connotation of noselessness was the inscription, rather than the avoidance, of sexual activity; the nose was often associated with its owner's illicit or unorthodox sexual practices – as Groebner remarks, '[t]he nose points downward'.[66] The removal of the nose and ears was thus also inscribed in the law codes of Cnut and his successors (including Henry I) as the fitting punishment for an unfaithful wife, who would further be sentenced to loss of property and public humiliation (*woruldsceame*).[67] This mutilation brings

61 Valentin Groebner, *Defaced: The Visual Culture of Violence in the Middle Ages*, trans. Pamela Selwyn (New York: Zone, 2004), p. 75.

62 Agamben, *Means Without End*, trans. Vincenzo Binetti and Cesare Casarino (Minneapolis: University of Minnesota Press, 2000), p. 100.

63 In the case of a number of virgin saints, this was also occasionally a tactic to avert marriage plans. Groebner makes the point, however, that although 'some medieval female saints threatened to cut off their noses to escape an unwanted marriage or a rape, as their hagiographers emphasize […] a severed nose was never the prominent feature of a venerable saint […] The severed nose's connotations of blemish, sin, and sexuality were apparently too strong for it to be a pious attribute' (pp. 76–7).

64 Carole Rawcliffe, *Leprosy in Medieval England* (Woodbridge: Boydell, 2006), p. 140.

65 Rawcliffe, *Leprosy in Medieval England*, pp. 194–5; Leslie Dunton-Downer, 'Wolf Man', in *Becoming Male in the Middle Ages*, ed. Jeffrey Jerome Cohen and Bonnie Wheeler, p. 210.

66 Groebner, *Defaced*, p. 73.

67 Cnut's second code specifies, 'Giyf be cwicum ceorle wif hig be oðrum were forlicge,

about the woman's public disgrace, which indicates that she is to remain in her community, on display, rather than be thrown out of it.

What is more significant than simple nasal deficiency, though, is that, according to Marie, several of the wife's offspring are similarly afflicted. The idea of female noselessness, itself one of Marie's inheritances from pre-Conquest sources, now becomes an inheritance in her story as well, passing down through the female line. She insists:

> Plusurs [des] femmes del lignage,
> C'est verité, senz nes sunt nees
> E si viveient esnasees (vv. 312–14)

> Many of the women in the family, I tell you truly, were born without noses and lived noseless (p. 72)

As Bynum states in her analysis of identity, metamorphosis and shape in the narrative: 'It is her body finally that (however unfair we may feel it is) carries the story.'[68] The physical attributes that provoke characters to action in the *lai* literalise the trope of symbolic difference as it relates to the dynamic of exile, more so in the case of the wife's nose than in that of Bisclavret's wolfish shape. What is also apparent, however, is that not only does the wife's noseless shape 'carry' the story, but her female, specifically her maternal 'shape', carries the noseless female offspring who supply the striking coda. The mark of her exile becomes bound up with the evidence of her maternity, an aspect of social abjection that is only hers, not shared with Bisclavret nor with her new husband.

That it is only the female offspring – those who may in turn come to represent the Kristevan 'maternal entity' – who are afflicted underlines this reproductive cast to her exile. Further, it is not an act of sovereignty but of maternity that precipitates their abjection. Agamben's crucial fascination with Greek *zoē* – bare life – might be taken further through Kristeva's focus on the reproductive body, the womb Aretaeus of Cappadocia (in a moment of weird parallelism with the zoomorphic sins of *Ancrene Wisse*) called *zōon en zōōi*, 'an animal inside an animal'.[69] Whereas Agamben does not encompass the wife in his reading, for Kristeva (and 'devotees of the abject'), the establishment of the threshold between self and other that is staged in abjection

7 hit open weoyrðe, geweoeorðe heo to woruldsceame syððan hyre sylfre, 7 hæbbe se riht wer eall þæt heo ahte; 7 heo þonne þolige nasae 7 earena' (If, during her husband's lifetime, a woman lies with another man, and it becomes known, let her afterwards become herself a public scandal, and her rightful husband is to have all that she owned, and let her then lose her nose and ears: Liebermann, I. 348). Translations from Old English are my own unless otherwise indicated.

68 Bynum, *Metamorphosis and Identity*, p. 173.

69 Quoted in Helen King, *Hippocrates' Woman: Reading the Female Body in Ancient Greece* (London: Routledge, 1998), p. 222.

– 'the misfire of identification with the mother as well as with the father' – is deeply bound up in the recognition of and separation from the maternal body, to the extent that 'the advent of one's own identity demands a law that mutilates'.[70] The sovereign thus becomes less focal than the mother, and the wandering wolf is replaced by a wandering nose. Interestingly, although Bisclavret wanders in singular exile before being welcomed back into the fold, the wife suffers banishment in which her new husband and their offspring share. As the generations multiply, the shunned couple spawn a collection of descendants likewise exiled from their noses. In this weird community based on inherited, shared exile, expedited by mutilation, the *esnesees* exist both without the body politic and yet within it. In turn, their bodies are marked as being both outside the political order and also constitutive of it – without community and yet within it.

THE WIFE AND HER WOLF

This subtle proximity between the exile and those with whom she formerly belonged bespeaks the threshold state that is ironically maintained by the exile's significance to the society that has abjected her, and her adherence to its customs (precisely by remaining in exile). In this, Marie's *lai* echoes a long tradition that has fascinated scholars of a different genre – the Old English elegies, in which 'exile itself, as one constant tradition in the Anglo-Saxon world, can affirm that world and be as dearly clung to as the seemingly more positive aspects of life'.[71] Yet even the 'constant tradition' of poetic exile has its outsiders.

The Anglo-Saxon narrative poem *Wulf and Eadwacer*, an elegiac composition found in the Exeter Book, is notoriously difficult to render in modern English. Slippery and evasive, loaded with double meanings and ambiguous terms, the sense of the poem is by no means clear. Benjamin Thorpe (in his 1842 edition) was famously flummoxed by 'Riddle I', as he called it, which he leaves untranslated and reproduces with the disclaimer, 'Of this I can make no sense, nor can I arrange the verses.'[72] To quote the standard 'arrangement' will give an idea of the scope for different senses:

> Leodum is minum   swylce him mon lac gife;
> willað hy hine aþecgan,   gif he on þreat cymeð.
>   Ungelic is us.
> Wulf is on iege,   ic on oþerre.

[70] Kristeva, *Powers of Horror*, p. 54.

[71] Robert Bjork, '*Sundor æt rune:* The Voluntary Exile of the Wanderer', *Neophilologus* 73.1 (1989), 119–29 (p. 119).

[72] *Codex Exoniensis: A Collection of Anglo-Saxon Poetry*, ed. and trans. Benjamin Thorpe (London: Society of Antiquities, 1842), p. 527, n. 380.

Fæst is þæt eglond, fenne biworpen.
Sindon wælreowe weras þær on ige;
willað hy hine aþecgan, gif he on þreat cymeð.
Ungelice is us.
Wulfes ic mines widlastum wenum dogode,
þonne hit wæs renig weder, ond ic reotugu sæt,
þonne mec se beaducafa bogum bilegde,
wæs me wyn to þon; wæs me hwæþre eac lað.
Wulf, min Wulf, wena me þine
seoce gedydon, þine seldcymas,
murnende mod, nales meteliste.
Gehyrest þu, Eadwacer? Uncerne earne hwelp
bireð wulf to wuda.
Þæt mon eaþe tosliteð þætte næfre gesomnad wæs,
uncer giedd geador.[73]

The mysterious text appears to centre around three people: two presumably male characters, Wulf and Eadwacer, and a third, to whom they are both bound either romantically or legally. This is the speaker – an anonymous female.

[73] Quotations are taken from *The Exeter Book,* ed. George Krapp and Elliott van Kirk Dobbie, *ASPR 3* (New York: Columbia University Press, 1936), pp. 179–80; subsequent references will be given in parentheses. See also *The Old English Elegies: A Critical Edition and Genre Study,* ed. Anne L. Klinck (Montreal: McGill-Queens University Press, 1992), p. 92. I offer my own translation of *Wulf and Eadwacer* below, but the play of words in this poem presents a challenge that has attracted many more poetic renderings; see Paul Muldoon's version in *The Word Exchange: Anglo-Saxon Poems in Translation,* ed. Greg Delanty and Michael Matto (New York: W. W. Norton & Co., 2012), p. 51; Kevin Crossley-Holland's in *The Battle of Maldon and Other Old English Poems* ed. Bruce Mitchell (London: Macmillan, 1965), pp. 78–9; Dolores Frese's in *Wulf and Eadwacer*: The Adulterous Woman Reconsidered', *Notre Dame English Journal* 15.1 (1983), 1–22. (Subsequent translations are my own unless otherwise indicated).

To my people it is as if they have been given a gift.
They will consume him if he comes into the troop.
There is a difference between us.
Wulf is on an island, I am on another.
The island is fastened, bounded by fen.
There are cruel men there on the island.
They will consume him if he comes into the troop.
There is a difference between us.
Wulf's wide-tracks I have dogged in my imagination.
When the weather was rainy, and I sat in tears,
then the battle-bold one wrapped me in his arms –
there was pleasure in that; yet it was loathsome to me, too.
Wulf, my Wulf, hoping for you
Has made me sick; it is your seldom-coming,
My mourning mind, not lack of food.
Do you hear, Eadwacer? Our wretched whelp
Wulf bears to the woods.
It is easy to slit apart that which never was joined,
Our song together.

She laments Wulf – who, as his name might suggest, appears to be shunned by the community – and though she is sick in mind and body through his continued absence, fears retribution from her community should he return. Their separation appears to be the focus of her grief, and twice she repeats the refrain, 'Ungelic is us' (there is a difference between us, ll. 3, 8). Towards the end of the poem, she appears suddenly to switch her attention from Wulf to someone else, saying, 'Gehyrest þu, Eadwacer? Uncerne earne hwelp bireð Wulf to wuda' (Do you hear, Eadwacer? Wulf will bear our wretched whelp to the woods, l. 16). The poem ends with a mournful prognosis for their tenuous connection, inverting Matthew 19.6 to predict, 'Þæt mon eaþe tosliteð þætte næfre gesomnad wæs, / uncer giedd geador' (One can easily tear asunder that which was never joined: our song together, l. 18).[74]

The poem is most often grouped with the Exeter Book elegies, and in the manuscript it gets sandwiched between *Deor* and the riddles. It has also been connected with and analysed through other traditions, significantly the *frauenlieder*, which Patricia Belanoff accesses through feminist semiotic theory. Meditating on whether this poem (or a partner text, *The Wife's Lament*) could have been female-authored, Belanoff argues that 'the language is different because the poems are women's songs, a genre which inevitably entails a differentness of language'.[75] The poem is distinguished by interruptions and transgressions of the (masculine-inflected) rules of Old English poetry – in stress, metre, structure, theme – which, when examined through the lens of Kristevan symbolic and semiotic theory, mark it as different both in gender and genre from the elegies with which it is often anthologised. While Belanoff draws on Kristeva to accentuate *Wulf and Eadwacer*'s linguistic uniqueness and refusal to conform, Helen Bennett's reading of the same two poems uses the Kristevan semiotic and the concept of the abject to emphasise the difference in the narrators' circumstances: 'by both their physical being and the absence of reconciliation to the social structure', she argues, 'the wife and the speaker in *W&E* fit Kristeva's description of the abject – the exile – in ways that the male exiles do not'.[76]

When it comes to the narrative, critical riddlings may affect translations and the overall tone of the poem to the tune of anything from a minor semantic quibble to an overhaul of the story.[77] Often, the one leads to the other, the most prevalent examples being, in fact, the two nouns *Wulf* and

74 In the Vulgate, the verse reads, 'Quod ergo Deus conjunxit, homo non separet' (What therefore God has joined together, let not man put asunder). Quotation and translations are taken from the Douay-Rheims version.

75 Belanoff, 'Women's Songs, Women's Language', pp. 193–203 (p. 194).

76 Bennett, 'Exile and the Semiosis of Gender', p. 48.

77 For an overview of critical interpretations, see Klinck, *The Old English Elegies*, pp. 168–77.

Eadwacer: it is by no means certain that they represent two different people.[78] The speaker – almost always taken to be female – has neither name nor epithet. Although 'reotogu' (l. 10) seems to provide one hard fact in the poem's mass of unknown quantities (being declined feminine), she remains as elusive as the men, and as anonymous. While successive editions of the poem have been named for Wulf and/or for Eadwacer, the nameless speaker almost never impinges on the title. The language of the poem, too, is famously – purposely – indirect and contradictory. Its refrain, 'willað hy hine aþecgan, gif he on þreat cymeð. / Ungelic[e] is us' (ll. 2–3, 7–8), is an unusual feature in elegiac poetry and one that has drawn comparisons with ballad forms and Norse poetry; it also typifies the stylistic and semantic overlaps that create the poem's many doubled meanings.[79] The first line of the refrain can be rendered 'they will kill (or consume) him if he comes with/into the troop', but equally, 'they will receive him if he comes with/into the troop'. The figure under discussion

78 *Wulf*, of course, is a common element in Anglo-Saxon names (Cynewulf was once thought to be the suitably wolfish author of 'Riddle I'). Fanagan and Kerling both take Wulf and Eadwacer as distinct persons but diverge when it comes to the issue of who is meant to be the *beaducafa*. Fanagan argues for a correlation with Eadwacer, making him the warrior with whom the speaker, married to Wulf, has a fling; see John Fanagan, '*Wulf and Eadwacer*: A Solution to the Critics' Riddle', *Neophilologus* 60.1 (1976), 130–7; Johan Kerling, 'Another Solution to the Critics' Riddle: *Wulf and Eadwacer* Revisited', *Neophilologus* 64.1 (1980), 140-3. Kerling points out that 'semantically *wulf* "wolf" and *beaducafa* "the one brave in battle" are closer to each other than *wulf* and *eadwacer* "one watchful of property"' (p. 140). By contrast, John F. Adams, in '*Wulf and Eadwacer:* An Interpretation', *Modern Language Notes* 73.1 (1958), 1–5, suggests that *eadwacer* is not a proper but a common noun here, used satirically – 'an epithet: an ironic reference to Wulf, who is the woman's lover and the father of her child, but who is not her husband' (p. 2). Richard Giles proposes that this is indeed irony but directed by the speaker at herself: 'she asks, "Hearest thou, Property-Watcher?"' having been 'given, unwillingly, the task of protecting their "wretched whelp"'; see Giles, '*Wulf and Eadwacer*: A New Reading', *Neophilologus* 65.3 (1981), 4689–72; (p. 470). Dolores Frese concentrates on the plight of the speaker's son ('*Wulf and Eadwacer*: The Adulterous Woman Reconsidered', p. 16); Stanley Greenfield, meanwhile, cuts the whelp out altogether, along with the second male character: 'in my reading the "whelp" does not exist. Rather, I see it as a metaphor for Wulf's and the speaker's joy in love, which is metaphorically also "our *giedd* together"': see Greenfield, *Hero and Exile: The Art of Old English Poetry* (London: Hambledon, 1989), p. 190.

79 The verb *aþecgan* is usually translated as 'destroy' or 'kill', but it may also mean 'serve', 'consume' or 'receive'. With shades of *homo sacer*, the word *gife* – which would seem to apply to the same thing or person to be destroyed, received, consumed or otherwise treated – may connote a gift but also a sacrifice, something set entirely apart. Finally, *on þreat* can be taken as either 'with' or 'into' the troop or host (depending on whether the noun is amended with a dative inflection). For a discussion of the lexicon of *Wulf and Eadwacer*, see Belanoff, 'Ides [...] geomrode giddum: The Old English Female Lament', in *Medieval Woman's Song: Cross-Cultural Approaches*, ed. Anne L. Klinck and Ann Marie Rasmussen (Philadelphia, PA: University of Pennsylvania Press, 2002), pp. 29–46, 214–18 (pp. 39–41); also Frese's translation, which maintains these conflicting interpretations in suspension (p. 17).

might be as easily absorbed into the group as abjected by it. It is interesting to consider if the second line of the refrain comments on this ambiguous figure. It can be translated as 'things are different with us' or, alternatively, 'there is a difference between us' – it has even been rendered (taking *un*- as an intensifier) 'we are too alike'.[80] How *ungelic* are Wulf and the speaker?

When contemplating the dynamic of exile in *Wulf and Eadwacer* – particularly when it comes to who is in exile and where – this question is pivotal. The speaker, who aligns herself with Wulf throughout the poem, is also an outcast on her island and may indeed be too much like the 'wolf' she addresses. It is hardly surprising that *Wulf* is often taken to refer to an outlawed character – this possibility is linked back to the evidence of Old Icelandic texts and other Germanic sources, and in particular yoked to expressions such as the one with which this chapter began, found in the *Leges Edwardi*: 'lupinum enim gerit caput a die utlagationis sue, quod ab Anglis uulfesheued nominatur' (for from the day of his outlawry he bears a wolf's head, which is called *wluesheued* by the English).[81] There is a need for historical precision here: E. G. Stanley, who traced the etymological roots of the tradition, notably concluded that it is not to be assumed that this name 'would have suggested to the Anglo-Saxons, as it has suggested to generations of Anglo-Saxonists, that Wulf was an outlaw'.[82] Stanley did not address the law codes in detail but their evidence is open to similar judgements: for example, while the *wluesheued* clause is often cited as an Anglo-Saxon source, the laws of Edward were not codified until after his death, when they were recorded in Latin by an anonymous writer, probably around the 1140s. In keeping with the Anglo-Norman claims of legislative conservation noted above, it was asserted they were recorded immediately after the Conquest at King William's request.[83] 'Wolf' as a legal trope may appear to be a genuine inheritance, a detail imported from Continental codes and attached to English ones, or a sort of false memory of Anglo-Saxon law

80 See Carole A. Hough, '*Wulf and Eadwacer*: A Note on 'Ungelic', *American Notes and Queries* 8.3 (1995), 3–6.

81 Liebermann, *Gesetze*, I. 631.

82 E. G. Stanley, 'Wulf, My Wolf!', in *Old English and New: Studies in Language and Linguistics in Honor of Frederick G. Cassidy*, ed. Joan H. Hall, Nick Doane and Dick Ringler (New York: Garland, 1992), pp. 42–62 (p. 53).

83 Although the poem's markers of exile – isolated location, ostracism from the general populace, a state of in-betweenness – tally with the association of the Anglo-Saxon *wulf* and the exile, it is worth noting as well that in Old English *utlag* also denotes an outlaw, while Æthelstan II refers to 'þam hlafordleasum mannum, ðe mon nan ryht ætbegytan ne mæg' (those lordless men of whom no law can be got) by the term *flyma* (Liebermann, 1. 150–2). Regarding the fate of a *flyma*, Æthelstan's code declares 'hine lecge for ðeof se þe him tocume' (let him slay him for a thief who can come at him); Æthelræd III. 10 later specifies 'ælc flyma beo flyma on ælcum lande, þe on aānum sy' (every *flyma* is a *flyma* in every land, who is so in one [Liebermann, 1. 230]). For the Norman composition, later medieval influence and eventual re-evaluation of the *Leges Edwardi*, see O'Brien, *God's Peace and King's Peace*.

reinforced by Anglo-Norman iteration. Although here is not the place to reassess the basis of the trope in Anglo-Saxon England, if it is an Anglo-Saxonist fantasy then it seems to have been an Anglo-Norman fantasy long before medievalists took it up.

On the other hand, the *werewolf* does make an appearance in pre-Conquest law. The compound is recorded in the ecclesiastical laws of Cnut (1016–35), composed appropriately enough by Wulfstan:

> Þonne moton þa hyrdas beon swyðe wacore 7 geornlice clypigende, þe wið þone þeodsceaðan folce sceolon scyldan: þæt syndan bisceopas 7 mæssepreostas, þe godcunde heorda bewarian 7 bewerian sceolon mid wislican laran, þæt se wodfreca werewulf to swyðe ne slite ne to fela ne abite of godcundre heorde.[84]

> Then the herdsmen should be very watchful and always calling out, who should shield the people from criminals: those are the bishops and mass-priests, who should watch and guard the godly flock with wise teachings, so that the ravening werewolf neither tears too much nor eats too many of the godly flock.[85]

Although the *werewulf* (probably connoting the devil) is a kenning unique to Wulfstan,[86] there is an interesting overlap between Wulfstan's rhetoric and *Wulf and Eadwacer*'s poetics. Not only do they share the image of the shunned wolf – equated to the þeodsceaða, the one who threatens the community – but also the dichotomous relation of *wulf* and *wacen*. Whereas the poem juxtaposes outcast *Wulf* and unsympathetic Ead*wacer*, Wulfstan counsels watchfulness (*wacore*) in the face of the menacing, madly consuming *werewulf*. In Wulfstan, too, the fate of the wretched is to be torn, slit, rent apart: while (as so often) it is not entirely clear what in the poem one may 'eaþe tosliteð' – is it 'uncer giedd geador' or a different connection? – here it is unambiguously the flock that is at risk of being torn asunder. Belanoff also identifies parallels between the *wulf* figure and the *sliten* action in a verse from *Maxims I*,[87] pointing out that 'if she is going to participate in the slitting of her *giedd*, she has taken on a trait of the wolf herself'.[88] While Wulfstan is likely writing some time after *Wulf and Eadwacer* was committed to parchment, the idea of a wolfish

84 Liebermann, *Gesetze*, 1. 306.

85 For this passage in Wulfstan's sermons, see *The Homilies of Wulfstan*, ed. Dorothy Bethurum (Oxford: Clarendon Press, 1957), p. 241.

86 See Jonathan Wilcox, 'The Wolf on Shepherds: Wulfstan, Bishops, and the Context of the *Sermo Lupi ad Anglos*', in *Old English Prose: Basic Readings*, ed. Paul E. Szarmach (New York: Garland, 2000), pp. 395–418 (p. 400).

87 Here again the verb *slitan* is associated with the wolf: 'Wineleas, wonsælig mon genimeð him wulfas to geferan, felafæcne deor. Ful oft hine se gefera sliteð' (The friendless, miserable man takes wolves for his comrades, very deceitful animals. Very often this companion slashes him, Krapp and Dobbie, *ASPR* 3, 161: 146–7)

88 Belanoff, 'Ides', pp. 41–3.

wordhoard is intriguing and the parallels between this female speaker and the Wulf she weeps for reinforced when she taps into it.

Parallel, too, are their respective geographical locations. She grieves that 'Wulf is on iege, ic on oþerre' (Wulf is on an island, I on another; l. 4); in informing the audience that one island is 'Fæst… fenne biworpen' (secured, surrounded by fens; l. 5), she is as ever ambiguous – it is not obvious to which island she refers. A physical embodiment of mental or spiritual isolation, the island is an eloquent feature of Anglo-Saxon topographical symbolism, echoing the biblical desert, to which prophets and saints retreated for periods of intense contemplation, or the wilderness, its poetic counterpart.[89] Inasmuch as it has both a geographical and a conceptual function, the island is a site of solitude or remoteness that may slide into exile and forgetting; if this is the province of the one who is cut off from the world, it might seem tempting to situate Wulf here. However, the symmetry of the fourth line suggests the speaker is not precluded from this same state of expulsion: if Wulf is identified with the figure of the exile, the speaker may be also. She appears to be living among her people, which may or may not include another man who may or may not be her husband, but she is also 'on an island', surrounded not by water or fens but by those who seem to abject her – the exile's double. Without the explicit threat of extermination, this is not an exact parallel – it could not be said that the speaker is a *mulier sacra*, and in contrast with the wife in *Bisclavret*, the speaker does not appear to be cast out through an act of violence – but the apparent suspension of her relationships keeps her in a zone of indistinction. She is not within, nor is she outside the influence of Eadwacer; she is not with Wulf, nor in her keening cry, 'Wulf, min Wulf', is she without him.

Elegiac exile itself might therefore be a platform for gendered generic difference. Stacy Klein suggests that 'while the male exile's movement symbolizes his spiritual progress […] the female exile's stasis symbolizes her spiritual inertia', while Bennett characterises the speaker as 'stationary, not storm-tossed, but [her] lack of movement does not reflect stability'.[90] While the Breton wolves are both obliged to wander to the margins of society – and, in the case of the female wolf, the story as well – the Anglo-Saxon female

[89] See Catherine A. M. Clarke, *Literary Landscapes and the Idea of England, 700–1400* (Cambridge: D. S. Brewer, 2006), pp. 7–36. It is not insignificant that monastic communities in Anglo-Saxon England were often built on or associated with islands: Bede describes Ely as being surrounded on all sides by water and fenland. Other examples include the Abbey of St Columba on Iona (mid-sixth century) and Thorney Abbey in the Cambridgeshire fens (*c.* 970); even Westminster Abbey was built on Thornege – the Isle of Thorns.

[90] See Stacy S. Klein, 'Gender and the Nature of Exile in Old English Elegies', in *A Place to Believe In: Locating Medieval Landscapes*, ed. Clare A. Lees and Gillian R. Overing (University Park, PA: Pennsylvania State University Press, 2006), pp.113–31 (p. 122); Bennett, 'Exile and the Semiosis of Gender', p. 45.

wolf-exile is static and confined. Shari Horner argues that in female-voiced elegies, 'textual emphasis on physical enclosure, paired with [...] "interior" journeys, signifies their status as women', which is certainly true of one island-bound exile here (although Wulf's 'other island' might problematise the femininity of internment).[91] The two remain bracketed together in their suspension and exceptions, and yet gender separates them: even if the speaker is at home and Wulf is at large, she (like Bisclavret's wife) is accompanied in exile.

The use of the word *hwelp* – a young animal, a puppy or cub – is telling: like 'Wulf' itself (and indeed 'Eadwacer'), this term has been mined for possible meanings and its connotations exercise critics and translators. It has been read entirely at face value, as an actual wolf's cub and as entirely metaphorical, as a parallel to the *giedd* of the final line.[92] Considering the 'wolves' in the text, however, lends support to the most common interpretation: that the whelp is the child of either Eadwacer or, more likely, Wulf (Pulsiano and Wolf argue that the *hwelp* must surely be the outlaw's child).[93] If the *hwelp* is the speaker's offspring with Wulf (and if her heartache is inspired by anyone, it seems unlikely to be anyone other than 'Wulf, min wulf'), it may well be the progeny of two wolves. Once again, exile becomes an inheritance: Klein writes that the speaker's yoking of Wulf and the whelp 'marks [the child] as destined for exile', and, in her apparent complicity, she reacts against the social structure of which she both is and is not part, seeking to 'annihilate one of the more potentially positive fruits of sexual difference: a child fully equipped to participate in society'.[94] The markers of exception and exclusion that indicate Wulf's separation also distinguish the speaker, neither with nor without her people: if the father of this whelp is identified with the wolf's head, it might logically follow that its mother is also, and the figure suffering abjection is once again aligned with the maternal body. Connected and yet disconnected from those around her, the speaker who misses Wulf so keenly becomes the counterpart he leaves behind – a 'wolf-headed' woman in the place of the exile.

SHE-WOLVES AND TEXTUAL BANISHMENT

The shifting interrelation between outlawry, exile and the wolf's head underpins the literary and cultural tropes that Marie de France and the

91 Shari Horner, 'En/closed Subjects: *The Wife's Lament* and the Culture of Early Medieval Female Monasticism', in *Old English Literature: Critical Essays*, ed. R. M. Liuzza (New Haven, CT: Yale University Press, 2002), pp. 381–91 (p. 384).

92 See Peter Orton, 'An Approach to *Wulf and Eadwacer*', *Proceedings of the Royal Irish Academy* 85 (1985), 223–58; Greenfield, *Hero and Exile*.

93 Philip Pulsiano and Kirsten Wolf, 'The "Hwelp" in *Wulf and Eadwacer*', *English Language Notes* 28.3 (1991), 1–9.

94 Klein, 'Gender and Exile', p. 129.

Exeter Book poet play with, and they in turn reveal this connection's nuances and limits. Although male figures in these texts are described as wolves, the women are just as wolfish, as outcast, held in as much suspense as the more obviously lupine and sacred male characters – in some ways more so. The male wolves are at the centre of these narratives – they are named (whether or not Wulf and Bisclavret begin as descriptors, they are typically applied in edited texts in the style of proper names), whereas the women are not. Despite the first-person narrative voice of *Wulf and Eadwacer*, both texts concern themselves more with the situation of the 'wolves' than of the women. Yet, in the context of exile and of Agamben's and Kristeva's theories, this is perhaps what makes the women, not the men of these stories, the wolves' heads. The wife in *Bisclavret* is throughout a more marginal figure than her husband, even before she is banished by the king; the speaker in *Wulf and Eadwacer*, on the other hand, occupies a liminal zone in which she can neither reveal nor conceal her own story. If the wolf's head is the one who is cast out and found in a sovereign sphere, a zone of indistinction, there seems to be a more complicated dynamic at work in both these texts concerning the nature and identity of their exiled figures.

Agamben's paradigm is useful in this regard: it shows the workings of power in *Bisclavret*, his exemplar, very clearly (although not in the way Agamben himself relates). *Bisclavret* is as much about return as it is about exile, and it poses the question, can the outlaw – the one whom the law has abandoned – ever lay claim to the law? It is true that Bisclavret finds that a wolf may look at a king: he is excused to the sovereign's chambers for his resumption of human clothing, while his wife is banished.[95] Yet, in one variation, an interesting development takes place with regard to the transformation scenes. Where other narratives turn on seemingly natural, or at least habitual, metamorphosis, as if it were some genetic fluke that the man-wolf himself merely accommodates, in *Melion*, *Guillaume de Palerne* and the Middle English adaptation *William of Palerne* the werewolf is changed by an enchanted ring. Moreover, while *Melion* attributes the magical properties to the ring (the knight himself uses it earlier in the story and it is used by the king for Melion's final transformation), *Guillaume* in particular emphasises the magical agency of Alphonse's stepmother. The 'witty werewolf', like Bisclavret, retains his courtly manners and harbours a desire for vengeance on the woman who transformed him.

[95] Nudity is a preoccupation in *Guillaume* and *William* just as it is in *Bisclavret*. The ex-werewolf's shame at his natural state is assuaged in these narratives by the queen who induced his physical changes (*Guillaume de Palerne*, vv. 7728–69; *William of Palerne*, ll. 4439–49). Derrida wonders about nudity as he considers how his cat constructs him as human. Whereas the human is ashamed of being 'naked as a beast', the animal – the cat who looks at the philosopher stepping out of the shower – 'is not naked because it is naked' (*The Animal That Therefore I Am*, pp. 4–5). That the werewolf's humanity coincides with the experience of shame might also be borne in mind in the analysis of the humiliation meted out to wives.

When his opportunity arises, however, though he similarly tries to spring on his enemy, he is prevented by his protégé, Guillaume, who has specifically sent for her for his friend's redemption. Alphonse's transformation is not secured through the torture of the woman responsible, but through Guillaume's detections and her own craft:

> L'anel qui fu de tel vertu
> Li a la dame au col pendu
> A .I. filet vermeil de soie.
> Molt en maine li leus grant joie
> De ce que la dame li fait.
> Dont a la dame .I. livre trait,
> Tant a porlit et conjuré
> La vassal a deffaituré
> Et tot remis en sa samblance.
>
> The ring that was so powerful
> The lady hung from his neck
> On a thread of red silk.
> The wolf displays great joy
> At what the lady is doing to him.
> Then the lady pulled out a book;
> She read it entirely and conjured until
> She changed the form of the vassal
> And totally restored his appearance.[96]

Here, the werewolf's woman is permitted to return to the fold through her restorative action. Yet this is also more than penance, for what it also reveals is that in the *homo sacer* pattern, Alphonse's stepmother conforms more to the figure of the sovereign than to that of the wolf-(wo)man. As the tale insists in its recognition scene (so similar to *Bisclavret*'s), she also conforms to the pattern of female antagonists: in all these tales, it is the woman who creates or takes advantage of the conditions that cause a knight to become a wolf's head. The exile that is imposed by a woman is the exile that must be undone in order to restore the sovereign sphere. Whereas the (male) werewolf always has someone to speak for him – indeed, the willingness of the sovereign to recognise his humanness and speak in his defence is often the chief point of

[96] *Guillaume de Palerne: Roman du XIIIe siècle*, ed. Alexandre Micha, Textes Littéraires Français (Genève: Droz, 1990); *Guillaume de Palerne: An English Translation of the 12th Century French Verse Romance*, ed. and trans. Leslie A. Sconduto (Jefferson, NC: McFarland & Co., 2004), vv. 7743–51.
The moment the queen produces the ring in the Middle English *William of Palerne* is almost exactly the same, from the specification of its virtues to the red silk thread on which it has hung (ll. 4421–31). She likewise reads to him from a book of sorcery (l. 4433). See *William of Palerne: An Alliterative Romance*, ed. G. H. V. Bunt (Groningen: Boumas Boekhuis, 1985).

the tale – the female outcast seldom does. For a woman to banish her husband is truly sovereignty, and truly unspeakable.

Yet the werewolf narrative also echoes Kristeva's principle in its concern with the wife's maternity: while for Agamben, bare life is abandoned by and yet guarantees political life, for Kristeva, the abject must be established before the individual psychosexual life forms.[97] Jeffrey Jerome Cohen's analysis of revenge and return in *Bisclavret* finds that '[t]he wife, not the werewolf, is the monster'.[98] The knight's wolfish guise is unsustainable for either the logic of the story (as he returns from the margins and establishes himself in the cultural powerbase) or the function of a true monster. Analyses of monstrosity, not least Cohen's own, emphasise the monster's marginal or threshold state – the *monstrum* is etymologically a being that shows or warns (as Kristeva also knows well: she named her second novel, a tale of creeping criminality and external threat, *The Old Man and the Wolves*). When the knight resumes his former appearance, his wife's wolfishness may fill the vacancy in the 'bare life' department but the matrilineal continuity of its physical inscription ensures that the wolves never truly disappear.

In the Old English tradition, meanwhile, the figure of the wolf is subject to conflicting forces and fluid identity politics. The speaker appears to be between two protagonists, not alone and unaccompanied, speaking in ambiguous terms encompassing multiple meanings and occupying a space that floats between genres. Through this equivocation, though, the effects of the same power structure that replaces Bisclavret with his wife are readily observed in the continual suspensions that come into play in the poem: although she is apparently surrounded, like the wife, she is also marginalised. It is worth noting David Clark's rereading, a 'somewhat tongue-in-cheek, alternative interpretation' that does not necessarily involve a woman at all: instead, the speaker is 'a young man [...] imprisoned on an island and socially ostracized for engaging in a sexual relationship with another man, Wulf' and reviled as an effeminate *hwelp*.[99] In order to do so, however, the hapax legomenon *reotugu* must undergo gender reassignment and become *reotig* (when language 'sets up a separation', Kristeva reminds us, it is done 'precisely

97 Agamben writes that, though the sacred man is created by and abandoned by the law, 'from the point of view of sovereignty *only bare life is authentically political*' (*Homo Sacer*, p. 106; original emphasis). From a psychosexual perspective, meanwhile, Kristeva suggests: 'There is nothing like the abjection of self to show that all abjection is in fact recognition of the *want* on which any being, meaning, language, or desire is founded', *Powers of Horror*, p. 5.

98 Jeffrey Jerome Cohen, 'Gowther among the Dogs: Becoming Inhuman c. 1400', in *Becoming Male in the Middle Ages*, ed. by Jeffrey Jerome Cohen and Bonnie Wheeler, pp. 219–44 (p. 231).

99 David Clark, *Between Medieval Men: Male Friendship and Desire in Early Medieval English Literature* (Oxford: Oxford University Press, 2009), p. 30.

by repressing maternal authority').[100] Clark admits such a reading seems unlikely to become widespread, yet I mention it because this challenge to heteronormative readings actually takes to its logical extreme the invisibility and precariousness of the female character – by writing her out of the poem altogether. While the multifarious readings of *Wulf and Eadwacer* reveal the 'desperate need to achieve closure in the act of reading' that approaches a kind of critical sovereignty,[101] the authorial persona resonates with the maternal body, sending forth a body of artistic work via the inscribed body of text. While the writers behind these texts are suspended in degrees of anonymity (Marie, named after an editorial convention, the wolf-poet without even a pen-name), literary creation likewise overlaps with the exiles' procreation. Even here, there is a suspension: the inscribed parchment that has fixed and replaced the spoken word, with the song of a wolf written on sheep's clothing.

When straying into the territories of the animal, it becomes increasingly difficult to locate our protagonists except in suspension – they are not within, not outside; neither subject to the law, nor protected from it; not in one place, nor in another. The exile's sphere is the outside or, rather, the exile is to be found outside a particular sphere. Yet in being outside, they are necessarily inside, occupying one distinct space that is defined against (but that defines) all that it is without: be it a sovereign sphere of exception or a process of abjection. The place of this place seems to be particularly inflected by gender in the case of these metaphoric wolves, perhaps because the narratives also invoke the compulsion to abject the 'maternal entity'. In *Bisclavret*, the wolfishness of the wife becomes as clear as the nose (not) on her face, but she is not alone in her exile as she and her future progeny (the marks of her maternity) are expelled from the social sphere. In *Wulf and Eadwacer*, though – a poem in which the reader may theorise out of existence any one of the four persons of a deeply ambiguous story – a subtler, more fluid construction of culturally determined exile emerges. Here there is no literalised inscription of wolfish appearance, but in this earlier literary reflex *place* is even more crucial in marking the (female) wolf's head and her song-whelp. Through the evocation of her confinement, her song feeds into a tradition of mobility – poetry that was transmitted by performance and bequeathed by word of mouth.

'MORE THAN I CAN TELL'

In a typically auto-authenticating move, Marie de France finishes the tale of *Bisclavret* by detailing the nobleman's fortunes after his last transformation:

100 Kristeva, *Powers of Horror*, p. 72.

101 Marilynn Desmond, 'The Voice of the Exile: Feminist Literary History and the Anonymous Anglo-Saxon Elegy', *Critical Inquiry* 16.3 (1990), 572–90 (p. 589).

> Si tost cum il pot aver aise,
> Tute sa tere li rendi;
> Plus li duna ke jeo ne di.
> La femme ad del païs ostee [...]
> L'aventure ke avez oïe
> Veraie fu, n'en dutez mie.

> It was not long before [the king] restored his land to him; he gave him more than I can tell and banished the woman from the kingdom [...] The adventure you heard actually took place, do not doubt it (vv. 302–6, 315–16).

At the end of the *lai*, there is so much going on that Marie cannot even tell it all; it escapes the reach of language. It is this challenge to the sovereignty of language that lends *Bisclavret* its depth and makes *Wulf and Eadwacer* so magnificently opaque but so completely fascinating. Both foster an air of Heideggerian mystery, the unshowable, untellable part that lurks in language but will not be contained by it. The attempt to impose order on this shifting mass of unspeakables is fated only to increase it. In much the same fashion as the critical literature surrounding Chaucer's Pardoner, the plethora of possible *ménages* that might be inferred from *Wulf and Eadwacer* all work to tangle up the very question they all strive to straighten out. The comparison of this poem with the riddles is never more apt than when the attempt is made to find 'the answer'. The source of these answers, and the root of their varying plausibility, is, naturally, the semantic slippage always at work in the text, and like Marie's word-games, it is unlikely that any of this ambiguity is accidental. It is this riddle-like quality that says without saying – or hints without giving it away – that is at work in *Bisclavret*, too, naming the werewolf and yet not naming him, putting him in the power of the sovereign even at the heart of the forest.

In Kristeva's abject, where speech and the need to locate the self coincide in the same compulsion, the exile is the one who asks, '"*Where* am I?" instead of "*Who* am I?" For the space that engrosses the deject, the excluded, is never *one*, nor *homogenous*, nor *totalizable*, but essentially divisible, foldable, and catastrophic'.[102] The end of the *lai* (which, we are to understand, will continue to be 'written' on the faces of noseless descendants) is more than Marie can tell, and the final interpretation of the elegy that generated so many readings will never be heard. Where the forests and wanderings of Bisclavret and Wulf are typical of the out-of-bounds space of exiled wolves or sacred men, for banished women, the strange suspension between community and solitude (created in part through their own fecundity) evokes a different kind of exile, distinguished from the settled, socialised sphere in a way that is far less clear-cut [...] and perhaps, consequently, rather more wolfish. Yet, even when effectively silenced by their circumstances – whether it be a complicated love

102 Kristeva, *Powers of Horror*, p. 8 (original emphasis).

triangle or the unfortunate detail of having become a wolf – the protagonists are able to speak from this place of the unspeakable. Poetically, in the cadence of the *frauenlied*, or performatively, through an act of retribution, the incidents that show the repressed, the outlawed and the abjected as the lingering, constitutive presence of the unspeakable do not reinscribe this quality; they defy it. Banishment is what you make of it: for man, woman or wolf, the language of the exile can overcome the exile from language.

4

TAKING THE WORDS OUT OF HER MOUTH: GLOSSING GLOSSECTOMY IN TALES OF PHILOMELA

Every February, Padua celebrates a saint's day nicknamed the Feast of the Tongue, honouring the sublimely eloquent St Anthony of Padua by genuflecting to the part of him still residing in the city: his miraculously preserved tongue, just as it was found by St Bonaventure upon the first translation of the saint's remains in 1263. Gorgeously housed in a reliquary, the tongue still stands in for the saint, now 750 years young and reputedly incorrupt, conjuring the power of Anthony's oration. It recalls, too, stories of saints who could not be silenced, where the removal of the tongue is no guarantee that the victim will cease to speak and, indeed, generally fails parlously in this objective. The substitution of an individual's tongue for their speech is by no means limited to stories of medieval saints, however, nor to those whose speech is beyond reproach: as the locus and instrument of speech, the tongue of a medieval subject whose speech proved corrupt was also liable to be punished or removed. Law codes and penitentials advocated speech be conditioned or curtailed; unruly speech – a sin of the tongue – was tameable but in some cases the only guarantor of governance is removal of the tongue, cutting off speech permanently. This chapter considers how tongue tearing might be contextualised and gendered in medieval culture, before examining the narrative of another tongueless orator – the late medieval reflexes of the Philomela legend. The story of the raped and maimed princess tells of speech that is torn away and then restored, but the proxies and prosthetics woven into Philomela's unexpected performance challenge the relation between silencing and silence. Does the one really lead to the other? The final metamorphosis into a nightingale, rather than causing Philomela's exclusion from (physical) speech, brings with it the return of her tongue – a songbird's tongue. By the end of her story, though, this has already become a superfluous reattachment, a relic of a conventional variety of speech that is no longer required when the secret of the unspeakable crime has been 'spoken' and exposed and the voice of the victim has returned through extraordinary and unforeseen means. Karma Lochrie argues, à la Foucault, that the usefulness of silencing and secrecy – medieval no less than modern – is that they are 'positively verbose, and this verbosity can tell us much about ourselves, our histories, our social world [...] and perhaps most importantly, the workings of power and individual resistance'.[1] However, even as power may operate in

1 Lochrie, *Covert Operations*, p. 5.

and through secrecy, the reverse discourse of revelation (or confession) – even the possibility of such a disclosure – simultaneously works to undermine it. In this tale, Philomela performs where she can no longer speak, in a peculiarly feminine form of expression – one that might be termed écriture féminine – which is both provoked by and comes to undermine the masculine economy of violence it opposes, and asks how is the unspeakable engendered? How is it gendered? How is it overcome?

A CLIP OF THE TONGUE

In order to stand in for a speaking subject, the tongue is often figured as an object: a common expression in late medieval England, for example, declared that 'your tongue is your sword'.[2] Biblical tongues are compared to a 'piercing arrow' (Jeremiah 9.8), 'choice silver' (Proverbs 10.20) or 'the pen of a scrivener that writeth swiftly' (Psalms 44.2): a compliant and pious tongue is a choice attribute. The transgressive tongue, on the other hand, is also objectified but it is objectified in order to correct its owner's insubordinate subjectivity. It is addressed as if it were another person altogether, as in Psalms 51: 'Thou hast loved all the words of ruin, O deceitful tongue. Therefore will God destroy thee forever: he will pluck thee out, and remove thee from thy dwelling place: and thy root out of the land of the living' (Psalms 51.6–7).[3] The tongue's seeming independence of its owner here leads to its destruction: while the obedient tongue is a useful possession, the unruly or impious tongue must be disavowed, cast out, removed.[4]

This is the logic behind the punishments meted out to those guilty of deviant speech or 'sins of the tongue'. As Bettina Lindorfer puts it, in the penitentials of the later Middle Ages the 'slitting, slicing, boring, cutting and tearing out of the tongue treats this organ as if it itself independently committed the verbal misbehavior'.[5] The sins of the tongue were enumerated

2 Similarly, in John Trevisa's translation of *On the Properties of Things*, the tongue is 'þe instrument of taast and of spekinge [...] moist and hoot in complexioun and euelong in disposicioun, and þynne, ischape as a swerd'. See 'De proprietatibus linguae bone et male' (Capitulum 21m), in *On the Properties of Things: John Trevisa's Translation of Bartholamæus Anglicus, De Proprietatibus Rerum; A Critical Text*, ed. M. C. Seymour, 2 vols (Oxford: Clarendon, 1975); pp. 206–9.

3 See Proverbs 16.1; Psalms 70.24.

4 For the destruction of the impious tongue, see Proverbs 10.31–2; Psalms 11.1–5; 2 Maccabees 7.1–4.

5 Lindorfer, '*Peccatum Linguae* and the Punishment of Speech Violations', in *Speaking in the Medieval World*, ed. Jean E. Godsall-Myers (Leiden: Brill, 2003), pp. 23–43 (p. 39). Along with Lindorfer, Edwin D. Craun and Sandy Bardsley have looked at deviant speech and sins of the tongue in late medieval Europe: see Craun, *Lies, Slander and Obscenity: Pastoral Rhetoric and the Deviant Speaker* (Cambridge: Cambridge University Press, 1997); Bardsley, *Venomous Tongues: Speech and Gender in Late Medieval England* (Philadelphia, PA: University of Pennsylvania Press, 2006).

early in the thirteenth century in William Peraldus's *Summa vitiis et virtutibus*, which followed the traditional seven deadly sins with an eighth book dedicated to twenty-four sins of the tongue. These ranged from lying to slander and gossip to swearing and blasphemy, and it was a model that gained many adherents among penitential writers. The vocal vices were also subject to painful yet spectacular symbolic punishments both before and after death: Robert Mannying's *Handlyng Synne*, for example, details a particularly graphic posthumous penalty for backbiters and those '[þ]at kunne nat kepe here tungë ry3t' (that cannot control their tongues), featuring the shade of a monk who:

> shette hys tunge before þe grecys,
> And gnoghe hyt ynwarde al to pecys.
> Hys tunge was brennynge þat he so gnoghe,
> Yn to hys mouþe a3en he hyt droghe;
> And eft, outë he dede hyt shete,
> And gnoghe hyt eft wyþ peynës grete.[6]

> (in front of the steps, thrust his tongue out and gnawed it inwardly all to pieces. His tongue that he gnashed in this way was burning, and he drew it again into his mouth; and afterwards, out he stuck it again and then gnawed it in great pain.)

As might be expected, however, the greatest sin of the tongue is blasphemy, for which the harshest punishments are found not in church law but in the temporal law codes of medieval Europe. Mutilation of the tongue, the lips and the teeth were deemed fit retribution for blaspheming, cursing, swearing and bearing false witness, appearing in town statutes, charters and royal decrees across Europe.[7] It is worth noting, however, that the frequency with which violent punishments were actually inflicted, even when convictions were secured, may not have been high. Lindorfer makes the point that alternatives (such as fasting or paying fines) not only existed but were the more

6 *Robert of Brunne's Handlyng Synne and Parts of its French Original*, ed. Frederick J Furnivall, EETS o.s. 119 (London: Trübner, 1901), pp. 125, 123. This spectacle also features in the *Prick of Conscience*, whose prediction for backbiters reads, 'Ilk ane salle gnaw þair awen tonges in sonder' (Each one shall knaw their own tongue into pieces); see *The Pricke of Conscience*, ed. Richard Morris (Berlin: Philogical Society, 1863), p. 200.

7 Lindorfer notes a variety, including statutes from Italy, Germany and France ('*Peccatum Linguae*', pp. 32–8). The thirteenth-century directive of Louis IX (St Louis) stated that blasphemy should be punished with mutilation of the lips, tongue and teeth (p. 32); other less-saintly rulers issued similar decrees, including Charles V of France, who advocated an ascending tariff of oral punishment for repeat offenders, starting with fasting and the stocks, moving through 'splitting of the upper lip, splitting of the lower lip and severing of both lips' and finally on to tongue removal for a fifth offence: see Hunt Janin, *Medieval Justice: Cases and Laws in France, England and Germany, 500–1500* (Jefferson, NC: Macfarland, 2004), p. 40.

likely penalty, and wonders 'were the cruelest punishments even ever really carried out'?[8]

When sins of the tongue were punished, however, whereas Sandy Bardsley has recorded the propensity for women to be punished as scolds and gossips (by means of fasting or being put in the stocks), the blasphemers were more often male than female. Gerd Schwerhoff's study of sins of the tongue in late medieval German legal codes records several cases of corporal punishment meted out to male offenders;[9] likewise David Lawton suggests most blasphemers convicted by the Spanish Inquisition were male.[10] In England, meanwhile, Derek Neal suggests that, although 'far more women than men were prosecuted for speech offenses, especially in the form of "scoldings" [...] [m]en were more generally expected to enact specific forms of disorderly speech: swearing (cursing) and blasphemy'.[11]

At the other end of the sanctity scale, however, one more place one might expect to find incidents of tongue tearing is in the hagiographic literature, and the saints do not disappoint. St Terentian, St Leger and Theodore, bishop of Corinth all suffered the removal of their tongues, while Pope Leo III was once attacked in Rome by assailants who attempted to gouge his eyes and remove his tongue. (Leger also endured eye boring in concert with tongue cutting.) However, the suffering and survival of tongue torture takes on a different cast in the passion of one of its most famous subjects, St Christina. A virgin martyr whose life was widely circulated in the fourteenth century (thanks in part to its inclusion in de Voragine's *Legenda Aurea*, one of the most extensively disseminated texts of the late medieval period), Christina epitomises saintly defiance in the face of her tormentors. Her many tortures include the shearing of her tongue in a particularly literal example of the standard attempt made on the part of the pagan tyrant to shut up his Christian victim. The indomitable Christina is not subdued but continues to speak, condemning her oppressors. (This is a feat Leger also achieves: despite his enemies having 'coruen of is

8 Lindorfer, '*Peccatum Linguae*', p. 38. Susanna Burghartz estimates that 73 per cent of blasphemy cases in late fourteenth-century Zurich were punished, but in most cases by fines (quoted in Lindorfer, '*Peccatum Linguae*', p. 38).

9 Punishments noted by Schwerhoff include those of Knoepflin der Stubekneht (who in 1357 swore not to return to Strasbourg before his tongue was then cut out), Heinrich der Swertfurb (pilloried first, then punished by tongue removal and banned and from Augsburg in 1368) and Ulrich Gleissenhammer, who lost his tongue in Nurnburg in 1465. See Gerd Schwerhoff, '"Blasphemare, dehonestare et maledicere Deum": Über die Verletzung der göttlichen Ehre im Spätmittelalter', *Verletzte Ehre: Ehrkonflikte in gesellschaften des Mittelaltersund der Fruhen Neuzeit*, ed. Klaus Schreiner and Gerd Schwerhoff (Koln: Bohlau, 1995), pp. 252–78 (p. 263).

10 David Lawton, *Blasphemy* (Philadelphia, PA: University of Pennsylvania Press, 1993), p. 92.

11 Derek G. Neal, *The Masculine Self in Late Medieval England* (Chicago: University of Chicago Press, 2008), p. 175.

tongue', nevertheless 'he prechede faste / And al-so wel as he dude er'.)[12] Impressively, her tongue serves as a weapon even when it is not in her mouth: she throws the detached organ in the eye of Julian, one of her torturers, and it blinds him. This is depicted with particular relish in William Paris's account of the legend:

> Julian wondrede who she myghte
> In hir grete tormentes jangill so.
> Therefore he bade a wykkyd wighte,
> 'Kytte oute hir tonge! It dos me woo.'
> And whan hir tonge lay at hir too,
> She spake als wele, that maydyn brighte,
> As never it had be kytt hir froo.
> Thei herd and seye, all men, with sight.
> She toke hir tonge upe, where it lay,
> And even sche caste it at Julian eye,
> That aftir nevermore alway
> On that syde myght he noght see.
> For she hyme hite, softely smylide she.[13]

Karen Winstead remarks of Paris's representation that, though Christina 'had always been a pugnacious saint', he appears to take considerable enjoyment in making his Christina even wittier and more confrontational – in the episode above, Christina 'actually pauses to admire her marksmanship'.[14] Julian's 'woe' is only increased once the tongue ceases to 'jangle' within Christina's mouth: once it is discharged, both the tongue and the saintly, feminine speech of which it is metonymic continue to wear down his authority until he must acknowledge theirs. Regarding the appendage with his one remaining eye, he speaks 'the tonge unto', complaining that it has now 'wrought [him] woo' through both its word and its blows.[15] In addressing her tongue, rather than the saint herself, Julian surrenders the vestiges of his influence and is forced to concede that, despite his attempts to undo Christina's speech, she and her language of female sanctity are mutable but not to be muted.[16]

12 Leodegar in *The Early South English Legendary, or Lives of Saints*, EETS o.s. 87 (London: Trübner, 1887), ed. Karl Horstmann pp. 82–3.

13 'Christina of Bolsena' in *Middle English Legends of Women Saints*, ed. Sherry L. Reames (Kalamazoo, MI: Medieval Institute Publications, 2003), pp. 227–42 (ll. 457–69).

14 Karen A. Winstead, *Virgin Martyrs: Legends of Sainthood in Late Medieval England* (Ithaca, NY and London: Cornell University Press, 1997), p. 84.

15 St Christina, ll. 474, 476.

16 Christine de Pizan also appropriates the story in the *Cité des Dames* to illustrate the challenge, the danger and the spectacle of autonomous female speech (and writing). As well as being Christine's own patron saint (and namesake), for her particular project of writing and defending women, the legend is 'peculiarly poised to represent the problems of Christine's own female authority', as Maureen Quilligan argues. Independent speech can be won, but not without risk: 'the narrative fact of the severed tongue continues to

In the saintly subject, then, the tongue may speak as well when it is ejected from the body as it does when it is still attached – if saintly relics like Anthony's tongue possess, even in death, their own kind of eloquence, Christina's *vita* supplies the model, *par excellence*, of the body part that continues to speak after repeated attempts to silence its owner. The spat tongue may, as in the case of Christina's linguistic blinding, disempower the oppressor by inflicting injury directly, or (or in addition) render him impotent by exposing the inefficacy of bodily torture on the saint. The tortured subject is able to maintain control over the will by demonstrating just how little the body can be made to mean – and, in doing so, how much.

(EN)GENDERING SILENCE

The image of the apparatus of speech being forcibly suppressed is a shocking one – perhaps even dumbfounding – not least because, in demonstrating so unequivocally that speech has been made impossible, the held tongue or sealed lips obligate an audience to contemplate what utterance might otherwise be possible. Perhaps the most infamous episode of (female) tongue snipping in medieval literature is the tale of Philomela, a story that again evokes the illusory autonomy of the tongue and defiance in the face of its removal, with a return to expression that overturns the presumption that language may be reduced to the physical apparatus that produces it and supersedes the primacy of the tongue in a succession of unpredictable ways. The tale of Tereus, Procne and the ill-fated Philomela has fascinated poets from antiquity onwards. Though the myth is told by several classical Greek authors – among them Sophocles, Philocles and Aristophanes – it is perhaps most famously depicted in Latin in Ovid's *Metamorphoses*, from whence it was adopted by writers from Chrétien de Troyes (in his poem *Philomena*) to Shakespeare (whose *Titus Andronicus* represents one of the earliest of his frequent raids on Ovid).[17] As an exemplary tale, it also appears in Chaucer's

enact the painful price paid for that authority [...] St. Christine's cut-off tongue represents both the power and precariousness of female speech'. See Quilligan, *The Allegory of Female Authority: Christine de Pizan's* Cité des Dames (Ithaca, NY: Cornell University Press, 1991), pp. 213, 221. For Christine's retelling, see *The 'Livre de la Cité des Dames' of Christine de Pisan: A Critical Edition*, ed. Maureen C. Curnow, PhD diss. (Nashville: Vanderbilt University, 1975), p. 1009, or *The Book of the City of Ladies*, trans. Earl Jeffrey Richards (New York: Persea Books, 1982), pp. 239–40.

17 For a systematic exploration of different expressions of the legend found in the late medieval period to the Renaissance, see *Representing Rape in Medieval and Early Modern Literature*, ed. Elizabeth Ann Robertson and Christine M. Rose (New York and Basingstoke: Palgrave Macmillan, 2001). Four essays in this volume form a cohesive Philomela suite: 'Raping Men: What's Motherhood Got to Do With It?' by Jane E. Burns (pp. 127–60); 'The Daughter's Text and the Thread of Lineage in the Old French *Philomena*' by Nancy A. Jones (pp. 161–88); '"O, Keep Me From Their Worse

Legend of Good Women. However, it is the considerably longer version by his contemporary, John Gower, to which I turn first.

Gower's *Confessio Amantis* is a text that speaks with many voices. It survives in forty-nine complete or near-complete manuscripts to *Legend of Good Women*'s (still robust) twelve, and they vary considerably. Forty-one were known to Macaulay, editor of the EETS version that remained standard for many years (though he relied primarily on a single manuscript).[18] Much scholarly ink has been spilled on the subject of how best to date, classify and categorise: the use, appearance or absence of illustrations or Latin passages in the text form the basis of two taxonomies, but these are only the most readily observable differences. One of the principal distinctions is the perceived shift in political allegiance that separates 'Ricardian' versions of the text (inflected by praise of Richard II and some of which contain a claim to be written at his request) from revised 'Lancastrian' versions (celebrating Henry of Derby – later Henry IV). Macaulay argued that Gower issued three recensions of the text,[19] differing in their references not only to Richard and Henry but also to Chaucer (who is name-checked in earlier versions), although more recent scholarship has challenged some of Macaulay's premises.[20] Whatever the rationale, the need for revision reflects a complex text that, famously attempting to carve a 'middel weie' through the learned and the likeable in poetry, is poised between confession and consolation, history lesson and sermon, real life and mythic legends. By balancing 'lust' and 'lore', the poet hopes his book will find favour – 'That of the lasse or of the more / Som man mai lyke of that I wryte' (*CA* Prol. 17–21). In traversing this middle way, the structure of the *Confessio* takes both its protagonist – Amans, the lover – and its audience through an extended sequence of stories as Genius, the confessor, dispenses his wisdom. A repository of transgressions, grouped around the seven deadly sins – a guide showing what not to do – the tales that form the bulk of the *Confessio* combine to make up not only a sort of

Than Killing Lust": Ideologies of Rape and Mutilation in Chaucer's *Physician's Tale* and Shakespeare's *Titus Andronicus*' by Robin L. Bott (pp. 189–212); and 'Rape and the Appropriation of Progne's Revenge in Shakespeare's *Titus Andronicus*, Or, Who Cooks the Thyestean Banquet?' by Karen Robertson (pp. 213–40).

18 *The English Works of John Gower*, ed. G. C. Macaulay, 2 vols, EETS e.s. 81, 82 (Oxford: Oxford University Press, 1900–01). Subsequent quotations from *Confessio Amantis* (hereafter *CA*) will be taken from this version and cited in parentheses by book and line number.

19 See Macaulay, *English Works* vol. 1, pp. cxxviii–cxxxviii.

20 See, for example, Peter Nicholson, 'Gower's Revisions in the *Confessio Amantis*', *The Chaucer Review* 19 (1984), 123–43. Joyce Coleman has more recently looked at the issue of patronage in both Chaucer and Gower, arguing for the primacy of Gower's first, rather than third, recension. See '"A bok for king Richardes sake": Royal Patronage, the *Confessio*, and the *Legend of Good Women*' in *On John Gower: Essays at the Millennium*, ed. R. F. Yeager, Studies in Medieval Culture 46 (Kalamazoo, MI: Medieval Institute Publications, 2007), pp. 104–23.

erotic psychomachia but also a multi-layered, subtle text. In this simultaneous appraisal of national wellbeing and orchestration of the many voices in his work, tongues and their functions are as crucial to Gower as they are to the story of Philomela.

In contrast to his other major works, the *Mirour de l'Omne* and *Vox Clamantis* – written in French and Latin respectively – Gower chose English for the *Confessio*. The decision to write in the vernacular is one the Prologue takes up, famously explaining:

> for that fewe men endite
> In oure Englissh, I thenke make
> A bok for Engelondes sake (*CA* Prol. 22–4)

Woven through the text, however, there is also a series of glosses and headings in Latin, the poem's other tongue – though whether these tongues are harmonious or equivocal might be a matter for debate.[21] As Gower's own oeuvre underlines, the three languages of post-Conquest England might be used and interwoven to create a vast poetic resource, but equally significant was the oral culture that went with it. As the discourse on confession suggests, the regulation of speech was a subject for debate and concern, but while in liturgical situations emphasis was placed on the extraction of utterances, in social and legal contexts problematic speech and 'sins of the tongue' were liable to be suppressed.[22] In Gower's 'Tale of Tereus', however, this paradigm is dramatically overturned. The competing voices of the *Confessio* as a whole

[21] While the glosses might be seen as an authorising element, for some scholars they often do far more to destabilise the text, introducing, as Sîan Echard calls it, 'a cacophony of potentially authoritative voices'. Moreover, as Winthrop Wetherbee points out, while '[t]he inclusion of the Latin materials is sometimes treated as if it were an end in itself, Gower's way of advertising his poem as sufficiently substantial and learned to be worthy of learned exposition', their individual merit and usefulness to the reader varies wildly. 'The marginalia oscillate between the poles of authoritative commentary [...] and a dogged, schoolmasterly moralism, pompous and at times ludicrously irrelevant', while the 'disembodied voice of the head-verses' is often good only for 'gnomic pronouncements on love, virtue and vice, whose calculated ambiguity points up the complexities of Gower's treatment of human love'. See Echard, 'Glossing Gower: In Latin, in English, and *in absentia*: the Case of Bodleian Ashmole 35', in *Re-Visioning Gower*, ed. R. F. Yeager (Asheville, NC: Pegasus Press, 1998), pp. 237–56 (p. 239); Winthrop Wetherbee, 'Classical and Boethian Tradition in the *Confessio Amantis*', in *A Companion to Gower*, ed. Sîan Echard (Cambridge: D. S. Brewer, 2004), pp. 181–96 (p. 183). See also Kurt Olsson, 'Reading, Transgression, and Judgment: Gower's Case of Paris and Helen', in *Re-Visioning Gower*, ed. R. F. Yeager, pp. 67–92.

[22] Though actual removal of the tongue seems to have been rare, as Bardsley shows in her study of 'scolding', a gendered and 'highly adaptable' category that functioned as a catch-all crime for the outspoken, the vast majority of defendants were women (*Venomous Tongues*, p. 6). While late medieval punishments for women convicted of scolding were often humiliating, as in the case of the cucking stool, or costly (fines were most often levied), the infamous 'scold's bridle', which locked around the head and

are reflected again in this tale, where the Latin heading gives an incomplete version of events, leaving the way clear for the mother tongue to surpass the language of patriarchy in representing a tale of female silence. Though a prevailing misogyny is vigorously expressed in the retelling of the Philomela legend, the spectacle of the raped woman whose tongue is cut out precipitates both an unspeaking performance and unspeakable consequences.

The themes of Genius's exemplar of 'Ravine' (*CA* V. 5551–6052) are violence and silence, but the one does not achieve the other. The tragic, vengeance-packed and frequently disturbing tale tells of the Thracian king Tereus, his wife Procne and her sister Philomela. Married off to Tereus, Procne begins to pine for her younger sister, who is living with their father, Pandion of Athens. At his wife's request, Tereus journeys to Greece to fetch Philomela. Though Pandion and (in Gower's version) his wife are reluctant to let their daughter go, they entrust her to Tereus and the two return to Thrace. At this point, Tereus – hitherto presented (in the best courtly love tradition) as a 'worthi king of hih lignage, / A noble kniht eke of his hond' (*CA* V. 5566–7) – begins to deviate dramatically from the laudable mission he has undertaken for his lady, and finds himself instead lusting after her sister. Within the space of a few lines, the noble brother-in-law becomes a bestial attacker, falling from grace and abandoning his wedding vows in his sudden, overwhelming compulsion to ravish Philomela. He does so at the first opportunity, robbing her first of her virginity and then – upon her threat to reveal his crime – of her tongue, which he cuts out with a pair of shears. Not taking any chances, he then imprisons her and returns home to tell Procne her sister is dead.

Having thus recounted the first part of the story (covering the same ground as the Latin gloss, which abruptly skips to the *deus ex machina* after the rape scene), the second half of the (English) tale takes up the cause of the wounded, feminine parties, dealing with reaction, returns and revenge. If the set-up is grisly, the pay-off is even more so. The incarcerated Philomela prays to Jupiter for guidance and deliverance, and eventually hits on a plan to tell Procne of her imprisonment: she weaves a message into a silk tapestry, which she has a messenger deliver to her sister privately. Upon receiving it, Procne is first distraught and then incensed, swearing vengeance. She liberates Philomela, but her rage consumes her to such an extent that, in order to extract sufficient retribution, she forgets her womanly and maternal pity (as completely as Tereus abandoned his masculine chivalry) and slays her own son, and Tereus's heir, Itys. In a brutal twist, she cooks the boy in a stew she then serves to her husband. When Tereus discovers the fate of his heir, he attempts to kill both sisters; however, the gods intervene, transforming the trio into birds.

suppressed the tongue – sometimes with a metal barb in place to inflict pain in talking – was not introduced until the sixteenth century (pp. 142–4).

It is, as Genius's narration emphasises, significant that at the same point at which Philomela is raped and defiled sexually she is also defiled facially. Diane Watt observes that 'Tereus [...] render[s] Philomela the more impotent by denying her the only power that remains to her – the power of speech – in what amounts to no less than a symbolic castration'.[23] In the need to maintain Tereus's masculine identity, Philomela in her eloquent femininity is viciously silenced, and her hitherto inviolate body is left wordless, bleeding and lacking. As she languishes in her prison, she prays to Jupiter and wishes she had never been born. Yet, though her powers of physical speech have been removed, Philomela does not remain silent; it is precisely as she contemplates her soundless state and craves her sister's help – 'speaking' with her in her heart (*CA* V. 5758) – that she devises her alternative strategy.

If Foucault's claim in *The History of Sexuality* – that 'silence and secrecy are a shelter for power, anchoring its prohibitions' – appears to be at work here, then so too is his subsequent qualification that the same 'silence and secrecy [...] loosen its holds'.[24] Tereus's performative bodily inscription of unspeakability on Philomela fails to silence her. Although Gower does not include the passage from Ovid describing how Philomela's tongue, even after it is severed, continues to move, the failure of masculine control is implied nevertheless.[25] The reader instead hears the speech '[w]ithinne hir herte' (*CA* V. 5740), as Philomela, cast away and abjected in her prison, prays that Jupiter 'do vengance / And schape [hir] deliverance' (*CA* V. 5751–2). Derek Pearsall singles out this development of a 'mental reality', as opposed to Ovid's 'physical reality' as the area in which Gower improves most on his source material, his (in)famous morality making Ovid's version 'look like a high-powered shocker'.[26]

As well as an inner monologue, Philomela also has at her disposal another particularly feminine form of expression – she sends to Procne a 'tokninge' of her husband's crimes, a piece of silk on which they are embroidered '[w]ith lettres and ymagerie' (V. 5765, 5771). If the speech of her heart is audible only to the gods and the reader, this piece of needlework attests unspoken speech

23 Watt, *Amoral Gower*, p. 94.

24 Foucault, *The History of Sexuality I*, p. 101.

25
> radix micat ultima linguae,
> ipsa iacet terraeque tremens immurmurat atrae,
> utque salire solet mutilatae cauda colubrae,
> palpitat et moriens dominae vestigia quaerit. (VI. 557–60)

(The mangled root quivers, while the severed tongue lies palpitating on the dark earth, faintly murmuring; and, as the severed tail of a mangled snake is wont to writhe, it twitches convulsively, and with its dying movement it seeks its mistress's feet.)
Ovid, *Metamorphoses, Books I–VIII*, trans. Frank Justus Miller, Loeb Classical Library (London: William Heinemann, 1916); hereafter *Met.* Subsequent references will be given in parentheses by book and line number, with translations from the same volume.

26 Derek Pearsall, 'Gower's Narrative Art', *PMLA* 81.7 (1966), 475–84 (p. 478).

intelligible only to other women, perhaps especially aristocratic women.[27] However, Philomela's last bid to reassert herself proves that, in the masculine discourse of violence, actions speak louder than words: in the most eloquent but 'unspeakable' act of the story, when Tereus has finished gorging on Itys stew, '[t]o schewen him the child was ded, / This Philomene tok the hed / [...] And [sette] it upon the bord' (*CA* V. 5909–13).[28] Though the supposedly passive, suppressed Philomela cannot speak, through her performance of unspeakable modes of discourse, she never stops being heard. Her name – 'love of song' – prophetically pre-empts the compensation for her speechlessness, which comes in one last 'unspeakable' discourse, namely the meddled sorrow and mirth in the song of the nightingale she becomes (*CA* V. 5989–90).

Chaucer also puts his spin on the story in the *Legend of Good Women* (written *c.* 1380–87, probably before *Confessio*). The poem relates a dream vision in which the narrator is reproved by the God of Love and his queen, Alceste, for writing ill of women in his previous works. She singles out *Troilus and Criseyde* and Chaucer's translation of the *Roman de la Rose*, but lists others of his work besides; why can he not write well of women, as well as evilly? The narrator defends himself against charges of having committed crimes against love, and agrees to the poetic penance the queen suggests – the making of a glorious legend of good and true women. For all his ensuing praise for the virtues of his feminine exemplars, however we may take this, Chaucer's final prompt in the opening of the *Legend of Good Women* is none of these models but instead the God of Love, who instructs him, 'At Cleopatre I wol that thow begynne, / And so forth, and my love so shalt thow wynne' (*LGW* Prol. F 566–7; G 542–3). Though Alceste commissions the poem, the narrator's labour is performed to gain the God of Love's approval.[29]

27 On the link between embroidery and aristocratic women in medieval Europe, see Margaret Wade Labarge, 'Stitches in Time: Medieval Embroidery in its Social Setting', *Florilegium* 16 (1999), 77–96; Jane E. Burns, *Sea of Silk: A Textile Geography of Women's Work in Medieval French Literature* (Philadelphia, PA: University of Pennsylvania Press, 2009); Valerie L. Garver, *Women and Aristocratic Culture in the Carolingian World* (Ithaca, NY: Cornell University Press, 2012).

28 In contrast with Ovid's heroine, Gower's Philomela does not play a major role in the domestic at the end of the tale. She does not take part in the murder of Itys, despite the fact that Ovid hands her the final blow (*Met.* VI. 643–4); however, she still gets the final 'word'.

29 On the narrator's tense relationship with the God of Love and male homosocial desire as a key theme of the *Legend*, see R. Barton Palmer, 'Chaucer's *Legend of Good Women*: The Narrator's Tale', in *New Readings of Chaucer's Poetry*, ed. Robert G. Benson and Susan J. Ridyard (Cambridge: D. S. Brewer, 2003), pp. 183–94; Elaine Tuttle Hansen, 'The Feminization of Men in Chaucer's *Legend of Good Women*', in *Seeking the Woman in Late Medieval and Renaissance Writings*, ed. Sheila Fisher and Janet E. Halley (Knoxville, TN: University of Tennessee Press, 1989), pp. 51–70.

The legend of Philomela is the eighth of the ten heroines who made it into the unfinished poem (*LGW* VII. 2228–393).[30] It differs significantly from Gower's presentation, most obviously in the fact that it is much shorter (165 lines to Gower's 523); the *Legend of Good Women* has been called a 'performable' text, but Chaucer's version makes crucial omissions, stopping short of telling the whole tale.[31] A habit of the narrator for muffling or silencing women's voices is signalled in most of the tales in the *Legend of Good Women*, and indeed in the unfinished state of the manuscript (though it is hardly the only work Chaucer left uncompleted). Chaucer's frequent expressions of deference or inexpressibility have often been noted in the *Legend of Good Women*, where his instances of *occupatio* become progressively cruder, and his tendency to note that he will abbreviate for reasons of time or space eventually gives the impression, for some readers, that he is simply tiring of his subject. By the eighth tale, the narrator declares himself 'agroted' and resolves to henceforth 'passe shortly' (*LGW* VIII. 2454–8), but he has been doing so since the beginning. Cleopatra's 'routhe' is such that 'ther is tonge non that may it telle' (*LGW* I. 669–70); none could write Thisbe's 'dedly cheere' (*LGW* II. 869–70); it is impossible to tell Lucrece's woe (*LGW* V. 1839).

This tendency becomes especially noticeable when it comes to the women of the legends having their say, or even writing it down. Amanda Holton details the extent of Chaucer's 'swingeing cut', which sees Philomela speak only three lines.[32] Ariadne's vital advice to Theseus, regarding the thread, is capped with the somewhat irritable 'What sholde I lenger sarmoun of it make?' (*LGW* VI. 2025), and her tale is brought to a halt with the declaration that it is 'an hevy thing' that is, in any case, also told elsewhere (*LGW* VI. 2218–21). The letters of the legendary ten are habitually included, only to be impatiently abbreviated. Thus, while Chaucer includes ten lines for the beginning of Dido's

30 Geoffrey Chaucer, 'The Legend of Good Women', in *The Riverside Chaucer*, 3rd edn (Oxford: Oxford University Press, 1987), pp. 587–630; hereafter *LGW*. Subsequent references will be given in parentheses by line number. Although the prologue and ballade seem to indicate a wider project, and were apparently revised, only ten of the nineteen good women Chaucer names are dealt with. It has also been hypothesised that the work may have been completed but that part of it was lost. See M. C. Seymour, 'Chaucer's *Legend of Good Women*: Two Fallacies', in *The Review of English Studies* 37 (1986), 528–34; also Julia Boffey and A. S. G. Edwards, '*The Legend of Good Women*' in *The Cambridge Companion to Chaucer*, 2nd edn, ed. Piero Boitani and Jill Mann (Cambridge: Cambridge University Press, 2001), pp. 112–26 (pp. 113–14). Boffey and Edwards note that, given the wide variation in the surviving manuscript evidence as regards the number of 'good women', '[s]ome of the manuscripts suggest that the poem may have existed, or, at least, was once believed by Chaucer's near contemporaries to have existed, in a much fuller form at an early point in its textual history. If so, we can only speculate about what was lost' (p. 113).

31 See William A. Quinn, *Chaucer's Rehersynges: The Performability of the Legend of Good Women* (Washington, DC: Catholic University of America, 1994).

32 Amanda Holton, *The Sources of Chaucer's Poetics* (Aldershot: Ashgate, 2008), p. 50.

suicide note, he soon breaks off, with the narrator's direction for those who are concerned with the letter to 'Rede Ovyde, and in hym he shal it fynde' (*LGW* III. 1367). Hypsipyle's letter to her husband is paraphrased briefly (*LGW* IV. 1566–75), since it is 'to longe to wryten and to sen' (*LGW* IV. 1565); the same legend includes six lines of Medea's letter (*LGW* IV. 1672–7), as the rest is too long and can be read in Ovid (IV. 1678). Phyllis's letter is condensed to 'a word or tweyne' (*LGW* VIII. 2489), though ironically hers does get the fullest attention of the writings of the 'good women' (VIII. 2496–512). The narrator still cannot let it pass without mentioning his own intervention ('her and ther in rym I have it layd / There as me thoughte that she wel hath sayd', *LGW* VIII. 2516–17). The narrator does at times become 'wery' of some of his male protagonists, too – including Tereus (*LGW* VII. 2258) – but in these cases his concern for concision does not extend to such obtrusive remarks and is more in keeping with a focus on the good women, rather than the bad men.

One of the heftiest cuts in Chaucer's *Legend of Good Women* is to Philomela's story: while Tereus and Procne's marriage, the journey to Athens, paternal perspective (there is no mother mentioned here) and Philomela's ordeal are all accounted for, the legend stops short after Philomela is set free from her prison. There are clearly dire consequences brewing: although Chaucer allows the scene to fade on the reunited sisters weeping innocuously in each others' arms, Procne is hardly less angry when she receives the news than she is in Gower; she is, indeed, speechless with rage (*LGW* VII. 2374). Despite having left little about Philomela's rape to the imagination, Chaucer refuses to address the end of the tale, declaring that '[t]he remenaunt is no charge for to telle' (*LGW* VII. 2383).

Elsewhere, however, the Chaucerian version provides more detail, rather than less. The representation of gender roles is particularly interesting when compared with the episode in the *Confessio*. In common with Genius's narration, Chaucer has his Tereus 'caste his fyry herte upon [Philomela]' through his own agency (*LGW* VII. 2292).[33] His burgeoning desire is not that of a courtly lover ensnared against his will by the sudden emergence of a siren, rather it is his own hand 'casting' his heart, just as Genius makes the point of his Tereus that sets 'his oghne herte on fyre' (*CA* V. 5622). However, if this is something of a reversal of the typical male–female roles, the actions of Tereus and Philomela thereafter do more to reinforce the norm than to undercut it. Philomela's skill in weaving – a point picked up by Chrétien[34] – is

33 While Genius lays the blame squarely at Tereus's door, in Ovid, a combination of Philomela's wondrous looks and Tereus's 'Thracian' nature – an innate lust ('innata libido') – work to fire up his desire (*Met.* VI. 455–60).

34
Avuec c'iert si bone ovriere
D'ovrer une porpre vermoille
Qu'an tot le mont n'ot sa paroille.
Un diaspre ou un baudequin
Nes la mesniee Hellequin

highlighted again in Chaucer's tale, where the description of the needlework and equipment is more detailed than in Gower:

> This woful lady lerned hadde in youthe
> So that she werken and enbroude couthe,
> And weven in hire stol the radevore
> As it of wemen hath be woned yore.
> [...]
> She coude eek rede and wel ynow endyte,
> But with a penne coude she nat wryte.
> But letters can she weve to and fro,
> So that, by that the yer was al ago,
> She hadde ywoven in a stamyn large
> How she was brought from Athenes in a barge,
> And in a cave how that she was brought;
> And al the thyng that Tereus hath wrought,
> She waf it wel, and wrot the storye above,
> How she was served for hire systers love. (*LGW* VII. 2350–65)

Gower, by contrast, keeps it brief:

> Sche waf a cloth of Selk al whyt
> With lettres and ymagerie,
> In which was al the felonie
> Which Tereüs to hire hath do. (*CA* V. 5770–3)

Tereus, meanwhile, becomes hyper-masculine: his strength and might are emphasised (*LGW* VII. 2326), he is compared to the wolf or the eagle in the act of slaughter (*LGW* VII. 2318–19), while the chopping of the tongue is achieved with a phallic swipe of the sword.

The animalistic imagery used to describe Tereus appears again in Gower – in both cases, the particulars are drawn straight from Ovid – indeed, Gower takes the theme of metamorphosis further: in his version, the characters are undergoing subtle but dramatic changes well before the intervention of the gods. Watt argues for Genius's rejection of a construction of rape that is centred on the injury to patriarchal values – Gower does not include the passages in Ovid in which Philomela and then Procne reflect on the wrong done to their *father* by Tereus; in fact, he undercuts Pandion's original role with the addition of a royal mother[35] – choosing instead to 'reinstate women

> Seüst ele an un drap portreire.

(Also, she was so skilled a worker of red *poupre* that in all the world she had no equal. In *diaspre* or in *baudequin*, she could in cloth portray even the followers of Harlequin). *Philomena: Conté raconté d'après Ovide,* ed. C. de Boer (Paris: Librairie Paul Geuthner, 1909), vv. 188–93.

35 Ovid mentions only Pandion, whose solemn speechifying as Tereus makes ready to transport Philomela – asking him to watch over her and see to her safe return – reminds

as the real victims of rape, and to counter the misogyny so common in this sort of narrative'.[36] On this point, the *Legend of Good Women* makes much of the determination of its classical female examplaria to either preserve their maidenhead at all costs or to remain faithful and prefer death to taking a new lover (*LGW* Prol. G 289–95). Philomela and Lucrece, however, cannot claim this type of honour, having been deprived of sexual autonomy by their rapists.[37] Mary Flannery raises the disquieting question of whether 'female honour [may] exist securely in the same context with male honour, which is so often won and preserved through aggression?'.[38] In a similar vein, Christine Rose surveys the use of and erasure of rape in Chaucer's works, coming to the troubled conclusion that: 'The more I explore the alarming occurrence of rape and violence against women in his works, the more convinced I become that one of the solutions to the problem of "woman" as Chaucer explored it *was* rape.'[39]

The possibility that Chaucer himself could have been a rapist has caused consternation over the century and a half since the discovery of a record in the close rolls of 4 May 1380, in which Chaucer is named by Cecily Chaumpaigne in a release following a charge she describes as 'raptu meo'.[40] Complex explanations of the episode have been offered in the past, from those who maintain the word *raptus* must mean abduction, to those who insist it is certainly rape.[41] For the purposes of Chaucer's own approach to the *Legend*, it is worth dwelling on Christopher Cannon's reopening of the case, in which he reinvestigates the

his son-in-law of the contract not only between he and his wife, but with his wife's father as well (*Met.* VI. 496–501).

36 Watt, *Amoral Gower*, p. 91.

37 On Chaucer and the raped women of the *Legend*, see Corinne J. Saunders, 'Classical Paradigms of Rape in the Middle Ages: Lucretia and Philomela', in *Rape in Antiquity*, ed. Susan Deacy and Karen F. Pierce (London: Classical Press of Wales, 1997), pp. 243–66; Richard Ireland, 'Lucrece, Philomela (and Cecily): Chaucer and the Law of Rape', in *Crime and Punishment in the Middle Ages*, ed. T. S. Haskett (Victoria, BC: University of Victoria, 1998), pp. 37–61; Corinne J. Saunders, *Rape and Ravishment in the Literature of Medieval England* (Cambridge: D. S. Brewer, 2001), pp. 265–311.

38 Mary C. Flannery, 'A Bloody Shame: Chaucer's Honourable Women', *RES* 62 (2011), 337–57 (p. 357).

39 Christine M. Rose, 'Reading Chaucer, Reading Rape', in *Representing Rape*, ed. Robertson and Rose, pp. 21–60 (p. 34).

40 The release is first noted in F. J. Furnivall, 'Literary Gossip', *Athenæum*, 29 November 1873, 698–9. See *Chaucer Life-Records*, ed. Martin M. Crow and Clair C. Olson (Oxford: Clarendon Press, 1966), p. 343.

41 See P. R. Watts, 'The Strange Case of Geoffrey Chaucer and Cecilia Chaumpaigne', *Law Quarterly Review*, 63 (1947), 491–513; T. F. T. Plucknett, 'Chaucer's Escapade', *Law Quarterly Review* 64 (1948), 33–6; Paul F. Baum, *Chaucer: A Critical Appreciation* (Durham, NC: Duke University Press, 1958), p. 42; Donald R. Howard, *Chaucer: His Life, His Works, His World* (New York: Fawcett Columbine, 1989), p. 317; Derek Pearsall, *The Life of Geoffrey Chaucer: A Critical Biography* (Oxford: Blackwell, 1992), pp. 135–8.

context of this problematic document. Cannon's argument hinges on the discovery of the second record of this case, copied as a memorandum in the rolls of the Court of the King's Bench, which would be on view more often than the entry in the close rolls.[42] Cannon points out that the word *raptus* is not only ambiguous in its meaning, but extremely rare in the formulaic language of the rolls records.[43] Its appearance should therefore give readers pause, despite the disagreements as to its connotation. This caution is borne out by the composition of the King's Bench record – where the word *raptus* is no longer included, conspicuous in its absence. As a term it is not to be glossed over but is, argues Cannon, 'so bold that three days later, whether by coercion, persuasion, or some more complicated manipulation in the court of the king, this strong word – this mention of rape – had to be quietly, but emphatically, retracted'.[44] If Cecily Chaumpaigne's injury was not an unspeakable crime, it seems to be one that should nevertheless not be mentioned.

While Chaucer evokes conventional sympathy for virginal Philomela's assault, and by changing the ending ensures she remains a 'good woman' rather than an accomplice to child murder, Gower's account of Tereus's crime engages with its challenges to masculinity, rather than femininity. Here the narrative exposes not a simple contrast between violated feminine virtue and unambiguous, controlling virility, but rather the boundary-crossing excess of rape. It is this (especially in contrast with the purity of the victim here), as much as its violence that makes it abhorrent, and as such rape does not only lead to a final, mythical metamorphosis, but effects just as dramatic a transformation of the very gender boundaries it would seem to underpin. The exceeding of gender boundaries may engender unspeakable actions – rape, incest, infanticide – but these actions also destabilise gender itself. Tereus's identity is in crisis throughout the text. Besides being described first in courtly terms (as a knight), then in bestial ones, and finally as a kind of stooge to the sisters' perverted course of justice – jumping up from the table and chasing them with a sword when he realises what has happened – the brute force of his masculinity seems to be diminished, not galvanised, by the act of rape. Where Philomela is thoroughly overwhelmed by his strength before the attack occurs, being of 'to litel myht' to fend him off (*CA* V. 5637), when Tereus forces her to the ground again in preparation for her glossectomy, the narrator notes disparagingly that it is 'a fieble dede of armes' (V. 5688). He even pulls her hair (V. 5686) and, interestingly, the tongue is not slashed with a sword (as in Chaucer), but snipped out with a pair of 'scheres' – the implement of tailors, barbers and seamstresses (V. 5690–1).

42 Christopher Cannon, '*Raptus* in the Chaumpaigne Release and a Newly Discovered Document Concerning the Life of Geoffrey Chaucer', *Speculum* 68.1 (1993), 74–94.

43 Cannon, '*Raptus* and the Chaumpaigne Release', p. 77.

44 Cannon, '*Raptus* in the Chaumpaigne Release', p. 94.

However, it is the ground Chaucer does not care to tread that proves most fertile for Gower's critique of rape. Carolyn Dinshaw looks at the divergences in Chaucer from the Ovidian sources in terms of 'narrative origins', the knowledge of which is 'denied the female because such knowledge is potentially disruptive of linear masculine order [...] the silenced woman's story remains between the two sisters, in prison, weeping in each other's arms'.[45] The spectre of infanticide appears to be a problem for Chaucer: it arises not only in the tale of Philomela but in the omission of both Philomela and Medea from the narrator's roster of 'good women' in the Balade (*LGW* Prol. 247–69).[46] Sheila Delany remarks that, in deliberately leaving out 'the one thing Medea is best known for', Chaucer makes this event 'as conspicuous in absence as it could be in presence, surely a deliberate cliff-hanger'.[47] In like manner, the curtailing of Philomela's story and Procne's revenge is one of the most significant abridgements in a work full of prominent omissions, and as Amanda Holton points out, Chaucer's expurgated version of this well-known tale will fool no one.[48] It is certainly interesting to consider that this may be part of the point. For Chaucer, it would seem, some things are indeed unspeakable.

In Gower's judicious treatment of the revenge scenario Chaucer omits, however, he takes full advantage of the opportunity to exploit the tale's shifting balance of power and unstable gender paradigms. Instead of letting the curtain fall on a tableau of sisterly sobbing, Gower takes on the climactic finale of infanticide, cannibalism and metamorphosis.[49] Juxtaposed with the effeminate tyrant is the virago mother. While her husband's dissipated lust unmans him, Procne's unconstrained (blood-)lust 'un-womans' her. Forgetting 'insihte of moderhede', she is ruthless in the execution of her revenge (*CA* V. 5891–7), and her impassioned condemnation of Tereus takes no prisoners: 'of thi dede', she tells him, 'The world schal evere singe and rede / In remembrance of thi defame' (*CA* V. 5923–5). Even after her transformation into a swallow, she continues to rail against the crimes of false men, and Tereus in particular

45 Dinshaw, *Chaucer's Sexual Poetics*, p. 81.

46 The other subjects of the legends are included: Cleopatre (Prol. 259), Thisbe (261), Dido (263), Hypsipyle (266), Lucrece (257), Ariadne (268), Phyllis (264), Hypermnestra (268). On the medieval responses to and adaptations of the Medea legend, see Ruth Morse, *The Medieval Medea* (Cambridge: D. S. Brewer, 1996).

47 Sheila Delany, *The Naked Text: Chaucer's Legend of Good Women* (Berkeley, CA: University of California Press, 1994), p. 200. Delany notes Christine de Pizan's similar treatment of Medea (p. 99).

48 Holton, *Chaucer's Poetics*, p. 15. On the rewritten ending, see also Gila Aloni, 'Palimpsestic Philomela: Reinscription in Chaucer's "Legend of Philomela"', in *Palimpsests and the Literary Imagination of Medieval England*, ed. Leo Carruthers, Raeleen Chai-Elsholz and Tatjana Silec (New York: Palgrave Macmillan, 2011), pp. 157–73.

49 On cannibalism in medieval literature, see Heather Blurton, *Cannibalism in High Medieval English Literature: Conquest and Identity in High Medieval England* (Basingstoke: Palgrave Macmillan, 2007).

(V. 6011–22). While the virile Procne achieves a comprehensive (though arguably pyrrhic) victory, Tereus ends up the victim of his own transgressive actions. The wounded woman who is the sign of his disintegrating manhood may be silent and enclosed, but Tereus cannot shut her up.

DISPLACED TONGUES

Tongueless in her prison, Philomela's isolation would seem complete. Not only has her potentially damaging speech been (literally) cut off, foreclosed, but she herself becomes cut off from her sister, her family, the outside world – enclosed in a cell where all she can do is sew and pray. Her absent tongue, however, continues to wag as surely as it does when it wriggles on the ground at her feet: while her physical tongue is no longer resident in her mouth, her speech – her other 'tongue' – though it does not pass through her lips, nevertheless escapes the narrow confines of her body, her prison and her enclosure. Like the executioners of tongues imagined in penitential literature, Tereus locates expression exclusively in the tongue, an oversight that is compounded throughout the remainder of the narrative. Of yet another omission in the *Legend of Good Women* – this time of Philomela's threats to expose her rapist – Corinne Saunders remarks that 'For Chaucer, the silencing of Philomela has already occurred in Tereus' action.'[50] In Gower, however, Philomela throws out her accusation – or her confession – into the world, from the folk in the country to the gods in heaven, just as she threatened she would do after Tereus's attack, in spite of the fact that Tereus took her at her own suggestion and clapped her in a cell, 'withinne wall / Of Stones closed' (*CA* V. 5665–6). In one way or another, she continues to speak to audiences both seen and unseen: to Jupiter, to whom she prays silently (*CA* V. 5741–52); to Procne, who receives the coded message in her embroidery; to the messenger, to whom somehow she communicates her wish to send her sister the cloth (V. 5777–81); and finally to Tereus, who cannot fail to read his rout in the ghastly token Philomela tosses onto the table (V. 5909–13).

To this list, there is another audience to add, namely the reading (or listening) audience, which through the poet-narrator – Genius shriving Amans, or Gower addressing his literary following – is privy to Philomela's inner monologue, and can hear how '[h]ire herte spekth' (*CA* V. 5758). Before Philomela hits on the idea of sewing her way to salvation, it is her inward thoughts that supply the place of her speaking voice: the premeditated substitution of the needlework for her utterance comes only after her instinctive substitution of her 'herte' for her tongue. Indeed, even her final speech to Tereus before the cutting of her tongue is uttered '[w]ith wofull herte' (*CA* V. 5654). These exchanges form a theme that runs through the text; not only

50 Saunders, 'Classical Paradigms of Rape', p. 261.

do they permit Philomela to broadcast her indictment of Tereus, but they also situate both his crime and the crime that follows in a broader context of symbolic violence, bloodlines and blood rites.[51]

From the moment Tereus cuts away Philomela's tongue, its role is taken up by a series of body doubles and stand-ins. The same tongue is associated with a variety of other body parts belonging to both Philomela and Tereus, starting with the site of Philomela's other injury – her violated maidenhead. Philomela herself draws attention to the parallels between her concurrent injuries, when she laments her losses in her prayers to Jupiter:

> I wolde I hadde noght be bore,
> For thanne I hadde noght forlore
> Mi speche and mi virginité. (*CA* V. 5747–9)

The loss of her tongue and her powers of speech are yoked with the equally grievous loss of her virginity, vital to her elite status as much as her sense of self. In Ovid's *Metamorphoses*, this rupture also threatens to have severe consequences for Philomela's relationship with her sister, to whom she is so devoted but whose marriage she has now (however unwillingly) encroached upon. By raping Philomela, Tereus also commits incest. In the Ovidian original, Philomela's grief and outrage is as much for her family as for herself:

> lugenti similis caesis plangore lacertis
> intendens palmas 'o diris barbare factis,
> o crudelis' ait, 'nec te mandata parentis
> cum lacrimis movere piis nec cura sororis
> nec mea virginitas nec coniugialia iura?
> omnia turbasti; paelex ego facta sororis,
> tu geminus coniunx, hostis mihi debita Procne!'

> like one in mourning, beating and tearing her arms, with outstretched hands she cried: 'Oh, what a horrible thing you have done, barbarous, cruel wretch! Do you care nothing for my father's injunctions, his affectionate tears, my sister's love, my own virginity, the bonds of wedlock? You have confused all natural

51 Peggy McCracken, 'Engendering Sacrifice: Blood, Lineage, and Infanticide in Old French Literature', *Speculum* 77.1 (2002), 55–75, looks at the spilling of blood in Chrétian's version of the legend, evaluating this act of symbolic bloodletting in the tradition of sacrifice. She argues for an ethics of sacrificial bloodshed that diverges along gendered lines:

> Medieval narratives about sacrifice suggest that [...] the relationship of the sacrificer to the offering symbolically genders the blood of sacrifice. Blood shed by the father is paternal blood – it demonstrates lineage and loyalty between men or between men and God [...] The blood shed by the mother is maternal blood; it recalls menstruation and the blood of parturition. It is then, in many medieval discourses, a polluting blood, a blood that cannot serve a higher good. Mother's blood, blood shed by a mother, is not sacrificial blood, and a mother's murder of her child can only be explained as a demonic act of vengeance. (p. 74)

> relations: I have become a concubine, my sister's rival; you, a husband to both. Now Procne must be my enemy.' (*Met.* VI. 532–8).

In reminding Tereus of the extent to which he has abused the trust of both his wife and father-in-law, Philomela seems to indict herself as well for having been the other party in Tereus's adultery. Not only has Tereus deprived her of her virginity, he has also forced her into a position where she might find herself cast out from her sister's affections, too. Her hitherto secure identity suddenly becomes unstable and ill-defined – although she sends her woven message to her sister, she appears to anticipate rage as well as a rescue: even when the anguished Procne bursts into her prison to liberate her, Philomela is 'unable / to look her straight in the eyes' (non attollere contra sustinet haec oculos, *Met.* VI. 605–6). It is not simply because her tongue has been cut out that she imagines that she will not be able to speak with her sister, but because she has been (repeatedly and incestuously) raped.

Gower does not include this apprehension. Though taken as one of the worst forms of lust, and thoroughly unnatural, incest is not unmentionable in the way that sodomy or (for Chaucer) infanticide is.[52] Whereas modern narratives emphasise the trauma and the difficulties of representation presented by cases of incest, later medieval texts, on the other hand, do not appear to struggle with the expression of incest in the same way.[53] Royal marriages were not infrequently within the degrees of consanguinity (even after the degrees of permitted kinship were reduced in the canons of Lateran IV), and near-incest is a popular motif among medieval writers, as Elizabeth Archibald points out. Moreover, 'incest, as a particularly heinous form of lust, offered a splendid opportunity for propaganda about contrition and penance as the roads to salvation'.[54] Despite the distress about incest, adultery and fornication that Ovid's Philomela suffers, Gower's heroine is never in doubt of her sister, itself unusual in the *Confessio*.[55] Philomela's shame is still present, however, as shown at the end of the tale when, as a bird, she hides herself away to conceal her despoiled 'maidenhiede' and contemplates her former 'wommanhiede'

52 Elizabeth Archibald observes that incest is only just below the 'unspeakable' sin in taxonomies such as *The Book of Vices and Virtues*; Chaucer's Pardoner includes it between fornication and sodomy. See '"Worse Than Bogery": Incest Stories in Middle English Literature', in *Incest and the Medieval Imagination*, ed. Elizabeth Barnes (Oxford: Clarendon Press, 2001), pp. 17–38 (p. 40).

53 See *Incest and the Literary Imagination*, ed. Elizabeth Barnes (Gainesville, FL: University Press of Florida, 2002), pp. 2–3.

54 Elizabeth Archibald, 'Incest in Medieval Literature and Society', *Forum for Modern Language Studies*, 25.1 (1989), 1–15 (p. 2). See also Archibald, '"Worse Than Bogery"', pp. 17–38.

55 Watt compares this episode with others in the *Confessio Amantis*, particularly the tale of Jason and Medea also found in Book V, noting that the concept of 'sosterhode' is usually invoked ironically by Gower (Watt, *Amoral Gower*, pp. 94–5).

(*CA* V. 5955–6). The humiliated 'blushes' of the red-cheeked nightingale serve as the lasting sign of her previous debasement, while her identity crisis continues – she is neither bird, nor woman, and incontrovertibly 'ne [...] yit a maide', as her perpetual song sighs (*CA* V. 5979).

By contrast, the slicing of her tongue is partly resolved in her avian state – the nightingale's song takes the place of her human voice. However, the Philomela-nightingale's tongue is not straightforwardly restorative: as a bird she can once again talk, but though she makes good on her promise to tell of her violation, she can only confirm that she is indeed bereft of 'such thing as men sein / mai neveremor be yolde agein' (*CA* V. 5647–8). Tereus takes away Philomela's power to assert herself through language at the same time as he takes away her maiden status – she is damaged goods, neither married nor marriageable, and her chances of improving her situation are further reduced by her mutilation and imprisonment. Taken out of the marriage and family equation (symbolically castrated, as Watt puts it), her circumstances prefigure those of Tereus, whose dynasty is ended with the murder of Itys – a decapitation in place of castration, but which effectively performs the same function.

This concept is of course borrowed from Hélène Cixous, who argues that the effects of castration anxiety in a masculine-ordered social structure are revisited on its women in a particular form, which she figures as a threat of decapitation. For Cixous, this figurative decapitation is both precluded by and refigured as unspeaking compliance:

> [I]f [women] don't actually lose their heads by the sword, *they may only keep them on condition that they lose them* – lose them, that is, to complete silence [...] If man operates under the threat of castration, if masculinity is culturally ordered by the castration complex, it might be said that the backlash, the return, on women of this castration anxiety is its displacement as decapitation, of woman, as loss of her head.[56]

Though Cixous – if she is thinking of literal decapitation – is not thinking of the punishments of the Middle Ages, the stifling of female speech – the loss of a female 'head' to masculine law – may truly be reckoned a symbolic decapitation. However, in this story the dismemberments are at one anatomical remove: Philomela loses not her head but her tongue, and Tereus, to whom revenge is a dish served stewed, loses not his member but his progeny. In Tereus's case, his 'symbolic castration' is nonetheless achieved: the sign of his dynasty and his masculinity is annihilated. As Carolyn Dinshaw puts it, by feeding him his heir, Procne 'makes him literally reinforce his self, his physical being – in the same act as that in which he destroys that flesh and blood'.[57] Itys's death thus represents both the tearing of Tereus's 'own flesh' – the loss

56 Hélène Cixous, 'Castration or Decapitation?', *Signs: Journal of Women in Culture and Society* 7 (1981), 41–55 (p. 43, original emphasis).

57 Carolyn Dinshaw, 'Rivalry, Rape, and Manhood: Chaucer and Gower', in *Violence*

of his 'own' head – and the end of his bloodline. Burns further points out of the Old French version that, although Procne's reinscription of power and gender relations does destroy a part of herself, 'in killing Tereus's son [she] also kills the fetishized phallus, redefining the child as hers to both produce and destroy'.[58] Indeed, in Ovid, Procne's frenzied thought processes when planning her husband's just deserts run rapidly through the possibilities of burning Tereus in his palace, cutting out *his* tongue (and eyes), and finally emasculation (*Met.* VI. 615–17). The murder and cooking of Itys, however, manages to combine the regicidal element of the first option with the latter themes of mutilation and castration. To this buffet of vengeance, Gower adds one more proof of the twisted perfection of Procne's choice: the consumption of human flesh is as perverse and unnatural – 'agein kinde' – as Tereus's rape of his own sister-in-law (*CA* V. 5905–6).

Tereus is thus made less than natural, less than a king, less than a man. Grabbing his sword when he realises his unwitting self-destruction (*CA* V. 5930) does him no good; the matter is long since out of his hands and in those of the two women, who engineered his downfall and who now 'unto the goddes crie' (V. 5932), invoking their earlier prayers to Venus, Apollo and Jupiter. Having consumed his flesh and blood moments before, his last remaining resort is unceremoniously cut off by the intervention of the gods, who transform him into a bird. Deprived of his bloodline – and in Lacanian terms his phallus – he is denied even his capacity to wield phallic weaponry, castrated twice over.

If Tereus ultimately falls foul of the same symbolic violence he inflicts on Philomela, she herself refuses to surrender her will – her 'head' – to the bloody economy that has taken her tongue. Though she is mute and mutilated, she does not consent to quiet her vengeful thoughts, whatever her tongue might (not) say. From the first lines after her ordeal, despite having plunged from her exalted royal position to the abject misery and isolation of her new accommodations, Gower has her remaining philosophical:

> Whan sche cam into prison ferst,
> It thoghte a kinges douhter strange
> To maken so soudein a change
> Fro welthe unto so grete a wo. (*CA* V. 5734–7)

Subdued as she is, her focus does not waver from the course of action she spelled out to Tereus; instead, she starts to engineer her 'comeback', working on two fronts – first praying to Jupiter, then contemplating how to send a message to Procne. Her tongueless silence is overcome in the appropriation of

Against Women in Medieval Texts, ed. Anna Roberts (Gainesville, FL: University Press of Florida, 1998) pp. 137–60 (pp. 145–6).

58 Jane E. Burns, *Bodytalk: When Women Talk in Old French Literature* (Philadelphia, PA: University of Pennsylvania Press, 1993), p. 143

a series of prostheses and mouthpieces – her heart; her needlework; Procne's outspoken outrage; Itys's silent, accusatory head. In the symbolic economy to which a silent woman should have no access, the stroke that removes Itys's head both unmans and 'beheads' Tereus (whom Itys so resembles).[59] Though Philomela loses her tongue, she keeps her head.

SEWING DISORDER – UNSPEAKABLE CRIMES AND BLIND PASSION

If the way around speechlessness is to be found in this alternative kind of 'writing', Philomela's tongue might be most powerfully substituted when its task is taken up by her needle. Luce Irigaray, discussing how discourses might be gendered and productively contrasted – even revolutionised – comments that, as long as political and philosophical discourses are classically the preserve of the masculine, 'women are left the so-called minor arts: cooking, knitting, embroidery, and sewing; and, in exceptional cases, poetry, painting, and music. Whatever their importance, these arts do not currently make the rules, at least not overtly.'[60] Her call for a radical overhaul of the ways in which sexual difference relates to these arts provides a useful point of departure for thinking through the unpredictable denouement of Philomela's narrative. While masculine silencing at first seems to dictate the situation, it is (if not entirely overturned) severely disrupted by the 'minor arts' employed by the two sisters – rewriting the rules by sewing and cooking.

Thus Philomela, unable to recount the unspeakable, represents it instead, stitching together to tell of what has been torn asunder. The account of this woven message is given slightly differently depending on which source is being consulted: the exact style of Philomela's communication is not uniform. While Ovid and Chaucer describe the embroidery as script – although the Latin *notas* might also mean signs, marks, tokens – Chrétien depicts it as a pictographic scene (Karen Casebier notes that he uses the verb *escrire*, connoting painting or drawing, for Philomena's actions, as well as detailing the colours of the threads, 'evok[ing] an embroidered picture').[61] Gower, meanwhile, covers himself both ways with 'lettres and ymagerie'. However, the interpretation of this textile-text-tableau *is* universally represented: Procne realises the truth as soon as she lays eyes on it. Though there is an implication that Philomela is literate or can at least read (as in Chaucer, *LGW* VII. 2356–7), the emphasis is on the fact of Procne's *seeing* the cloth, rather than reading it. Gower and Chaucer phrase the episode in almost exactly the same way, in fact, both using

59 'A! Quam / Es similis patri!' ('Ah! How like your father you are!' *Met.* VI. 621–2).

60 Luce Irigaray, 'Sexual Difference', in *An Ethics of Sexual Difference*, trans. Carolyn Burke and Gillian C. Gill (New York: Continuum, 2005), pp. 7–19 (p. 8).

61 Karen Casebier, 'Ovid's Medieval Metamorphosis: Techniques of Persuasion in Chrétien de Troyes' *Philomena*', *Philological Quarterly* 80.4 (2001), 441–65 (p. 449).

the word 'beheld' to describe how Procne sees and understands almost simultaneously (*CA* V. 5791; *LGW* VII. 2373). The woven message communicates visually what cannot be said in words. Indeed, Procne herself is struck dumb by its contents in both Chaucer (*LGW* VII. 2374) and Ovid (*Met.* VI. 583–5). Sight here both supplies the place of speech and takes it away.[62]

This synaesthetic understanding of the 'text' acts to subvert and in one sense negate Tereus's actions. Weaving, when cast as an archetypal female occupation, is positioned as the counterpart to the war and war games of men.[63] The working of tapestry and embroidery, in particular, is also an indicator of Philomela's aristocratic class and personal accomplishment, and it is crucially not only a solitary activity but one that brings in, connects to, incorporates other women: the drawing together of the threads holds a significance in itself, beyond the images that may be picked out in the threads, as Patricia Klindienst observes. Philomela weaves not only to express her suffering, but 'to speak to and be heard by her sister [...] [weaving] re-members or mends what violence tears apart: the bond between the sisters, the woman's power to speak, a form of community and communication'.[64] It is a particularly feminine form of expression that Tereus fails to anticipate: as Cixous's insistent characterisation suggests, 'a feminine text [that] can't be predicted, isn't predictable, isn't knowable and is therefore very disturbing [...] femininity is written outside anticipation: it really is the text of the unforeseeable'.[65]

62 Casebier remarks that this impression is made with particular emphasis in *Philomena*: 'The *Metamorphoses* further support this conclusion [that Ovid uses *notas* to mean letters or script] by informing the reader that Procne will actually read the tapestry's "inscription" and understand it ("carmen miserabile legit / Et [mirum potuisse!] silet" [6.582–3]). In comparison, Chrétien's queen merely looks at and comprehends the work ("Si la regarde et conut l'uoevre" [1237]).' Casebier, 'Ovid's Medieval Metamorphosis', p. 449.

63 Carolyn Dinshaw draws out the threads in the *Legend of Good Women*, comparing Philomela to the equally unfortunate and abandoned Ariadne, the subject of the preceding narrative in Chaucer (*LGW*, VI. 1886–2227): 'Ariadne's "thred" [...] becomes, in the next legend, Philomela's "cloth." The *Legend of Ariadne* parabolically articulates principles of a male-centered tradition as it shows the appropriation of the truth of the text and demonstrates the necessary separation of women from each other. The *Legend of Philomela* elaborates on these patriarchal literary techniques. Philomela is a prime example of a woman denied the "proper" means of making meaning, signifying: Ariadne wanders around the island, able only to produce an echo from the hollow rocks, but Philomela's very *glossa* is removed by Tereus.' Dinshaw, *Chaucer's Sexual Poetics*, pp. 80–1. The difference here, of course, is that Ariadne is deserted by her sister; Phedra is not at hand to receive any kind of message, woven or otherwise, and indeed participates in her sister's betrayal.

64 Patricia Klindienst, 'The Voice of the Shuttle is Ours', in Lynn A. Higgins and Brenda R. Silver, *Rape and Representation* (New York: Columbia University Press, 1991), pp. 35–64 (p. 51).

65 Hélène Cixous, 'Castration or Decapitation?', *Signs: Journal of Women in Culture and Society* 7 (1981), p. 53.

It is in Cixous's 'The Laugh of the Medusa', her 'classic (wo)manifesto', that she first sets out the parameters of women's writing, or rather the parameters that must be transgressed, burst open, 'flown' through.[66] The conventional strictures of language – the lack, the substitutions found in the Lacanian symbolic – are to be overwritten by a text that evades and transcends signs, relocating speech and writing back in the body. As Cixous puts it, '[t]heir 'symbolic' exists, it holds power – we, the sowers of disorder, know it only too well. But we are in no way obliged to deposit our lives in their banks of lack.'[67] Overhauling conventional expectation, the fabric-ation of alternative signifiers reinterprets the traditional tools of the spinster (or the medieval aristocratic embroiderer) – the needle becomes a pen mightier than a sword.

A 'sew-er' of disorder, Philomela takes up her thread in the *Confessio* (and in Ovid) in order to fashion her own symbolic breakthrough, and her woven message creates an unexpected, unforeseeable text. This idea of the *unseen* and *unforeseen* has particular force in the *Metamorphoses*, where significantly more is made of the distinction between what people can and cannot see. All three main protagonists, in fact, are described as seeing imperfectly – 'what blind night rules in the hearts of men!' (quantum mortalia pectora caecae / noctis habent!, *Met.* VI. 472–3) the narrator laments as Tereus sets about his duplicitous seduction – and their vision becomes more impaired as the narrative goes on, just as it was foretold. As Tereus's obsession with Philomela grows, he not only becomes fixated with her every feature and motion but 'pictures at will what he has not yet seen' (fingit, quae nondum vidit, *Met.* VI. 492). Later, Philomela's inability to 'lift her eyes' (sustinet haec oculos, *Met.* VI. 606) to look her sister in the face is inverted in Procne's calculating look at Itys. She 'regard[s] him with pitiless eyes' (oculisque tuens immitibus, *Met.* VI. 621) as she cooks up her revenge – she turns her eyes to her wronged sister when she begins to experience maternal qualms about killing the boy, and when she looks at her son she sees only Tereus's punishment. Finally, when Tereus munches on his meal, it is 'in the utter blindness of his understanding' (tantaque nox animi est, *Met.* VI. 652) that he calls, with gruesome irony, for Itys to be brought to him. Even the gods seem to be having problems with their eyes – Philomela's last utterance before the loss of her tongue is to swear he will suffer retribution, 'if those who dwell on high see these things' (si tamen haec superi cernunt, *Met.* VI. 542). Blind lust leads Tereus to his unspeakable crime, but the aftershock of Philomela's speechlessness threatens to render everyone blind.

[66] Sandra M. Gilbert, 'Introduction: A Tarantella of Theory', in Hélène Cixous and Catherine Clément, *The Newly Born Woman*, trans. Betsy Wing (London and New York: I B Tauris, 1996), pp. ix–xviii (p. x).

[67] Hélène Cixous, 'The Laugh of the Medusa', trans. Keith Cohen and Paula Cohen, *Signs: Journal of Women in Culture and Society*, 1.4 (1976), 875–93 (p. 884).

The connection between a severed tongue and blindness – reminiscent of Christina's passion, as discussed at the beginning of this chapter – also recalls the *imagos* of the Lacanian *corps morcelé*, representing 'the elective vectors of aggressive intentions [...] castration, mutilation, dismemberment, dislocation, evisceration, devouring, bursting open of the body' in which the synthesised, specular entity of the *Gestalt* cannot be recognised.[68] The dismembered body has the potential to dismember those who look on it, break them down, siphon away their power, and even figuratively castrate them. Without the 'pure mirror of an unruffled surface' with which to identify,[69] the interruption in the *Gestalt* represented by the *corps morcelé* threatens the subject's illusion of unity; bringing the subject into relation with the other, however, marks the entry into the symbolic order that governs language. Such is not the case in Cixous. Breaking *out* of the symbolic, into a female voice independent of the 'discourse of man', requires these crises of dismemberment not to be resolved and brought under control, but embraced and promoted:

> If woman has always functioned 'within' the discourse of man, a signifier that has always referred back to the opposite signifier which annihilates its specific energy and diminishes or stifles its very different sounds, it is time for her to dislocate this 'within,' to explode it, turn it around, and seize it; to make it hers, containing it, taking it in her own mouth, biting that tongue with her very own teeth to invent for herself a language to get inside of.[70]

Evading the symbolic, spitting out its 'tongue', Christina-like, and thereby escaping the site of silence, the '"repressed" of [...] culture' perform their fragmentation, dismemberment and upheaval in order to stage 'an explosive, *utterly* destructive, staggering return'.[71]

Cixous's outline of a female textual discourse, an écriture feminine, is relevant here (despite the passing decades) as it relocates the text away from linearity, closure, concern with origin. It is one capable of finding new modes

68 Jacques Lacan, 'Aggressivity in Psychoanalysis', in *Écrits*, pp. 9–32 (p. 13).

69 Lacan, 'Aggressivity in Psychoanalysis', in *Écrits*, p. 17.

70 Cixous, 'The Laugh of the Medusa', p. 887.

71 Cixous, 'The Laugh of the Medusa', p. 886 (original emphasis). Judith Butler looks at the success of sexual difference as a strategy in her essay 'The End of Sexual Difference?' in *Undoing Gender* (New York and London: Routledge, 2004), pp. 174–203. Reviewing the shape of feminism at the turn of the millennium, she finds 'zones of contestation [...] questions about what woman is, how we are to say "we,?" who is to say it and in the name of whom?' (p. 175). Though she observes that '[i]t seems that feminism is in a mess, unable to stabilize the terms that facilitate a meaningful agenda' (p. 175), she does not intend (as her title might imply) to declare sexual difference therefore finished, but rather explore the idea that '[s]exual difference is not a given [...] it is not that which we have already encountered and come to know; rather, as *a question* that prompts feminist inquiry, it is something that cannot quite be stated, that troubles the grammar of the statement, and that remains, more or less permanently, to interrogate' (p. 178).

of expression, 'inventing forms for women on the march [...] "in flight"'.[72] The metaphor of flight is one that begins with 'The Laugh of the Medusa', where Cixous declares that 'Flying is woman's gesture [...] It's no accident that *voler* [to fly; to steal] has a double meaning, that it plays on each of them and thus throws off the agents of sense.'[73] A 'woman-text' need not necessarily be one written by a woman (Cixous cites James Joyce's *Ulysses* as an exemplar),[74] nor is it necessarily readable only by women. It is perhaps significant that the turning point of Philomela's tale comes when she entrusts her woven SOS to a male messenger who is unaware '[w]hat it amonteth' (*CA* V. 5778). We never learn where he appears from or how she conveys the recipient without benefit of a tongue (or, apparently, any means of communication other than needlework). How, indeed, would the courier understand sewn speech designed to be read only by another woman? While Chaucer elaborates a little on Philomela's directions to a knave (though only to the extent that she conveys 'by signes', *LGW* VII. 2367), Gower's messenger appears from nowhere, knows nothing of the cloth save its destination, and disappears into the ether 'riht as he cam' five lines after his debut (*CA* V. 5781). And yet he is the vital link between the unspeakable act on an unspeaking princess and its acknowledgement and response in Philomela's speaking (and equally 'unspeakable') correspondent. He joins one language – the audible one from which Philomela has been cut off – to another: the spectacle of the cloth that Procne will read. At one level, he is a writerly convenience – barely more than a sign himself. At another, he articulates and translates two deeply gendered and deeply hostile speakers and languages, understanding 'speech' he cannot hear even though his gender seems to preclude his doing this in the logic of the narrative before simply disappearing at the end of this impossible negotiation – and of course, we never hear him speak.

In order to break out of silence, to make a mark and assume command of one's position in relation to language and the (masculine) symbolic, there must be speech that defies the imperative to be 'simple or linear or "objectified," generalized', but which is, rather, inflected by 'that element which never stops resonating [...] the song'.[75] The resonance of Cixous's rhetoric with the flight and song of the Philomela-nightingale (and the Procne-swallow) – particularly in Gower, who describes at length their speech and song – is

72 Cixous, 'Castration or Decapitation?', p. 52.

73 Cixous, 'The Laugh of the Medusa', p. 887.

74 Cixous, 'The Laugh of the Medusa', p. 884. Ian Blyth and Susan Sellers, responding in *Hélène Cixous: Live Theory* (New York and London: Continuum, 2004) to charges of essentialism sometimes levelled at Cixous, comment that 'it is also worth noting that general ambivalence towards "meaning" is an essential feature of Cixous's vision of écriture feminine [...] when reading Cixous, particularly the Cixous of the 1970s, words such as 'masculine' and 'feminine' need to be thought of as extremely fluid concepts – their meaning constantly shifting, unstable and unresolved' (p. 24).

75 Cixous, 'The Laugh of the Medusa', p. 881.

coincidental but striking.[76] The two sisters effect a process of overthrow that first sews disorder, then rends the fabric (and fabrications) of which Tereus's patriarchal order is composed, sneaking the outcast back into his palace, robbing him of his heir and presenting him with a severed bloodline, a dislocated castration, a mangled symbol of everything with which he has attempted to subdue and silence Philomela. Like Julian, Christina's tormentor, who talks to a tongue that will not stop jangling, Tereus finds himself shouted down by a speech whose nature he cannot recognise. Unlike Julian, however, he does not admit his loss (or his lack) to the women in question; in fact, in the *Confessio* he says nothing at all, for while the two sisters are transformed into singing birds, Tereus the lapwing utters not a twitter. Though Philomela has regained a voice, when the tongues come back, Tereus has no answers.

TALKING TO THE TONGUE: LOSING SPEECH, GAINING VOICES

Philomela's silent, feminine text(ile) comes as a shock to Procne's system, but a greater one to Tereus's. The evidence that the singular removal of the apparatus for physical speech does not inhibit the appearance of a transgressive, sensuous, plural expression is a possibility he did not even consider: the logic of his cruelty runs directly from *no tongue* to *no speech* – no communication, no access to language (and for him, no consequences). Subverting his logic, Philomela's re-entry into the sphere of language – of tongues – is truly an 'unforeseeable' text.

The comparison of different versions of this tale circulating in fourteenth-century England reveals gaps, dissonances and mysteries – things are missing. Chaucer's text is especially quick to cut, with the effect of cutting off his putative heroines before they can say too much in their own words. In Gower's rendering, the events at Pandion's palace, the Bacchanalian cover for Procne's rescue and what Macaulay calls 'the more shocking details connected with the death of Itys' are left out.[77] The rape scene and the excision of the tongue are also abridged (for Macaulay, Gower is to be 'commended for omitting the tasteless lines') in favour of a greater emphasis on the thoughts and prayers of the sisters, and especially the aftermath of the avian metamorphosis: although

[76] Animals are also a feature of some of Cixous's more recent work. In 'Jacques Derrida as a Proteus Unbound', trans. Peggy Kamuf, in *The Late Derrida*, ed. W. J. T. Mitchell and Arnold I. Davidson (Chicago: University of Chicago Press, 2007), pp. 171–205, Cixous again uses the speech of animals to make her point and mark her own position. As well as a singular excursion on hedgehogs, Cixous considers her two cats: '[n]ot to cite them here would be to show, I believe, a lack of respect toward Jacques Derrida. I would seem to be pretending to be a Heideggerian, whereas I am a Derridean, and so are my cats [...] Whoever cannot hear the cat's speech is just one step from not hearing a woman's speech or a Jew's or an Arab's or that of the subject of one of those species that bear the destiny of banishment' (pp. 178–9).

[77] Macaulay, *The English Works of John Gower*, vol. 2, p. 504.

the further wagglings of the physical tongue are left out of Gower's narrative, the message of the birdsong is given far more prominence.

Where the conflicting discourses of the tale prior to metamorphosis leave the violence of Tereus's actions ironically silenced by the victim on whom they were inflicted, the additional spectacle of the three birds compounds his loss of purchase on orality and authority. Gower specifies that the three are turned into birds, of which 'After thastat that thei were inne, / Here formes were set atwinne' (*CA* V. 5941–2), and in terms of their relative access to speech this condition seems to hold true. To make his point, Gower does what Ovid does not: he describes the birdsongs.[78] Procne, the swallow, lies low in winter, like the nightingale, but in summer makes it her business to '[chit] out in hir langage / What falshod is in mariage', both screeching ('chitting') like a bird and complaining like a scold (*CA* V. 6011–12). Philomela, the nightingale, now 'makth hir pleignte' with her restored tongue (*CA* V. 5978). (It is worth adding that, in omitting the end of the tale, Chaucer does not just skip the bloody revenge – he also abandons the tale before Philomela is given another voice.) Tereus, the lapwing, of whom it is said that he is 'the brid falseste of alle', sings nothing (*CA* V. 6047).

The point where Philomela is once more endowed with a physical voice is also the point at which the reader is reminded that Tereus, for all his brutal action, has never had one. In contrast with Ovid and Chrétien, who include passages of seduction and sly tricks on Tereus's part – incorporating, especially in the latter, instances of direct speech – Gower's Tereus apparently has no voice as a bird, and is 'heard' in Gower's multitude of voices only once (this when he agrees to fetch Philomela to see Procne, *CA* V. 5587–9). Both Philomela and Procne are heard in long passages of both direct speech and internal monologue or prayer, most powerfully in Philomela's threat to Tereus – her 'last words' (*CA* V. 5655–83) – and in Procne's later condemnation (V. 5915–25). Tereus, on the other hand, rapes, mutilates, imprisons, lies and threatens to kill all in apparent silence – or rather, in words that are apparently not worthy of record. Though Gower's narrating voice (unlike Chaucer's) does not call attention to the speech he silences, we do not hear the words with which Tereus convinces Philomela to trust him, or Procne that her sister is dead, only the report that these words were believed. If speech is not an option for the women, neither does it appear to be for Tereus.

More so than the violent but oddly silent Tereus (who recalls the eerie wordlessness of 'monstrous' figures such as *Beowulf*'s Grendel or the outlandish

[78] Chrétien also includes the songs, most notoriously the Old French rendering of Philomena's cry, 'Oci! Oci!' (Kill! Kill! *Philomena*, v. 1467). Casebier observes that 'If Chrétien's moral is more explicit than Ovid's, both metamorphoses reflect the animal logic to which the characters abandoned themselves by incorporating the vestiges of their worst human qualities in their changed forms.' Casebier, 'Ovid's Medieval Metamorphosis', pp. 460–1.

races of Mandeville), and even than the vociferous, raging Procne, it is the speech of mute Philomela that is most firmly impressed upon the reader, and which provides the tale with its 'voice'. Likewise, more strikingly than Ovid and more powerfully than paraleptic Chaucer, Gower throws the eloquence of Philomela's silent performance into sharp relief against Tereus's dumbness. Metamorphosis does not make her any more 'vocal' than she has already become: though 'symbolically castrated' in Tereus's eyes, she is far from impotent in actuality, opting for 'unforeseen' feminine tactics instead. Though she cannot overcome her other loss – her maidenhead – but merely restate it, her legend becomes the 'voice' of femininity, the nightingale the symbol of poetry and song.[79]

Cixous's vision of flight and song that supersedes the stifling structure of convention and the symbolic is reflected in the legend's reworking of ornithological reality: Philomela's voice is heard even though the real female nightingale does not sing.[80] The singing female of myth occupies the same position as the vocal male of nature; indeed, she displaces him. In her own way, Philomela's 'voice' – multiple, mutable, inventive, inscriptive – takes over Tereus's vocal presence in the tale according to Gower. Likewise, Cixous is adamant that words are not the only weapons in the struggle for intelligibility and self-expression. Speaking not only despite but *through* unspeakability here brings back an invisible, incarcerated woman; Gower's tale of revenge (in a way unlike Chaucer's) is also one of redemption and reversal. The tale inverts the proper order of familial and parental relations, of love and consumption, even punishment: the obedient, innocent Philomela suffers the abuse of the tongue normally reserved for liars and impious speakers; Tereus's mutilation casts the truth she threatens to tell as a crime, a sin of the tongue. Unlike Chaucer, Gower highlights not only the unnaturalness of Tereus's crime – his 'unkinde' act – but the expendability of language and the queerness of the sisters' performance, as they speak with dismembered bodies and write male ruin with the tools of feminine art. In performance, even a deed as unspeakable as Tereus's (or Procne's) is far from silent but is instead irrepressibly expressive. Even a tale as repressive as Philomela's, in the hands of a 'moral' writer such as Gower, can be made to speak in different tongues. In 'sewing' disorder, the tale effects an exchange: while Philomela shakes loose the constraints imposed on her by a violence that privileges only verbal,

79 See Jeni Williams, *Interpreting Nightingales: Gender, Class, History* (Sheffield: Sheffield Academic Press, 1997); also Catherine Maxwell, *The Female Sublime from Milton to Swinburne: Bearing Blindness* (Manchester: Manchester University Press, 2001).

80 Cixous, 'The Laugh of the Medusa', pp. 881–7. Williams emphasises, '[t]he very fact that the real singing-bird is the male of the species while the female does not sing is itself significant. The transposition of the gender of the literary figure thus implies that it carries qualities that mark it out as "feminine" over and above the actual sex of the bird and which therefore highlight the constructed nature of gender itself.' Williams, *Interpreting Nightingales*, p. 11.

physical speech – speaking through her stitches – Tereus's failure to anticipate or recognise the speech of the silent leads to his downfall, and the tying of his own tongue. The inscription on Philomela's unspeaking body is overwritten by the stitches that weave her 'tongue' back together; Tereus's mouth is sewn up in the tapestry that damns him.

CONCLUSION: AFTER WORDS

When we speak of the unspeakable today, it is often with a sense of distance and disbelief: at bombings, mass shootings, torture, war crimes and, in particular, terrorism. Unspeakable acts are those committed by other people, they are what the 'other' does. For this reason, Naomi Mandel writes specifically 'against the unspeakable', since to call something unspeakable is to take a moral high ground that is 'not a thoughtful response to atrocity, horror, trauma, and pain' but instead 'an exculpatory mechanism'.[1] She argues that it is in the interest of the literary critic to resist the 'seductive eloquence' of the unspeakable and recognise that 'all of us [...] are the producers and the products of our cultures and hence always already complicit in the ugliest aspects of our histories'.[2] To cleave to the unspeakable is to endorse a sense of 'we' and 'they' or 'now' and 'then'. It also risks passing over the ways in which 'speakable' or legitimated legal processes, social conventions and institutional powers render the behaviour and testimony of marginalised groups unmentionable or inexpressible. Silence in the face of violence (when it serves a specific set of values), ignored or rewritten testimony, and the persistence of codes and euphemism, still collude to obstruct the voices of women, people identifying as non-heterosexual or non-cisgender, people with disabilities, people of colour. The insistence that something is unspeakable and should not be mentioned reinforces both the non-speaker's power and the target's lack of power and lack of speech. Yet the unspeakable and unsayable also collapse binaries, and make clear the impossibility of their ever having obtained in the first place. To show who the unspeakable works for and who it works on brings the margins to the centre and the silent into the conversation; it also shows how the authority that vocalises what is unspeakable is also stymied by the paradoxes of the unspeakable, that are likewise constituted in language that has no guarantees for its users. Turning inside and outside, within and without in on themselves, the unspeakable challenges the voiceless to overcome silence.

Exploring these challenges in this book, two themes emerged. The first developed around the divergence between the apparent fluency of text or speech and the restless description-defying of its subjects – the Lacanian symbolic hiding, but failing to capture, the real; the second grew out of Foucauldian interest in the workings of power, the critical apparatus applied to the question of how power influences and controls speech. It also became a

1 Naomi Mandel, *Against the Unspeakable: Complicity, the Holocaust, and Slavery in America* (Charlottesville: University of Virginia Press, 2006), p. 217.

2 Mandel, *Against the Unspeakable*, p. 24.

survey of things that are unspeaking and/or incapable of vocalisation that are nevertheless more expressive than speech – this despite the fact that they are, as the examples above demonstrate, frequently and pointedly not only silent but absent. On the one hand, there is the missing item, the lacuna in the text, while on the other there is the overanalysed, multivalent passage.

The preceding chapters have worked through confession and sins of the mouth to the sins of the flesh that oral regulation is supposed to guard against. The book deals with the role of the flesh in unspeakability and the seal of confession, and moreover the role of gendered flesh. It looks at the role of language and bodies that are transformed into words, underpinning the process that results in the intolerance, persecution and punishment of unspeakable acts. It then moves to the role of the law and the body as construed by law, the denial of speech or the symbolic denial of reply for one judged to be outside the law, whose protests become unspeakable. Finally the unspeakable words are given new medium of expression in the tales of saints and victims of gendered violence, who visit silent but devastating revenge on their torturers, using silence and the unspeakable to their own ends. These chapters have taken the theme of flesh, gender, sex and sexuality in addressing what in other contexts is a more abstracted, intellectual pursuit, namely the negotiation and articulation of the unnameable and the unspeakable. While it is hardly possible to construe a secular equivalent to spiritual languages of apophasis, the exploration of the physical, material and corporeal offers a perspective that shows why the body is intimately bound up in the unspeakable, a pragmatic perspective in the vein of Barbara Newman's emphasis on medieval 'crossover'.[3] It is impossible to escape the influence of Christian ethics and philosophy, but it is likewise impossible to entirely exclude the body.

Listening for the unspeakable has frequently incorporated the pursuit of missing fragments, the search for what might be called the 'missing links' in the texts under consideration. Missing persons are encountered throughout these texts: the two 'wolves' of Chapter 3 are a case in point, but there are others that are equally notable (though perhaps less noticeable). Admittedly, puzzling absences are not a phenomenon exclusive to the Middle Ages. In a slightly different fashion, the pedigrees of theorists and critics can also reveal some eerie exclusions – Jean-Luc Nancy, for instance, has argued that Giorgio Agamben's *Homo Sacer* owes an unacknowledged debt to Jacques Derrida.[4]

[3] See Barbara Newman, *Medieval Crossover*, pp. 1–53.

[4] See Lorenzo Fabbri, 'Philosophy As Chance: An Interview with Jean-Luc Nancy', trans. Pascale-Anee Brault and Michael Naas, in *The Late Derrida*, ed. Mitchell and Davidson, pp. 209–22. Asked about Derrida's impact on Agamben's work, Nancy (a friend of both) replied that 'Agamben began at a certain point to reject Derrida in a radical way, which was of course his right, all the while taking back up many of Derrida's themes [...] To speak, as he did, of *différance* as a perpetual delay is to deliberately refuse to read

Likewise, Carolyn Burke makes the point that Luce Irigaray's erstwhile mentor remains an unnamed presence in *Speculum of the Other Woman* (though its very title shouts his influence), and wonders if Irigaray's work might in fact be 'haunted by Lacan'.[5] Being slightly haunted by Lacan too, throughout this book I have been seeking 'the response of the other', listening for what the 'other' of the Middle Ages has to say, even in places where this response is unspeakable. If it is speech that elicits this response from the other – and the Middle Ages seem so often to be 'othered' by modernity – then in looking at and sometimes touching on the end results of the unspeakable as it is performed, I am also making my way towards not just an end but another starting place, and asking what the unspeakable does for medieval studies.

What I hope to have shown here, writ large, is the processes that occur more minutely within the single texts. The first of these processes is that by which texts treating a subject that is controversial, mysterious or extraordinary – excessive, in any sense – are not just understood better with the support of other texts; they demand to be read alongside texts and contexts that are not there. Another, connected negotiation is the one that all medievalists know, the navigation of the silences in medieval literature and the space between what was said and what is now understood. Finally, my flash points throughout this book have come from the moments in which gender and sexuality are de/constructed by language and re/interpreted by readers – not only readers of texts but those protagonists who 'read' the performances and the silences within the texts of which they are part, and in so doing drive them. Gender and sexuality move in mysterious ways, but those manoeuvres in which they are presumed, assumed and inscribed (sometimes with force) are often those that are, at a stroke, unspoken, unspeakable and hugely telling. Taken together, these are processes that confront not only the medieval corpus but the inevitable and unavoidable paradox of language itself – that 'language *is* not what it means', but is, rather, a signpost to something else, something other, unreachable and unspeakable.[6]

Exploring the unspeakable incorporates not only what the unspoken might be and how to speak without speaking, but also the work the unspeakable might then perform. As such, the conclusion is also the starting point for another destination. This study has aimed to find a greater cross-section of ways in which the unspeakable is made to perform, how the unspeakable is not only a topic for the very good or the very bad but – especially with regard to gender and sexuality – one that affects everybody, and every body.

the texts. Or else to write about messianism after Derrida without mentioning him is aggressive and unscholarly (and I know that this was intentional)' (p. 217).

5 Carolyn Burke, 'Irigaray Through the Looking Glass', in *Engaging With Irigaray: Feminist Philosophy and Modern European Thought*, ed. Carolyn Burke, Naomi Schor and Margaret Whitford (New York: Columbia University Press, 1994), pp. 37–56 (p. 41).

6 Franke, *Philosophy of the Unsayable*, p.8.

The paradox of 'medieval' as a label is that it does not attach itself easily to a fixed period, or language, or dominant ideology. It is, in this sense, the exemplar of the sign that does not pin down what it is meant to describe and define (or Lacan's barred signifier). The literature of medieval England forms a far from static category; it is full of shifts, interruptions and disturbances – and free-floating fragments. The same label can be found on material from wildly different times and places – from Anglo-Saxon England to Chaucer's London, and beyond – that take in different languages and see a succession of upheavals in the dominant culture and centres of power and literary output. In looking at the unspeakable, there is the opportunity to (en)counter a mobile corpus with an equally flexible kind of analysis – one that makes a virtue of what cannot be said.

BIBLIOGRAPHY

PRIMARY TEXTS

Alain de Lille, *Anticlaudianus, or The Good and Perfect Man*, ed. and trans. James J. Sheridan (Toronto: Pontifical Institute of Medieval Studies, 1973).

Alain de Lille, *De Planctu Naturae*, ed. Nikolaus M. Häring, *Studi Medievali* 19 (1978), 797–879.

Alain de Lille, *The Plaint of Nature*, ed. and trans. James J. Sheridan (Toronto: Pontifical Institute of Medieval Studies, 1980).

Alberigo, J., et al., eds, *Conciliorum Oecumenicorum Decreta* (Freiberg: Verlag Herder, 1962).Aquinas, Thomas, *Summa Theologiæ*, ed. and trans. Thomas Gilby et al., 60 vols (London: Eyre and Spottiswoode, 1968).

Aristotle, *De Anima II–III*, trans. D. W. Hamlyn (Oxford: Clarendon Press, 1993).

Augustine, *On Christian Teaching*, trans. R. P. H. Green (Oxford: Oxford University Press, 1997).

Augustine, *De doctrina Christiana: de vera religione*, ed. J. Martin, Corpus Christianorum Series Latina, vol. 32 (Turnhout: Brepols, 1962).

Barnes, Jonathan, ed., *The Complete Works of Aristotle: The Revised Oxford Translation*, 2 vols (Princeton, NJ: Princeton University Press, 1984).

Bennett, J. A. W., and G. V. Smithers, eds, *Early Middle English Verse and Prose*, 2nd edn (Oxford: Oxford University Press, 1974).

Benson, Larry D., gen. ed., *The Riverside Chaucer*, 3rd edn (Oxford: Oxford University Press, 1987).

Bernard of Clairvaux, *Sermones super Cantica Cantorum*, *PL* 183, ed. J.-P. Migne (Paris: Garnier, 1841–55).

Bethurum, Dorothy, ed., *The Homilies of Wulfstan* (Oxford: Clarendon Press, 1957).

Bosworth, Joseph, *An Anglo-Saxon Dictionary*, ed. T. Northcote Toller et al. (Oxford: Clarendon Press, 1898).

Bowers, John M., ed., *The Canterbury Tales: Fifteenth Century Continuations and Additions* (Kalamazoo, MI: Medieval Institute Publications, 1992).

Brucker, Charles, ed., *Marie de France, Les Fables: Edition critique accompagné d'une introduction, d'une traduction, de notes et d'un glossaire* (Louvain: Peeters, 1991).

Bunt, G. H. V., ed., *William of Palerne: An Alliterative Romance* (Groningen: Boumas Boekhuis, 1985).

Burgess, Glyn S., and Keith Busby, trans., *The Lais of Marie de France* (London: Penguin, 1986).

Burgess, Glyn S., and Leslie C. Brook, eds, *Eleven Old French Narrative Lays* (Cambridge: D. S. Brewer, 2007).

Cain, Andrew, ed., *Jerome's Epitaph on Paula: A Commentary on the Epitaphium Sanctae Paulae* (Oxford: Oxford University Press, 2013).

Chrétien de Troyes, *Philomena: Conté raconté d'après Ovide,* ed. C. de Boer (Paris: Librairie Paul Geuthner, 1909).

Christine de Pizan, Jean Gerson, Jean de Montreuil, Gontier and Pierre Col, *Le Débat sur 'Le Roman de la Rose'*, ed. Eric Hicks (Paris: Editions Honoré Champion, 1977).

Crossley-Holland, Kevin, trans., *The Battle of Maldon and Other Old English Poems,* ed. Bruce Mitchell (London: Macmillan, 1965).

Crow, Martin M., and Clair C. Olson, eds, *Chaucer Life-Records* (Oxford: Clarendon Press, 1966).

Curnow, Maureen C., ed., 'The "Livre de la Cité des Dames" of Christine de Pisan: A Critical Edition', PhD diss. (Nashville: Vanderbilt University, 1975).

d'Ardenne, S. R. T. O., ed., Þe Liflade ant te Passiun of Seinte Iuliene, EETS o.s. 248 (Oxford: Oxford University Press, 1961).

Day, Mabel, ed., *The English Text of the Ancrene Riwle: edited from BM, MS Cotton Nero A. xiv,* EETS o.s. 225 (London: Oxford University Press, 1952).

Delanty, Greg, and Michael Matto, eds, *The Word Exchange: Anglo-Saxon Poems in Translation* (New York: W. W. Norton & Co., 2012).

Dembowski, Peter F., ed., *La Vie de Ste. Marie Egyptienne: Versions en Ancien et Moyen Français* (Geneva: Droz, 1977).

D'Evelyn, Charlotte, and Anna J. Mill, eds, *The South English Legendary,* EETS o.s. 235 (Oxford: Oxford University Press, 1956).

Donovan, Leslie, ed. and trans., *Women Saints' Lives in Old English Prose* (Cambridge: D. S. Brewer, 1999).

Furnivall, Frederick J., ed., *Robert of Brunne's Handlyng Synne and Parts of its French Original,* EETS o.s. 119 (London: Trübner, 1901).

Gardiner, Eileen, ed. and trans., *Visions of Heaven and Hell Before Dante* (New York: Italica, 1989).

——, ed. and trans., *Medieval Visions of Heaven and Hell: A Sourcebook* (London: Routledge, 1993).

Gower, John, *Confessio Amantis,* ed. Russell A. Peck, with Latin translations by Andrew Galloway, 3 vols, 2nd edn (Kalamazoo, MI: Medieval Institute Publications, 2013).

Gratian, *Decretum, Tractatus de Poenitentia, PL* 187, ed. J-P Migne (Paris: Garnier, 1841–55).

Guillaume de Lorris and Jean de Meun, *The Romance of the Rose,* trans. Charles Dahlberg (Princeton, NJ: Princeton University Press, 1971 and subsequent).

Guillaume de Lorris and Jean de Meun, *Le Roman de la Rose,* ed. Félix Lecoy, 3 vols, Societé des Anciens Textes Français (Paris: Firmin-Didot, Champion, 1914–24).

Hall, G. D. G., with M. T. Clanchy, eds, *Tractatus de legibus et consuetudinibus regni Anglie qui Glanvilla vocatur; The Treatise on the Laws and Customs of the Realm of England Commonly called Glanvill* (Oxford: Clarendon, 1993).

Hamer, R. F. S., ed., with Vida Russell, *Gilte Legende*, EETS o.s. 327, vol. 1 (Oxford: Oxford University Press, 2006).

Heldris de Cornuälle, *Le Roman de Silence*, trans. Regina Psaki, Garland Library of Medieval Literature 63 (New York and London: Garland, 1991).

Hopkins, Amanda, ed. and trans., *Melion and Biclarel: Two Old French Werewolf Lays*, Liverpool Critical Editions of French Texts, 10 (Liverpool: University of Liverpool, 2005).

Horstmann, Carl, ed., *The Early South English Legendary, or Lives of Saints*, EETS o.s. 87 (London: Trübner, 1887).

Hugh of Fouilloy, *De Bestis et Aliis Rebus, PL* 177, ed. J-P Migne (Paris: Garnier, 1841–55).

Jerome, *Commentarium in Epistolam ad Ephesios Libri III, PL* 26, ed. J-P Migne (Paris, Garnier, 1841–55).

Klinck, Anne L., ed. *The Old English Elegies: A Critical Edition and Genre Study* (Montreal: McGill-Queens University Press, 1992).

Krapp, George, and Elliott van Kirk Dobbie, eds, *ASPR 3: The Exeter Book* (New York: Columbia University Press, 1936).

Kunze, Konrad, ed., *Studien zur Legende der Heiligen Maria Aegiptiaca im Deutschen Sprachgebiet* (Berlin: Schmidt, 1969).

Lachance, Paul, ed. and trans., *Angela of Foligno: Complete Works*, The Classics of Western Spirituality (New York: Paulist Press, 1993).

Larson, Atria A., ed. and trans., *Gratian's Tractatus de penitentia: A New Latin Edition with English Translation* (Washington, DC: Catholic University of America Press, 2016).

Liebermann, Felix, ed. and trans., *Die Gesetze der Angelsachsen*, 3 vols (Halle: Niemeyer, 1903–16).

Macaulay, G. C., ed., *The English Works of John Gower*, 2 vols, EETS e.s. 81, 82 (Oxford: Oxford University Press, 1900–01).

Magennis, Hugh, ed. and trans., *The Old English Life of St Mary of Egypt* (Exeter: Exeter University Press, 2002).

Marie de France, *Lais*, ed. Alfred Ewert (Oxford: Blackwell, 1944).

Martin, Mary Lou, ed. and trans., *The Fables of Marie de France* (Birmingham, AL: Summa Publications, 1979).

Meech, Sandford Brown, and Hope Emily Allen, eds., *The Book of Margery Kempe*, EETS o.s. 212 (Oxford: Oxford University Press, 1940).

Micha, Alexandre, ed., *Guillaume de Palerne: Roman du XIIIe siècle*, Textes Littéraires Français (Genève: Droz, 1990).

Millett, Bella, and Jocelyn Wogan-Browne, *Medieval English Prose for Women* (Oxford: Oxford University Press, 1990).

Millett, Bella, ed., *Ancrene Wisse: A Corrected Edition of the Text in Cambridge, Corpus Christi College, MS 402 with Variants from other Manuscripts*, 2 vols, EETS o.s. 325, 326 (Oxford: Oxford University Press, 2005, 2008).

——, ed. and trans., Ancrene Wisse*: A Guide for Anchoresses* (Exeter: Exeter University Press, 2009).

Morris, Richard, ed., *The Pricke of Conscience* (Berlin: Philogical Society, 1863).

Morton, James, ed., *The Ancren Riwle; a Treatise on the Rules and Duties of Monastic Life, Edited and Translated from a Semi-Saxon MS. of the Thirteenth Century* (London: Camden Society, 1853).

Mynors, R. A. B., ed., *P. Vergili Maronis Opera* (Oxford: Clarendon, 1969).

O'Brien, Bruce R., ed. and trans., *God's Peace and King's Peace: The Laws of Edward the Confessor* (Philadelphia, PA: University of Pennsylvania Press, 1999).

Ovid, *Metamorphoses, Books I–VIII,* trans. Frank Justus Miller, Loeb Classical Library (London: William Heinemann, 1916).

Pepin, Ronald E., and Hugh Fleiss, eds, *Saint Mary of Egypt: Three Medieval Lives in Verse* (Kalamazoo, MI: Cistercian Publications, 2005).

Peraldus, Guilelmus, *Summa de virtubtibus et vitiis* (Venice: Paganino de Paganini, 1497).

Peter Damian, *Book of Gomorrah: An Eleventh Century Treatise Against Clerical Homosexual Practices*, ed. and trans. Pierre J. Payer (Waterloo, Ont.: Wilfrid Laurier University Press, 1982).

Reames, Sherry L., ed., *Middle English Legends of Women Saints* (Kalamazoo, MI: Medieval Institute Publications, 2003)

Richards, Earl Jeffrey, trans., *The Book of the City of Ladies* (New York: Persea Books, 1982).

Rothwell, Harry, ed., *English Historical Documents, 1189–1327* (London: Routledge, 1975).

Schiavone de Cruz-Sáenz, Michèle, ed., *The Life of Saint Mary of Egypt: An Edition and Study of the Medieval French and Spanish Verse Redactions* (Barcelona: Puvill, 1979).

Sconduto, Leslie A., ed. and trans., *Guillaume de Palerne: An English Translation of the 12th Century French Verse Romance* (Jefferson, NC: McFarland & Co., 2004).

Seymour, M. C., ed., *On the Properties of Things: John Trevisa's Translation of Bartholamæus Anglicus, De Proprietatibus Rerum; A Critical Text*, 2 vols (Oxford: Clarendon, 1975).

Shepherd, Geoffrey, ed., *Ancrene Wisse: Parts Six and Seven* (Exeter: Exeter University Press, 1985).

Tanner, Norman P., ed., *Decrees of the Ecumenical Councils* (Washington, DC: Georgetown University Press, 1990).

Thomas, A. H., ed., *Calendar of Select Pleas and Memoranda of the City of London, 1381–1412* (Cambridge: Cambridge University Press, 1932).

Thorpe, Benjamin, ed. and trans., *Codex Exoniensis: A Collection of Anglo-Saxon Poetry* (London: Society of Antiquities, 1842).

Thorpe, Lewis, ed., *Le Roman de Silence: A Thirteenth-Century Arthurian Verse-Romance by Heldris de Cornuälle* (Cambridge: W. Heffer & Sons, 1972).

O'Hara Tobin, Prudence Mary, ed., *Les Lais anonymes du XIIe et XIIIe siècles: édition critique de quelques lais bretons* (Geneva: Droz, 1976).

Tretheway, W. H., ed., *The French Text of the Ancrene Riwle: edited from Trinity College, Cambridge, MS R. 147*, EETS o.s. 240 (Oxford: Oxford University Press, 1958).

Virgil, *Eclogues, Georgics, Aeneid I–VI*, Loeb Classical Library, trans. H. Rushton Fairclough, rev. by G. P. Goold (Cambridge, MA: Harvard University Press, 1999).

Vitae Patrum, PL 73, ed. J.-P. Migne (Paris: Garnier, 1841–55).

Wada, Yoko, ed. and trans., *'Temptations' from* Ancrene Wisse (Osaka: Kansai University Press; Cambridge: D. S. Brewer, 1994).

Ward, Benedicta, *Harlots of the Desert: A Study of Repentance in Early Monastic Sources* (Kalamzoo, MI: Cistercian Publications, 1987).

White, T. H., ed. and trans., *The Book of Beasts: Being a Translation from a Latin Bestiary of the Twelfth Century* (Madison, WI: Parallel Press, 2002).

Woodbine, George E., ed. *Bracton, De legibus et consuetudinibus Angliæ: Bracton on the Laws and Customs of England,* 3 vols, trans. Samuel E. Thorne (Cambridge, MA: Harvard University Press, 1968).

Zettersten, Arne, ed., *The English Text of the Ancrene Riwle: edited from Magdalene College, Cambridge, MS Pepys 2498,* EETS o.s. 274 (London: Oxford University Press, 1976).

SECONDARY SOURCES

Acker, Paul, 'Horror and the Maternal in *Beowulf*', *PMLA* 121.3 (2006), 702–16.

Adams, John F., '*Wulf and Eadwacer:* An Interpretation', *Modern Language Notes* 73.1 (1958), 1–5.

Agamben, Giorgio, *Language and Death: The Place of Negativity*, trans. Karen E. Pinkus and Michael Hardt (Minneapolis: University of Minnesota Press, 1991).

——, *Potentialities: Collected Essays in Philosophy*, ed. and trans. Daniel Heller-Roazen (Stanford: Stanford University Press, 1999).

——, *Means Without End*, trans. Vincenzo Binetti and Cesare Casarino (Minneapolis: University of Minnesota Press, 2000).

——, *Homo Sacer: Sovereign Power and Bare Life*, trans. Daniel Heller-Roazen (Stanford: Stanford University Press, 2001).

——, *Remnants of Auschwitz*, trans. Daniel Heller-Roazen (New York: Zone Books, 2002).

——, *State of Exception*, trans. Kevin Attell, (Chicago: University of Chicago Press, 2005).

Aloni, Gila, 'Palimpsestic Philomela: Reinscription in Chaucer's "Legend of Philomela"', in *Palimpsests and the Literary Imagination of Medieval England*, ed. Leo Carruthers, Raeleen Chai-Elsholz and Tatjana Silec (New York: Palgrave Macmillan, 2011), pp. 157–73.

Allen, Peter L., 'The Ambiguity of Silence: Gender, Writing and *Le Roman de Silence*' in *Sign, Sentence, Discourse: Langauge in Medieval Thought and Literature*, ed. Julian N. Wasserman and Lois Roney (Syracuse, NY: Syracuse University Press, 1989), pp. 98–112.

Archibald, Elizabeth, 'Incest in Medieval Literature and Society', *Forum for Modern Language Studies* 25.1 (1989), 1–15.

——, '"Worse Than Bogery": Incest Stories in Middle English Literature', in *Incest and the Literary Imagination*, ed. Elizabeth Barnes, pp. 17–38.

Armstrong, Lawrin, *The Idea of a Moral Economy: Gerard of Siena on Usury, Restitution, Prescription* (Toronto: University of Toronto Press, 2016).

Bachelard, Gaston, *The Poetics of Space* (Boston, MA: Beacon Press, 1994).

Bardsley, Sandy, *Venonous Tongues: Speech and Gender in Late Medieval England* (Philadelphia, PA: University of Pennsylvania Press, 2006).

Baring-Gould, Sabine, *The Book of Werewolves* (London: Smith and Elder, 1865).

Barratt, Alexandra, 'The Five Wits and their Structural Significance in Part II of *Ancrene Wisse*', *Medium Ævum* 56.1 (1987), 12–24.

Bataille, Georges, *Death and Sensuality: A Study of Eroticism and the Taboo*, trans. Mary Dalwood (New York: Walker and Co., 1962).

Baum, Paul F., *Chaucer: A Critical Appreciation* (Durham, NC: Duke University Press, 1958).

Beckwith, Sarah, 'Passionate Regulation: Enclosure, Ascesis, and the Feminist Imaginary', *South Atlantic Quarterly* 93.4 (1994), 803–24.

Beidler, Peter G., ed., *Masculinities in Chaucer: Approaches to Maleness in the* Canterbury Tales *and* Troilus and Criseyde (Cambridge: D. S. Brewer, 1998).

Belanoff, Patricia A., 'Women's Songs, Women's Language: *Wulf and Eadwacer* and *The Wife's Lament*', in *New Readings on Women in Old English Literature*, ed. Helen Damico and Alexandra Hennessey Olsen (Bloomington, IN: Indiana University Press, 1990), pp. 193–203.

——, '"Ides … geomrode giddum": The Old English Female Lament', in *Medieval Woman's Song: Cross-Cultural Approaches*, ed. Anne L Klinck and Ann Marie Rasmussen (Philadelphia, PA: University of Pennsylvania Press, 2002), pp. 29–46, 214–18.

Benjamin, Walter, 'Critique of Violence', trans. Edmund Jephcott, in *Walter Benjamin: Selected Writings, Vol. 1, 1913–1926*, ed. Marcus Bullock and Michael W. Jennings (Cambridge, MA: Belknap Press, Harvard University Press, 1996), pp. 236–52.

Bennett, Harold, 'Sacer Esto', *Transactions and Proceedings of the American Philological Assocation* 61 (1930), 5–18.

Bennett, Helen, 'Exile and the Semiosis of Gender in Old English Elegies', in *Class and Gender in Early English Literature: Intersections*, ed. Britton J. Harwood and Gillian R. Overing (Bloomington, IN: Indiana University Press, 1994), pp. 43–58.

Bennett, Judith M., and Shannon McSheffrey, 'Early, Erotic and Alien: Women Dressed as Men in Medieval London', *History Workshop Journal* 77 (2014), 1–25.

Benson, C. David, 'Chaucer's Pardoner: His Sexuality and Modern Critics', *Mediaevalia* 8 (1982), 337–46.

Berger, Adolf, *Encyclopedic Dictionary of Roman Law: Transactions of the American Philosophical Society*, vol. 43, part 2 (Clark, NJ: The Lawbook Exchange Ltd., 2002).

Bernau, Anke, 'Virginal Effects: Text and Identity in "Ancrene Wisse"', in *Gender and Holiness*, ed. Samantha J. E. Riches and Sarah Salih (Cardiff: University of Wales Press, 2002), pp. 36–48.

Bernstein, Alan E., *Pierre d'Ailly and the Blanchard Affair: University and Chancellor of Paris at the Beginning of the Great Schism* (Leiden: Brill, 1978).

Bjork, Robert, '*Sundor æt rune:* The Voluntary Exile of the Wanderer', *Neophilologus* 73.1 (1989), 119–29.

Bliss, Jane, *Naming and Namelessness in Medieval Romance* (Cambridge: D. S. Brewer, 2008).

Bloch, R. Howard, *Etymologies and Genealogies: A Literary Anthropology of the French Middle Ages* (Chicago: University of Chicago Press, 1983).

——, *Scandal of the Fabliaux* (Chicago, University of Chicago Press, 1986).

——, *The Anonymous Marie de France* (Chicago: University of Chicago Press, 2003).

Blud, Victoria, 'Wolves' Heads and Wolves' Tales: Women and Exile in *Bisclavret* and *Wulf and Eadwacer*', *Exemplaria* 26.4 (2014), 328–46.

Blum, Martin, 'Negotiating Masculinities: Erotic Triangles in the Miller's Tale', in *Masculinities in Chaucer*, ed. Peter G. Beidler, pp. 37–52.

Blumreich, Kathleen M., 'Lesbian Desire in the Old French *Roman de Silence*', *Arthuriana* 7.2 (1997), 47–62.

Blurton, Heather, *Cannibalism in High Medieval English Literature: Conquest and Identity in High Medieval England* (Basingstoke: Palgrave Macmillan, 2007).

Blyth, Ian, and Susan Sellers, *Hélène Cixous: Live Theory* (New York, London: Continuum, 2004).

Boesel, Chris, and Catherine Keller, eds, *Apophatic Bodies: Negative Theology, Incarnation, and Relationality* (New York: Fordham University Press, 2010).

Boffey, Julia, and A. S. G. Edwards, '*The Legend of Good Women*' in *The Cambridge Companion to Chaucer*, 2nd edn, ed. Piero Boitani and Jill Mann (Cambridge: Cambridge University Press, 2001), pp. 112–26.

Bogdanos, Theodore, *Pearl: Image of the Ineffable. A Study in Medieval Poetic Symbolism* (University Park, PA, and London: Pennsylvania State University Press, 1983).

Boos, Sonja, *Speaking the Unspeakable in Postwar Germany: Toward a Public Discourse on the Holocaust* (Ithaca, NY: Cornell University Press, 2014).

Bossy, John, 'The Social History of Confession in the Age of the Reformation', *Transactions of the Royal Historical Society* 5.25 (1975), pp. 21–38.

Boswell, John, *Christianity, Social Tolerance and Homosexuality: Gay People in Western Europe from the Beginning of the Christian Era to the Fourteenth Century* (Chicago: University of Chicago Press, 1980).

Bott, Robin L., '"O, Keep Me From Their Worse Than Killing Lust": Ideologies of Rape and Mutilation in Chaucer's *Physician's Tale* and Shakespeare's *Titus Andronicus*' in *Representing Rape in Medieval and Early Modern Literature*, ed. Elizabeth Ann Robertson and Christine M. Rose (New York and Basingstoke: Palgrave Macmillan, 2001) pp. 189–212.

Brahney, Kathleen C., 'When Silence Was Golden: Female Personae in the *Roman de Silence*', in *The Spirit of the Court: Selected Proceedings of the Fourth Congress of the International Courtly Literature Society*, ed. Glyn S. Burgess and Robert A. Taylor (Cambridge: D. S. Brewer, 1985), pp. 52–61.

Breeze, Andrew, 'Welsh *Baban* "Baby" and *Ancrene Wisse*', *Notes and Queries* 40.1 (1993), 12–13.

Brundage, James, A., *Law, Sex, and Christian Society in Medieval Europe* (Chicago: University of Chicago Press, 1990).

Bullough, Vern L., and Bonnie Bullough, *Cross Dressing, Sex, and Gender* (Philadelphia, PA: University of Pennsylvania Press, 1993).

Burger, Glenn, 'Kissing the Pardoner', *PMLA* 107.5 (1992), 1143–56.

Burgess, Glyn S., *The Lais of Marie de France: Text and Context* (Manchester: Manchester University Press, 1987).

Burgwinkle, William E., *Sodomy, Masculinity, and Law in Medieval Literature: France and England, 1050–1230* (Cambridge: Cambridge University Press, 2004).

Burke, Carolyn, 'Irigaray Through the Looking Glass', in *Engaging With Irigaray: Feminist Philosophy and Modern European Thought*, ed. Carolyn Burke, Naomi Schor and Margaret Whitford (New York: Columbia University Press, 1994), pp. 37–56.

Burns, George, 'Margery Kempe Reviewed', *The Month* 171 (1938), 238–44.

Burns, Jane E., *Bodytalk: When Women Talk in Old French Literature* (Philadelphia, PA: University of Pennsylvania Press, 1993).

——, 'Raping Men: What's Motherhood Got to Do With It?' in *Representing Rape in Medieval and Early Modern Literature*, ed. Elizabeth Ann Robertson and Christine M. Rose (New York and Basingstoke: Palgrave Macmillan, 2001), pp. 127–60.

——, *Sea of Silk: A Textile Geography of Women's Work in Medieval French Literature* (Philadelphia, PA: University of Pennsylvania Press, 2009).

Burrus, Virginia, *The Sex Lives of Saints: An Erotics of Ancient Hagiography* (Philadelphia, PA: University of Pennsylvania Press, 2004).

Burson, Joshua, 'Gender Identity in Late-Medieval Germany: The Strange Case of Hans Hall' (unpublished).

Busby, Keith, 'Neither Flesh nor Fish nor Good Red Herring: The Case of Anglo-Norman Literature', in *Studies in Honour of Hans-Erich Keller: Medieval French and Occitan Literature and Romance Linguistics*, ed. Rupert T. Pickens (Kalamazoo, MI: Medieval Institute Publications, 1993), pp. 399–417.

Butler, Judith, *Bodies That Matter: On the Discursive Limits of 'Sex'* (New York and London: Routledge, 1993).

——, *Undoing Gender* (New York and London: Routledge, 2004).

Bynum, Carolyn Walker, *Holy Feast and Holy Fast: The Religious Significance of Food to Medieval Women* (Berkeley, CA: University of California Press, 1987).

——, *Fragmentation and Redemption: Essays on Gender and the Human Body in Medieval Religion* (New York: Zone, 1992).

——, *Metamorphosis and Identity* (New York: Zone, 2001).

Cadden, Joan, *Nothing Natural is Shameful: Sodomy and Science in Late Medieval Europe* (Philadelphia, PA: University of Pennsylvania Press, 2013).

Cameron, M. L., 'The Sources of Medical Knowledge in Anglo-Saxon England', *Anglo-Saxon England* 11 (1983), 135–55.

Campbell, Emma, *Medieval Saints' Lives: The Gift, Kinship and Community in Old French Hagiography* (Cambridge: D. S. Brewer, 2008).

——, 'Political Animals: Human/Animal Life in *Bisclavret* and *Yonec*', *Exemplaria* 25.2 (2013), 95–109.

Cannon, Christopher, '*Raptus* in the Chaumpaigne Release and a Newly Discovered Document Concerning the Life of Geoffrey Chaucer', *Speculum* 68.1 (1993), 74–94.

——, *The Grounds of English Literature* (Oxford: Oxford University Press, 2004).

——, 'Between the Old and the Middle of English', *New Medieval Literatures* 7 (2005), 203–21.

Casebier, Karen, 'Ovid's Medieval Metamorphosis: Techniques of Persuasion in Chrétien de Troyes' *Philomena*', *Philological Quarterly* 80.4 (2001), 441–65.

Castelli, Elizabeth A, ed., *Journal of the History of Sexuality* 10.2 (2001).

Cawsey, Kathy, *Twentieth Century Chaucer Criticism: Reading Audiences* (London: Rouledge, 2016).

de Certeau, Michel, *The Mystic Fable, Volume One: The Sixteenth and Seventeenth Centuries*, trans. Michael B. Smith (Chicago: University of Chicago Press, 1992).

Chase, Colin, 'Source Study as a Trick with Mirrors: Annihilation of Meaning in the Old English "Mary of Egypt"', *Sources of Anglo-Saxon Culture*, ed. Paul E. Szarmach, Studies in Medieval Culture 20 (Kalamazoo, MI: Medieval Institute, 1986), pp. 23–33.

Cixous, Hélène, 'Castration or Decapitation?', *Signs: Journal of Women in Culture and Society* 7 (1981), 41–55.

——, 'The Laugh of the Medusa', trans. Keith Cohen and Paula Cohen, *Signs: Journal of Women in Culture and Society* 1.4 (1976), 875–93.

——, 'Jacques Derrida as a Proteus Unbound', trans. Peggy Kamuf, in *The Late Derrida*, ed. W. J. T. Mitchell and Arnold I. Davidson (Chicago: University of Chicago Press, 2007), pp. 171–205.

Cixous, Hélène, and Catherine Clément, *The Newly Born Woman*, trans. Betsy Wing (London and New York: I. B. Tauris, 1996).

Clark, David, *Between Medieval Men: Male Friendship and Desire in Early Medieval English Literature* (Oxford: Oxford University Press, 2009).

Clarke, Catherine A. M., *Literary Landscapes and the Idea of England, 700–1400* (Cambridge: D. S. Brewer, 2006).

Clay, Rotha Mary, *The Hermits and Anchorites of England* (London: Methuen, 1914).

Clayton, Mary, 'Hermits and the Contemplative Life in Anglo-Saxon England', in *Old English Prose Saints' Lives and Their Contexts*, ed. Paul E. Szarmach (Albany, NY: State University of New York Press, 1996), pp. 147–76.

Cohen, Jeffrey Jerome, 'Gowther Among the Dogs: Becoming Inhuman c. 1400', in *Becoming Male in the Middle Ages* ed. Jeffrey Jerome Cohen and Bonnie Wheeler (New York: Garland, 2000), pp. 219–44.

——, *Medieval Identity Machines*, Medieval Cultures 35 (Minneapolis: University of Minnesota Press, 2003).

Coleman, Joyce, '"A bok for king Richardes sake": Royal Patronage, the *Confessio*, and the *Legend of Good Women*' in *On John Gower: Essays at the Millennium*, ed. R. F. Yeager, Studies in Medieval Culture 46 (Kalamazoo, MI: Medieval Institute Publications, 2007), pp. 104–23.

Collard, Franck, *The Crime of Poison in the Middle Ages,* trans. Deborah Nelson-Campbell (Westport, CT: Praeger, 2008).

Colledge, Eric, '*The Recluse*: A Lollard Interpolated Version of the *Ancren Riwle*', *RES* 15 (1939), 1–15, 129–45.

Collingwood, R. G., *The Idea of Nature* (New York and Oxford: Oxford University Press, 1945).

Conner, Randy, '"*Les Molles et les Chausses*": Mapping the Isle of Hermaphrodites in Premodern France', in *Queerly Phrased: Language, Gender, and Sexuality*, ed. Anna Livia and Kira Hall (New York and Oxford: Oxford University Press, 1997), pp. 127–46.

Cooper, Kate Mason, '*Elle* and *L*: Sexualised Textuality in *Le Roman de Silence*', *Romance Notes* 25.3 (1985), 341–60.Crane, Susan, *Animal Encounters: Contacts and Concepts in Medieval Britain* (Philadelphia, PA: University of Pennsylvania Press, 2012).

Craun, Edwin D., '"Inordinata Locutio": Blasphemy in Pastoral Literature, 1200–1500', *Traditio* 39 (1983), 135–62.

——, *Lies, Slander and Obscenity: Pastoral Rhetoric and the Deviant Speaker* (Cambridge: Cambridge University Press, 1997).

Curry, Walter Clyde, 'The Secret of Chaucer's Pardoner', *JEGP* 18 (1919), 593–606.

Curtius, Ernst Robert, *European Literature and the Latin Middle Ages* (London: Routledge & Keegan Paul, 1953).

Daston, Lorraine, and Fernando Vidal, eds, *The Moral Authority of Nature* (Chicago: University of Chicago Press, 2004).

Davis, Carmel Bendon, *Mysticism and Space: Space and Spatiality in the Works of Richard Rolle, "The Cloud of Unknowing" Author and Julian of Norwich* (Washington, DC: Catholic University of America Press, 2008).

Delany, Sheila, *The Naked Text: Chaucer's Legend of Good Women* (Berkeley, CA: University of California Press, 1994).

Derrida, Jacques, 'How to Avoid Speaking: Denials', in *Languages of the Unsayable*, ed. Budick and Iser, pp. 3–70.

——, *L'animal que donc je suis* (Paris: Éditions Galilée, 2006).

——, *The Animal That Therefore I Am*, trans. David Wills (New York: Fordham University Press, 2008).

Desmond, Marilynn, 'The Voice of the Exile: Feminist Literary History and the Anonymous Anglo-Saxon Elegy', *Critical Inquiry* 16.3 (1990), 572–90.

Deutscher, Penelope, 'The Inversion of Exceptionality: Foucault, Agamben, and "Reproductive Rights"', *South Atlantic Quarterly* 107.1 (2008), 55–70.

Dinshaw, Carolyn, *Chaucer's Sexual Poetics* (Madison, WI: University of Wisconsin Press, 1989).

——, 'Rivalry, Rape, and Manhood: Chaucer and Gower', in *Violence Against Women in Medieval Texts*, ed. Anna Roberts (Gainesville, FL: University Press of Florida, 1998) pp. 137–60.

——, *Getting Medieval: Sexualities and Communities, Pre- and Post-Modern* (Durham, NC: Duke University Press, 1999).

——, 'Queer Relations', *Essays in Medieval Studies: Out of Bounds* 16 (2002), 79–94.

Dobson, E. J., 'The Date and Composition of *Ancrene Wisse*', *Proceedings of the British Academy* 52 (1966), pp. 181–208.

——, *The Origins of* Ancrene Wisse (Oxford: Clarendon, 1976).

Dunton-Downer, Leslie, 'Poetic Language and the Obscene', in Jan M. Ziolkowski, ed., *Obscenity: Social Control and Artistic Creation* (Leiden: Brill, 1998), pp. 19–37.

——, 'Wolf Man', in *Becoming Male in the Middle Ages*, ed. Jeffrey Jerome Cohen and Bonnie Wheeler (New York: Garland, 2000), pp. 203–18.

Echard, Sîan, *Arthurian Narrative in the Latin Tradition* (Cambridge: Cambridge University Press, 1998).

——, 'Glossing Gower: In Latin, in English, and *in absentia*: the Case of Bodleian Ashmole 35', in *Re-Visioning Gower*, ed. R. F. Yeager (Asheville, NC: Pegasus Press, 1998), pp. 237–56.

Economou, George, *The Goddess Natura in Medieval Literature* (Cambridge, MA: Harvard University Press, 1972).

Evans, Ruth, 'The Production of Space in Chaucer's London', in *Chaucer and the City*, ed. Ardis Butterfield (Cambridge: D. S. Brewer, 2006), pp. 41–56.

Fabbri, Lorenzo, 'Philosophy As Chance: An Interview with Jean-Luc Nancy', trans. Pascale-Anee Brault and Michael Naas, in *The Late Derrida*, ed. W. J. T. Mitchell and Arnold I. Davidson (Chicago: University of Chicago Press), pp. 209–22.

Fanagan, John, '*Wulf and Eadwacer*: A Solution to the Critics' Riddle', *Neophilologus* 60.1 (1976), 130–7.

Farina, Lara, *Erotic Discourse in Early English Religious Writing* (Basingstoke: Palgrave Macmillan, 2006).

Flannery, Mary C., 'A Bloody Shame: Chaucer's Honourable Women', *RES* 62 (2011), 337–57.

Foucault, Michel, *Histoire de la sexualité 1: La volonté de savoir* (Paris: Éditions Gallimard, 1976).

——, *The History of Sexuality I: The Will to Knowledge*, trans. Robert Hurley (London: Penguin, 1976).

——, *The History of Sexuality III: The Care of the Self*, trans. Robert Hurley (London: Penguin, 1986).

——, *Society Must Be Defended*, trans. David Macey, ed. Mauro Bertani (London: Penguin, 2003).

Franke, William, *What Cannot Be Said: Apophatic Discourses in Philosophy, Religion, Literature, and the Arts*, 2 vols (Notre Dame: University of Notre Dame Press, 2007).

Franke, William, *A Philosophy of the Unsayable* (Notre Dame: University of Notre Dame Press, 2014).

Frantzen, Allen J., *The Literature of Penance in Anglo-Saxon England* (New Brunswick, NJ: Rutgers University Press, 1983).

——, *Desire for Origins: New Language, Old English, and Teaching the Tradition* (New Brunswick, NJ: Rutgers University Press, 1990).

——, 'The Disclosure of Sodomy in *Cleanness*', *PMLA* 111.3 (1996), 451–64.

——, *Before the Closet: Same-Sex Love from* Beowulf *to* Angels in America (Chicago: Chicago University Press, 1998).

Frese, Dolores W., '*Wulf and Eadwacer*: The Adulterous Woman Reconsidered', *Notre Dame English Journal* 15.1 (1983), 1–22.

Furnivall, F. J., 'Literary Gossip', *Athenæum*, 29 November 1873, 698–9.

Garver, Valerie L., *Women and Aristocratic Culture in the Carolingian World* (Ithaca, NY: Cornell University Press, 2012).

Gaunt, Simon, *Gender and Genre in Medieval French Literature* (Cambridge: Cambridge University Press, 1995).

Georgianna, Linda, *The Solitary Self: Individuality in the* Ancrene Wisse (Cambridge: MA, Harvard University Press, 1981).

Giffney, Noreen, Michelle M. Sauer and Diane Watt, eds, *The Lesbian Premodern* (Basingstoke: Palgrave Macmillan, 2011).

Giles, Richard F., '*Wulf and Eadwacer*: A New Reading', *Neophilologus* 65.3 (1981), 468–72.

Goldberg, Jeremy, 'John Rykener, Richard II and the Governance of London', *Leeds Studies in English* 45 (2014), 49–70.

Goodich, Michael, *The Unmentionable Vice: Homosexuality in the Later Medieval Period* (Oxford: Clio Press, 1978).

Gray, Jonathan Michael, *Oaths and the English Reformation* (Cambridge: Cambridge University Press, 2012).

Grayson, Janet, *Structure and Imagery in* Ancrene Wisse (Hanover, NH: University Press of New England, 1974).

Green, Richard F., 'The Pardoner's Pants (And Why They Matter)', *Studies in the Age of Chaucer* 15 (1993), 131–45.

Greenfield, Stanley B., *Hero and Exile: The Art of Old English Poetry* (London: Hambledon, 1989).

Griffin, Miranda, 'The Beastly and the Courtly in Medieval Tales of Transformation: *Bisclavret, Melion* and *Mélusine*', in *The Beautiful and the Monstrous: Essays in French Literature, Thought and Culture*, ed. Amaleena Damlé and Aurélie L'Hostis, Modern French Identities 87 (Bern: Peter Lang, 2010), pp. 139–50.

Groebner, Valentin, *Defaced: The Visual Culture of Violence in the Middle Ages*, trans. Pamela Selwyn (New York: Zone, 2004).

Gross, Gregory W., 'Trade Secrets: Chaucer, the Pardoner, the Critics', *Modern Language Studies* 25.4 (1995), 1–36.

Gudmarsdottir, Sigridur, 'Feminist Theology and the Sensible Unsaying of Mysticism', in *Apophatic Bodies: Negative Theology, Incarnation, and Relationality*, ed. Chris Boesel and Catherine Keller (New York: Fordham University Press), pp. 273–85.

Guynn, Noah D., *Allegory and Sexual Ethics in the High Middle Ages*, The New Middle Ages (Basingstoke: Palgrave, 2007).

Hanrahan, Michael, 'Speaking of Sodomy: Gower's Advice to Princes in the *Confessio Amantis*', *Exemplaria* 14.2 (2002), 423–46.

Hansen, Elaine Tuttle, 'The Feminization of Men in Chaucer's *Legend of Good Women*', in *Seeking the Woman in Late Medieval and Renaissance Writings*, ed. Sheila Fisher and Janet E. Halley (Knoxville, TN: University of Tennessee Press, 1989), pp. 51–70.

Hasenfratz, Robert, 'Eisegan stefne (*Christ and Satan* 36a), the *Visio Pauli*, and ferrea vox (*Aeneid* 6, 626)', *Modern Philology* 86.4 (1989), 398–410.

Heidegger, Martin, 'The Way to Language', in *Basic Writings: Revised and Expanded Edition*, ed. David Farrell Krell (London: Routledge, 1994), pp. 394–426.

Henderson, David, *Apophatic Elements in the Theory and Practice of Psychoanalysis: Pseudo-Dionysius and C. G. Jung* (London: Routledge, 2014).

Heron, Onnaca, 'The Lioness in the Text: Mary of Egypt as Immasculated Female Saint', *Quidditas* 21 (2000), 23–44.

Hiltunen, Risto, 'Telling the Anchorite Code: *Ancrene Wisse* on Language', in *Discourse Perspectives on English: Medieval to Modern*, ed. Risto Hiltunen and Janne Skaffari (Amsterdam: John Benjamins, 2003), pp. 57–86.

Hinds, Stephen, *Allusion and Intertext: Dynamics of Appropriation in Roman Poetry* (Cambridge: Cambridge University Press, 1998).

Hodges, Laura Fulkerson, *Chaucer and Clothing: Clerical and Academic Costume in the General Prologue to the Canterbury Tales* (Cambridge: D. S. Brewer, 2005).

Holton, Amanda, *The Sources of Chaucer's Poetics* (Aldershot: Ashgate, 2008).

Horner, Shari, 'En/closed Subjects: *The Wife's Lament* and the Culture of Early Medieval Female Monasticism', in *Old English Literature: Critical Essays*, ed. R. M. Liuzza (New Haven, CT: Yale University Press, 2002), pp. 381–91.

Hough, Carole A., '*Wulf and Eadwacer*: A Note on "Ungelic"', *American Notes and Queries* 8.3 (1995), 3–6.

——, 'Two Puns in *Ancrene Wisse*', *Notes and Queries* 54.2 (2007), 122–3.

Howard, Donald R., *Chaucer: His Life, His Works, His World* (New York: Fawcett Columbine, 1989).

Howie, Cary, *Claustrophilia: The Erotics of Enclosure in Medieval Literature* (Basingstoke: Palgrave Macmillan, 2007).

Huot, Sylvia, *The 'Romance of the Rose' and Its Medieval Readers: Interpretation, Reception, Manuscript Transmission* (Cambridge: Cambridge University Press, 1993).

Illingworth, R. N., 'La chronologie des *Lais* de Marie de France', *Romania* 87 (1966), 433–75.

Innes-Parker, Catherine, 'Fragmentation and Reconstruction: Images of the Female Body in *Ancrene Wisse* and the *Katherine* Group', *Comitatus* 26.1 (1995), 27–52.

Ireland, Richard, 'Lucrece, Philomela (and Cecily): Chaucer and the Law of Rape', in *Crime and Punishment in the Middle Ages*, ed. T. S. Haskett (Victoria, BC: University of Victoria, 1998), pp. 37–61.

Irigaray, Luce, *Speculum de l'autre femme* (Paris: Éditions de Minuit, 1974).

——, *Ce sexe qui n'en est pas un* (Paris: Éditions de Minuit, 1977).

——, *Speculum of the Other Woman*, trans. Gillian C. Gill (Ithaca, NY: Cornell University Press, 1985).

——, *This Sex Which Is Not One*, trans. Catherine Porter (Ithaca, NY: Cornell University Press, 1985).

——, *An Ethics of Sexual Difference*, trans. Carolyn Burke and Gillian C. Gill (London: Continuum, 1993).

Janin, Hunt, *Medieval Justice: Cases and Laws in France, England and Germany, 500–1500* (Jefferson, NC: Macfarland, 2004).

Jones, E. A., 'Anchoritic Aspects of Julian of Norwich', in *A Companion to Julian of Norwich*, ed. Liz Herbert McAvoy (Cambridge: D. S. Brewer, 2008), pp. 75–87.

Jones, Nancy A., 'The Daughter's Text and the Thread of Lineage in the Old French *Philomena*', in *Representing Rape in Medieval and Early Modern Literature*, ed. Elizabeth Ann Robertson and Christine M. Rose (New York and Basingstoke: Palgrave Macmillan), pp. 161–88.

Jordan, Mark D., *The Invention of Sodomy in Christian Theology* (Chicago and London: University of Chicago Press, 1997).

——, *The Silence of Sodom: Homosexuality in Modern Catholicism* (Chicago: University of Chicago Press, 2000).

Jordan, William Chester, 'The Pardoner's "Holy Jew"', in *Chaucer and the Jews*, ed. Sheila Delany (London: Routledge, 2002), pp. 25–42.

Joy, Eileen A., 'Goodbye to All That: The State of My Own Personal Schizoid Field of Anglo-Saxon Studies', *The Heroic Age* 11 (2008), available at http://www.heroicage.org/issues/11/foruma.php.

Karras, Ruth Mazo, and David Lorenzo Boyd, 'The Interrogation of of a Male

Transvestite Prostitute in Fourteenth Century London', *GLQ: A Journal of Lesbian and Gay Studies* 1 (1995), 459–65.

——, 'Ut Cum Muliere: A Male Transvestite Prostitute in Fourteenth Century London', in *Premodern Sexualities*, ed. Louise Fradenburg, Carla Freccero and Kathy Lavezzo (New York and London: Routledge, 1996), pp. 99–116.

Karras, Ruth Mazo, and Tom Linkinen, 'John/Eleanor Rykener Revisited', in *Founding Feminisms in Medieval Studies: Essays in Honor of Jane E Burns*, ed. Lainc E. Doggett and Daniel E. O'Sullivan (Cambridge: D. S. Brewer, 2016), pp. 111–21.Kay, Sarah, and Miri Rubin, eds, *Framing Medieval Bodies* (Manchester: Manchester University Press, 1994).

Keller, Catherine, 'The Cloud of the Impossible: Embodiment and Apophasis', in *Apophatic Bodies: Negative Theology, Incarnation, and Relationality*, ed. Chris Boesel and Catherine Keller (New York: Fordham University Press, 2010), pp. 25–44.

Kerling, Johan, 'Another Solution to the Critics' Riddle: *Wulf and Eadwacer* Revisited', *Neophilologus* 64.1 (1980), 140–3.

King, Helen, *Hippocrates' Woman: Reading the Female Body in Ancient Greece*, (London: Routledge, 1998).

Kirkpatrick, Robin, *Dante's Inferno: Difficulty and Dead Poetry*, Cambridge Studies in Medieval Literature, 1 (Cambridge: Cambridge University Press, 1987).

Kittredge, G. L., 'Chaucer's Pardoner', *The Atlantic Monthly* 72 (1893), 829–33.

Kleiman, Irit Ruth, ed., *Voice and Voicelessness in Medieval Europe*, The New Middle Ages (Basingstoke: Palgrave Macmillan, 2015).

Klein, Stacy S. 'Gender and the Nature of Exile in Old English Elegies', in *A Place to Believe In: Locating Medieval Landscapes*, ed. Clare A. Lees and Gillian R. Overing (University Park, PA: Pennsylvania State University Press, 2006), pp. 113–31.

Klindienst, Patricia, 'The Voice of the Shuttle is Ours', in *Rape and Representation*, ed. Lynn A. Higgins and Brenda R. Silver (New York: Columbia University Press, 1991), pp. 35–64.

Kristeva, Julia, *Powers of Horror: An Essay on Abjection*, trans. Leon S. Roudiez (New York: Columbia University Press, 1982).

Kuryluk, Ewa, *Veronica and Her Cloths: History, Symbolism and Structure of a 'True' Image* (Oxford: Blackwell, 1991).

Labarge, Margaret Wade, 'Stitches in Time: Medieval Embroidery in its Social Setting', *Florilegium* 16 (1999), 77–96.

Labbie, Erin F., 'The Specular Image of the Gender-Neutral Name: Naming Silence in *Le Roman de Silence*', *Arthuriana* 7.2 (1997), 63–77.

——, *Lacan's Medievalism* (Minneapolis: University of Minnesota Press, 2006).

Lacan, Jacques, Écrits: A Selection, trans. Alan Sheridan (London and New York: Routledge, 1977).

——, *The Four Fundamental Concepts of Psychoanalysis (The Seminar of Jacques Lacan, Book XI)*, trans. Jacques-Alain Miller (New York: W. W. Norton & Co., 1978).

——, *The Ego in Freud's Theory and in the Technique of Psychoanalysis (The Seminar of Jacques Lacan, Book II: 1954–1955)*, ed. Jacques-Alain Miller, trans. Sylvana Tomaselli (New York: W. W. Norton & Co, 1991).

——, *On Feminine Sexuality: The Limits of Love and Knowledge (The Seminar of Jacques Lacan, Book XX: Encore 1972–1973)*, ed. Jacques-Alain Miller, trans. Bruce Fink (New York: W. W. Norton & Co, 1998).

Larson, Atria A., *Master of Penance: Gratian and the Development of Penitential Thought and Law in the Twelfth Century* (Washington, DC: Catholic University of America Press, 2014).

Lawton, David, *Blasphemy* (Philadelphia, PA: University of Pennsylvania Press, 1993).

Lees, Clare A., 'Actually Existing Anglo-Saxons', *New Medieval Literatures* 7 (2005), 223–52.

Lees, Clare A., and Gillian R. Overing, *Double Agents: Women in Clerical Culture in Anglo-Saxon England* (Philadelphia, PA: University of Pennsylvania, 2001).

Lees, Clare A., and Diane Watt, 'Age and Desire in the Old English *Life of St Mary of Egypt*: A Queerer Time and Place?' in *Middle-Aged Women in the Middle Ages*, ed. Sue Niebrzydowski (Cambridge: D. S. Brewer, 2011), pp. 53–68.

Lewis, C. S., *The Allegory of Love: A Study in Medieval Tradition* (Oxford: Oxford University Press, 1936).

——, *Studies in Words* (Cambridge: Cambridge University Press, 1990).

Lindorfer, Bettina, '*Peccatum Linguae* and the Punishment of Speech Violations', in *Speaking in the Medieval World*, ed. Jean E Godsall-Myers (Leiden: Brill, 2003), pp. 23–43.

Lochrie, Karma, *Margery Kempe and Translations of the Flesh* (Philadelphia, PA: University of Pennsylvania Press, 1991).

——, 'Presumptive Sodomy', *Textual Practice* 13 (1999), 295–310.

——, *Covert Operations: The Medieval Uses of Secrecy* (Philadelphia: University of Pennsylvania Press, 1999).

——, 'Between Women', in *The Cambridge Companion to Medieval Women's Writing*, ed. Carolyn Dinshaw and David Wallace (Cambridge: Cambridge University Press, 2003), pp. 70–88.

——, *Heterosyncrasies: Female Sexuality When Normal Wasn't* (Minneapolis: University of Minnesota Press, 2005).

Macherey, Pierre, 'The Text Says What It Does Not Say', trans. G. Hall, in *Literature in the Modern World*, ed. Dennis Walder (Oxford: Oxford University Press, 1990), pp. 215–22.

Magennis, Hugh, 'St Mary of Egypt and Ælfric: Unlikely Bedfellows in Cotton Julius E. vii?', in *The Legend of Mary of Egypt in Medieval Insular Hagiography*, ed. Erich Poppe and Bianca Ross (Dublin and Portland, Oregon: Four Courts Press, 1996), pp. 99–112.

Malo, Robyn, 'The Pardoner's Relics (And Why They Matter the Most)', *The Chaucer Review* 43.1 (2008), 82–102.

Malone, Kemp, 'When Did Middle English Begin?', *Language* 6 (1930), 110–17.

Mandel, Naomi, *Against the Unspeakable: Complicity, the Holocaust, and Slavery in America* (Charlottesville, VA: University of Virginia Press, 2006).

Marion, Jean-Luc, *The Idol and Distance* (New York: Fordham Press, 2001).

Marvin, Julia, 'The Unassuming Reader: F. W. Maitland and the Editing of Anglo-Norman', in *The Book Unbound: Editing and Reading Medieval Manuscripts and Texts*, ed. Siân Echard and Stephen Partridge (Toronto: University of Toronto Press, 2004), pp. 14–36.

Maxwell, Catherine, *The Female Sublime from Milton to Swinburne: Bearing Blindness* (Manchester: Manchester University Press, 2001).

McAlpine, Monica E., 'The Pardoner's Homosexuality and How it Matters', *PMLA* 95.1 (1980), 8–22.

McAvoy, Liz Herbert, ed., *Rhetoric of the Anchorhold: Space, Place and Body within the Discourses of Enclosure* (Cardiff: University of Wales Press, 2008).

McAvoy, Liz Herbert, and Mari Edwards, eds, *Anchorites, Wombs and Tombs: Intersections of Gender and Enclosure in the Middle Ages* (Cardiff: University of Wales Press, 2005).

McCabe, T. Matthew N., *Gower's Vulgar Tongue: Ovid, Lay Religion, and English Poetry in the* Confessio Amantis (Cambridge: D. S. Brewer, 2011).

McCarthy, Conor, *Love, Sex and Marriage in the Middle Ages: A Sourcebook* (London: Routledge, 2004).

McCash, June Hall, 'Sidney Painter (1902–1960): The Issue of Patronage for Marie de France', in *The Reception and Transmission of the Works of Marie de France, 1774–1974*, ed. Chantal A. Maréchal (Lewiston, NY: Mellen Press, 2003), pp. 171–208.

McClellan, William, '"Ful Pale Face": Agamben's Biopolitical Theory and the Sovereign Subject in Chaucer's *Clerk's Tale*', *Exemplaria* 17.1 (2005), 103–34.

McCracken, Peggy, '"The Boy Who Was a Girl": Reading Gender in the *Roman de Silence*', *Romanic Review* 85.4 (1994), 517–36.

——, 'Engendering Sacrifice: Blood, Lineage, and Infanticide in Old French Literature', *Speculum* 77.1 (2002), 55–75.

——, 'Skin and Sovereignty in *Guillaume de Palerne*', *Cahiers de recherches médiévales et humanistes* 24 (2012), 361–75.

McGinn, Bernard, *The Foundations of Mysticism* (London: SCM Press, 1992).

——, *The Growth of Mysticism* (London: SCM Press, 1995).

——, *The Flowering of Mysticism* (New York: Crossroads, 1998).

McNamara, Jo Ann, 'The *Herrenfrage*: The Restructuring of the Gender System, 1050–1150', in *Medieval Masculinities: Regarding Men in the Middle Ages*, Medieval Cultures 7, ed. (Minneapolis: University of Minnesota Press, 1994), pp. 3–29.

Ménard, Phillippe, *Les Lais de Marie de France: contes d'amour et d'aventures du Moyen Age* (Paris: Presses Universitaires de France, 1979).

——, *'Les histoires de loup-garou au moyen âge': Symposium in Honorem Prof. Martin de Riquer* (Barcelona: Cuaderns Crema, 1985), 209–38.

Michelson, Peter, *Speaking the Unspeakable: A Poetics of Obscenity* (Albany, NY: State University of New York Press, 1992).

Mickel, Jr, Emanuel J., 'Antiquities in Marie's *Lais*', in *In Quest of Marie de France: A Twelfth-Century Poet*, ed. Chantal A. Maréchal (Lampeter, Wales: Edwin Mellon Press, 1992), pp. 123–347.

Milem, Bruce, *The Unspoken Word: Negative Theology in Meister Eckhart's German Sermons* (Washington, DC: Catholic University of America Press, 2002).

Millett, Bella, 'The Origins of the *Ancrene Wisse*: New Answers, New Questions', *Medium Ævum* 61.2 (1992), 206–28.

——, '*Mouvance* and the Medieval Author: Re-editing *Ancrene Wisse*', in *Late-Medieval Religious Texts and their Transmission: Essays in Honour of A I Doyle*, ed. A. J. Minnis (Cambridge: D. S. Brewer, 1994), pp. 9–20.

——, '*Ancrene Wisse* and the Conditions of Confession', *English Studies* 80.3 (1999), 193–215.

Mills, Robert, 'Sovereign Power and Bare Life in Poetry by François Villon', *Exemplaria* 17.2 (2005), 445–80.

——, 'Male–Male Love and Sex in the Middle Ages, 1000–1500', in *A Gay History of Britain: Love and Sex Between Men Since the Middle Ages*, ed. Matt Cook, with H. G. Cocks, Robert Mills and Randolph Turnbach (Oxford, Westport, CT: Greenwood World Publishing, 2007), pp. 1–44.

——, 'Gender, Sodomy, Friendship, and the Medieval Anchorhold', *Journal and Medieval Religious Cultures* 36.1 (2010), 1–27.

——, *Seeing Sodomy in the Middle Ages* (Chicago: University of Chicago Press, 2015).

Mitchell, W. J. T., and Arnold I. Davidson, *The Late Derrida* (Chicago: University of Chicago Press, 2007).

Morse, Ruth, *The Medieval Medea* (Cambridge: D. S. Brewer, 1996).

Mortley, Raoul, *From Word to Silence* (Bonn: Peter Hanstein, 1986).

Murray, Alexander, 'Confession Before 1215', in *Transactions of the Royal Historical Society*, 6.3 (1993), 51–81.

Murray, Jacqueline, 'Twice Marginal and Twice Invisible: Lesbians in the Middle Ages', in *A Handbook of Medieval Sexuality*, ed. Vern L. Bullough and James A. Brundage (New York: Garland, 1996), pp. 191–222.

Neal, Derek G., *The Masculine Self in Late Medieval England* (Chicago: University of Chicago Press, 2008).

Newman, Barbara, *God and the Goddesses: Vision, Poetry and Belief in the Middle Ages* (Philadelphia: University of Pennsylvania Press, 2003).

——, *Medieval Crossover: Reading the Secular Against the Sacred* (Notre Dame, IN: University of Notre Dame Press, 2013).

Nicholson, Peter, 'Gower's Revisions in the *Confessio Amantis*', *The Chaucer Review* 19.2 (1984), 123–43.

——, *Love and Ethics in Gower's* Confessio Amantis (Ann Arbor, MI: University of Michigan Press, 2005).

Noonan, John Thomas, *The Scholastic Analysis of Usury* (Cambridge, MA: Harvard University Press, 1957).

Norris, Robin, 'Vitas Matrum: Mary of Egypt as Female Confessor', *Old English Newsletter* Subsidia 33 (2005), 79–109.

Olsson, Kurt, 'Natural Law and John Gower's *Confessio Amantis*', in *Gower's* Confessio Amantis: *A Critical Anthology*, ed. Peter Nicholson (Cambridge: D. S. Brewer, 1991), pp. 181–213.

——, 'Reading, Transgression, and Judgment: Gower's Case of Paris and Helen', in *Re-Visioning Gower*, ed. R. F. Yeager (Asheville, NC: Pegasus Press, 1998), pp. 67–92.

Orlemanski, Julie, 'A Silence in the Family Tree: The Genealogical Subject in Heldris of Cornwall's *Silence*', in *Individualism: The Cultural Logic of Modernity*, ed. Zubin Meer (Lanham, MD: Lexington Books, 2011), pp. 33–46.

Orton, Fred, Ian Wood and Clare A. Lees, eds, *Fragments of History: Rethinking the Ruthwell and Bewcastle Monuments* (Manchester: Manchester University Press, 2007).

Orton, Peter, Margaret E., 'An Approach to *Wulf and Eadwacer*', *Proceedings of the Royal Irish Academy* 85 (1985), 223–58.

Owens, Margaret E., *Stages of Dismemberment: The Fragmented Body in Late Medieval and Early Modern Drama* (Cranbury, NJ: Associated University Presses, 2005).

Palmer, R. Barton, 'Chaucer's *Legend of Good Women*: The Narrator's Tale', in *New Readings of Chaucer's Poetry*, ed. Robert G. Benson and Susan J. Ridyard (Cambridge: D. S. Brewer, 2003) pp. 183–94.

Patterson, Lee, 'Chaucerian Confession: Penitential Literature and the Pardoner', *Medievalia et Humanistica* 7 (1976), 153–68.

——, 'Chaucer's Pardoner on the Couch: Psyche and Clio in Medieval Literary Studies', *Speculum* 76.3 (2001), 638–80.

Payer, Pierre J., *Sex and the New Medieval Literature of Confession, 1150–1300* (Toronto: Pontifical Institute of Mediaeval Studies, 2009).

Pearsall, Derek, 'Gower's Narrative Art', *PMLA* 81.7 (1966), 475–84.

——, 'Chaucer's Pardoner: Death of a Salesman', *Chaucer Review* 17.4 (1983), 358–64.

——, *The Life of Geoffrey Chaucer: A Critical Biography* (Oxford: Blackwell, 1992).

Peterson, Zina, 'Institution and Individual in Conflict: The Early Middle English *Ancrene Wisse* and the Authority of Speech Acts', *Journal of Historical Pragmatics* 6 (2005), 69–86.

Pigg, Daniel F., 'Performing the Perverse: The Abuse of Masculine Power in the *Reeve's Tale*', in *Masculinities in Chaucer: Approaches to Maleness in the Canterbury Tales and Troilus and Criseyde*, ed. Peter G. Beidler (Cambridge: D. S. Brewer, 1998), pp. 53–61.

Plucknett, T. F. T., 'Chaucer's Escapade', *Law Quarterly Review* 64 (1948), 33–6.

Pollock, Frederick, and Frederic William Maitland, *History of English Law before the Time of Edward I*, 2 vols (Cambridge: Cambridge University Press, 1898).

Poppe, Erich, and Bianca Ross, eds, *The Legend of Mary of Egypt in Medieval Insular Hagiography* (Dublin and Portland, Oregon: Four Courts Press, 1996).

Puff, Helmut, 'Female Sodomy: The Trial of Katherina Hetzeldorfer (1477)', *JMEMS* 30.1 (2000), 41–61.

Pulsiano, Philip, and Kirsten Wolf, 'The "Hwelp" in *Wulf and Eadwacer*', *English Language Notes* 28.3 (1991), 1–9.

Quilligan, Maureen, *The Allegory of Female Authority: Christine de Pizan's* Cité des Dames (Ithaca, NY: Cornell University Press, 1991)

Quinn, William A., *Chaucer's Rehersynges: The Performability of the Legend of Good Women* (Washington, DC: Catholic University of America, 1994).

Rawcliffe, Carole, *Leprosy in Medieval England* (Woodbridge: Boydell, 2006).

Robertson, Elizabeth, 'The Rule of the Body: the Feminine Spirituality of the *Ancrene Wisse*', in *Seeking the Woman in Late Medieval and Renaissance Writings: Essays in Feminist Contextual Criticism*, ed. Sheila Fisher and Janet E. Halley (Knoxville, TN: University of Tennessee Press, 1989), pp. 109–34.

Robertson, Elizabeth Ann, and Christine M. Rose, eds, *Representing Rape in Medieval and Early Modern Literature* (New York and Basingstoke: Palgrave Macmillan, 2001).

Robertson, Karen, 'Rape and the Appropriation of Progne's Revenge in Shakespeare's *Titus Andronicus*, Or, Who Cooks the Thyestean Banquet?', in *Representing Rape in Medieval and Early Modern Literature*, ed. Elizabeth Ann Robertson and Christine M. Rose (New York and Basingstoke: Palgrave Macmillan, 2001), pp. 213–40.

Robins, William, 'Three Tales of Female Same-Sex Marriage: Ovid's "Iphis and Ianthe", the Old French *Yde et Olive*, and Antonio Pucci's *Reina d'Oriente*', *Exemplaria* 21.1 (2009), 43–62.

Rollo, David, *Kiss My Relics: Hermaphroditic Fictions of the Middle Ages* (Chicago: University of Chicago Press, 2011).

Root, Jerry, *'Space to Speke': The Confessional Subject in Medieval Literature* (New York: Peter Lang, 1997).

Rose, Christine M., 'Reading Chaucer, Reading Rape', in *Representing Rape in Medieval and Early Modern Literature*, ed. Elizabeth Ann Robertson and Christine M. Rose (New York and Basingstoke: Palgrave Macmillan, 2001), pp. 21–60.

Rowland, Beryl, 'Animal Imagery and the Pardoner's Abnormality', *Neophilologus* 48.1 (1964), 56–60.

Rumsey, Lucinder, 'The Scorpion of Lechery and *Ancrene Wisse*', *Medium Ævum* 61.1 (1992), 48–58.

Salih, Sarah, *Versions of Virginity in Late Medieval England* (Cambridge: D. S. Brewer, 2001).

Salisbury, Joyce, *The Beast Within: Animals in the Middle Ages*, 2nd edn (London and New York: Routledge, 1994, 2011).

Saunders, Corinne J., 'Classical Paradigms of Rape in the Middle Ages: Lucretia and Philomela', in *Rape in Antiquity*, ed. Susan Deacy and Karen F. Pierce (London: Classical Press of Wales, 1997), pp. 243–66.

——, *Rape and Ravishment in the Literature of Medieval England* (Cambridge: D. S. Brewer, 2001).

Sautman, Francesca Canadé, and Pamela Sheingorn, *Same-Sex Love and Desire Among Women in the Middle Ages* (New York: Palgrave, 2001).

Savage, Anne, '"The Translation of the Feminine": Untranslatable Dimensions of Anchoritic Works', in *The Medieval Translator* 4, ed. Roger Ellis and Ruth Evans (Binghamton: NY: Medieval and Renaissance Texts and Studies, 1994), pp. 181–99.

——, 'The Communal Authorship of *Ancrene Wisse*', in *A Companion to* Ancrene Wisse, ed. Yoko Wada (Cambridge: D. S. Brewer), pp. 45–56.

Scala, Elizabeth, *Absent Narratives: Manuscript Textuality, and Literary Structure in Late Medieval England* (New York: Palgrave Macmillan, 2002).

Scanlon, Larry, 'Speaking the Unspeakable: Sexual Regulation and the Priesthood of Genius', *Romanic Review* 86.2 (1995), 213–42.

Elaine Scarry, *The Body in Pain: The Making and Unmaking of the World* (Oxford: Oxford University Press, 1985).

Schibanoff, Susan, 'Sodomy's Mark: Alain de Lille, Jean de Meun, and the Medieval Theory of Authorship', in *Queering the Middle Ages*, ed. Glenn Burger and Steven F. Kruger, Medieval Cultures 27 (Minneapolis: University of Minnesota Press, 2001), pp. 28–56.

Sells, Michael A., *Mystical Languages of Unsaying* (Chicago: Chicago University Press, 1994).

Sells, Michael A., and James Webb, 'Lacan and Bion: Psychoanalysis and the Mystical Language of "Un-Saying"', *Journal of Melanie Klein and Object Relations* 15.2 (1997), 243–64.

Seymour, M. C., 'Chaucer's *Legend of Good Women*: Two Fallacies', in *RES* 37 (1986), 528–34.

Scheps, Walter, 'Chaucer's Numismatic Pardoner and the Personification of Avarice', *Acta* 4 (1977), 107–23.

Scheil, Andrew P., 'Bodies and Boundaries in the Old English *Life of St. Mary of Egypt*', *Neophilologus* 84.1 (2000), 137–56.

Schwerhoff, Gerd, '"Blasphemare, dehonestare et maledicere Deum": Über die Verletzung der göttlichen Ehre im Spätmittelalter', in *Verletzte Ehre: Ehrkonflikte in gesellschaften des Mittelaltersund der Fruhen Neuzeit*, ed. Klaus Schreiner and Gerd Schwerhoff (Koln: Bohlau, 1995), pp. 252–78.

Seshadri, Kalpana Rahita, *HumAnimal: Race, Law, Language*, post humanities 21 (Minneapolis: University of Minnesota Press, 2012).

Shahar, Shulamith, *Childhood in the Middle Ages* (London: Routledge, 1990).

Sitwell, Gerard, 'Introduction', in *The Ancrene Riwle*, trans. M. B. Salu (London: Burns and Oates, 1955), pp. vii–xxiii.

Smith, Kirby Flower, 'An Historical Study of the Werewolf in Literature', *PMLA* 9.1 (1894), 1–42.

Stanley, E. G., 'Wulf, My Wolf!', in *Old English and New: Studies in Language and Linguistics in Honor of Frederick G. Cassidy*, ed. Joan H. Hall, Nick Doane and Dick Ringler (New York: Garland, 1992), pp. 42–62.

Steel, Karl, *How to Make a Human: Animals and Violence in the Middle Ages* (Columbus, OH: Ohio State University Press, 2011).

Stevenson, Jane, 'The Holy Sinner: The Life of Mary of Egypt', in *The Legend of Mary of Egypt in Medieval Insular Hagiography*, ed. Erich Poppe and Bianca Ross (Dublin and Portland, Oregon: Four Courts Press, 1996), pp. 19–50.

Stock, Lorraine Kochanske, 'The Importance of Being Gender "Stable": Masculinity and Feminine Empowerment in *Le Roman de Silence*', *Arthuriana* 7.2 (1997), 7–34.

Strohm, Paul, *Theory and the Premodern Text* (Minneapolis: University of Minnesota Press, 2000).

Sturges, Robert S., *Medieval Interpretation: Models of Reading in Literary Narrative, 1100–1500* (Carbondale, IL: Southern Illinois University Press, 1991).

——, *Chaucer's Pardoner and Gender Theory: Bodies of Discourse*, The New Middle Ages Series (Basingstoke: Palgrave Macmillan, 2000).

Sullivan, Karen, *Truth and the Heretic: Crises of Knowledge in Medieval French Literature* (Chicago: University of Chicago Press, 2005).

Swan, Mary, and Elaine M. Treharne, eds., *Re-Writing English in the Twelfth Century* (Cambridge: Cambridge University Press, 2006).

Tambling, Jeremy, *Confession: Sexuality, Sin, the Subject* (Manchester: Manchester University Press, 1990).

Tentler, Thomas N., *Sin and Confession on the Eve of the Reformation* (Princeton, NJ: Princeton University Press, 1977).

Thompson, Sally, *Women Religious: The Founding of English Nunneries after the Norman Conquest* (Oxford: Clarendon Press, 1991).

Tinkle, Theresa, *Medieval Venuses and Cupids: Sexuality, Hermeneutics, and English Poetry* (Stanford: Stanford University Press, 1996).

Tolkien, J. R. R., 'Ancrene Wisse and *Hali Meiðhad*', *Essays and Studies* 14 (1929), 104–26.

Torrance, John, ed., *The Concept of Nature* (Oxford: Clarendon Press, 1992).

Treharne, Elaine, *Living Through Conquest: The Politics of Early English, 1020–1220* (Oxford: Oxford University Press, 2012).

Trotter, David, 'Language Contact and Lexicography: The Case of Anglo-Norman', in *The Origins and Development of Emigrant Languages: Proceedings from the Second Rasmus Rask Colloquium, Odense University, November 1994*, ed. Hans R. Nielsen and Lene Schøsler (Odense: Odense University Press, 1996), pp. 21–39.

Turner, Denys, 'How To Read the Pseudo-Denys Today?', *International Journal of Systematic Theology* 7.4 (2005), 428–40.

Wada, Yoko, ed., *A Companion to* Ancrene Wisse (Cambridge: D. S. Brewer, 2003).

Warren, Ann K., *Anchorites and their Patrons in Medieval England* (Berkeley, CA: University of California Press, 1985).

Watt, Diane, *Amoral Gower: Language, Sex, and Politics* (Minneapolis: University of Minnesota Press, 2003).

——, *Medieval Women's Writing: Works by and for Women in England, 1100–1500* (Cambridge: Polity Press, 2007).

Watts, Ann Chalmers, 'Pearl, Inexpressibility, and Poems of Human Loss', *PMLA* 99.1 (1984), 26–40.

Watts, P. R., 'The Strange Case of Geoffrey Chaucer and Cecilia Chaumpaigne', *Law Quarterly Review*, 63 (1947), 491–513.

Webb, Diana, *Pilgrims and Pilgrimage in the Medieval West* (London: I. B. Tauris, 2001).

Wenzel, Siegfried, 'The Sources of Chaucer's Seven Deadly Sins', *Traditio* 30 (1974), 351–78.

Wetherbee, Winthrop, 'Classical and Boethian Tradition in the *Confessio Amantis*', in *A Companion to Gower*, ed. Sîan Echard (Cambridge: D. S. Brewer, 2004), pp. 181–96.

White, Hugh, *Nature, Sex, and Goodness in a Medieval Literary Tradition* (Oxford: Oxford University Press, 2001).

Whitman, Jon, 'Dislocations: The Crisis of Allegory in the *Romance of the Rose*', in *Languages of the Unsayable: The Play of Negativity in Literature and Literary Theory*, ed. Sanford Budick and Wolfgang Iser (Stanford, CA: Stanford University Press, 1996), pp. 259–79.

Wilcox, Jonathan, 'The Wolf on Shepherds: Wulfstan, Bishops, and the Context of the *Sermo Lupi ad Anglos*', in *Old English Prose: Basic Readings*, ed. Paul E. Szarmach (New York: Garland, 2000), pp. 395–418.

Williams, Jeni, *Interpreting Nightingales: Gender, Class, History* (Sheffield: Sheffield Academic Press, 1997).

Winstead, Karen A., *Virgin Martyrs: Legends of Sainthood in Late Medieval England* (Ithaca, NY and London: Cornell University Press, 1997).

Wittgenstein, Ludwig, *Tractatus Logico-Philosophicus*, trans. C. K. Ogden (London: Kegan Paul, Trench, Trubner & Co., 1922).

Wogan-Browne, Jocelyn [Price], '"Inner" and "Outer": Conceptualizing the Body in *Ancrene Wisse* and Aelred's *De Institutione Inclusarum*', in *Medieval English Religious and Ethical Literature: Essays in Honour of G. H. Russell*, ed. Gregory Kratzman and James Simpson (Cambridge: D. S. Brewer, 1986), pp. 192–208.

Wolfe, Cary, *Before the Law: Humans and Other Animals in a Biopolitical Frame* (Chicago: Chicago University Press, 2013).

Yeager, R. F., 'Learning to Read in Tongues: Writing Poetry for a Trilingual Culture', in *Chaucer and Gower: Difference, Mutuality, Exchange*, ed. R. F. Yeager (Victoria, BC: University of Victoria, 1991), pp. 115–29.

——, ed., *Re-Visioning Gower* (Asheville, NC: Pegasus Press, 1998).

Zettersten, Arne, *Studies in the Dialect and Vocabulary of the 'Ancrene Riwle'* (Lund: C. W. K. Gleerup, 1965).

Ziarek, Ewa Płonowska, 'Bare Life on Strike: Notes on the Biopolitics of Race and Gender', *South Atlantic Quarterly* 107.1 (2008), 89–105.

Ziolkowski, Jan M., *Alan of Lille's Grammar of Sex: The Meaning of Grammar to a Twelfth-Century Intellectual* (Cambridge, MA: Medieval Academy of America, 1985).

Žižek, Slavoj, *The Sublime Object of Ideology* (London and New York: Verso, 1989).

INDEX

GENDER IN THE MIDDLE AGES

- I *Gender and Medieval Drama*, Katie Normington, 2004
- II *Gender and Petty Crime in Late Medieval England: The Local Courts in Kent, 1460–1560*, Karen Jones, 2006
- III *The Pastoral Care of Women in Late Medieval England*, Beth Allison Barr, 2008
- IV *Gender, Nation and Conquest in the Works of William of Malmesbury*, Kirsten A. Fenton, 2008
- V *Monsters, Gender and Sexuality in Medieval English Literature*, Dana M. Oswald, 2010
- VI *Medieval Anchoritisms: Gender, Space and the Solitary Life*, Liz Herbert McAvoy, 2011
- VII *Middle-Aged Women in the Middle Ages*, edited by Sue Niebrzydowski, 2011
- VIII *Married Women and the Law in Premodern Northwest Europe*, edited by Cordelia Beattie and Matthew Frank Stevens, 2013
- IX *Religious Men and Masculine Identity in the Middle Ages*, edited by P. H. Cullum and Katherine J. Lewis, 2013
- X *Reconsidering Gender, Time and Memory in Medieval Culture*, edited by Elizabeth Cox, Liz Herbert McAvoy and Roberta Magnani, 2015
- XI *Medicine, Religion and Gender in Medieval Culture*, edited by Naoë Kukita Yoshikawa, 2015